MISS
RHYTHM

Oh, What a Dream . . . ! (Courtesy of Ruth Brown)

MISS RHYTHM

*The Autobiography of Ruth Brown,
Rhythm and Blues Legend*

RUTH BROWN

with Andrew Yule

DONALD I. FINE BOOKS

NEW YORK

DONALD I. FINE BOOKS
Published by the Penguin Group
Penguin Books USA Inc., 375 Hudson Street,
New York, New York 10014, U.S.A.
Penguin Books Ltd, 27 Wrights Lane,
London W8 5TZ, England
Penguin Books Australia Ltd, Ringwood,
Victoria, Australia
Penguin Books Canada Ltd, 10 Alcorn Avenue,
Toronto, Ontario, Canada M4V 3B2
Penguin Books (N.Z.) Ltd, 182–190 Wairau Road,
Auckland 10, New Zealand

Penguin Books Ltd, Registered Offices:
Harmondsworth, Middlesex, England

Published in 1996 by Donald I. Fine Books,
an imprint of Penguin Books USA Inc.

1 3 5 7 9 10 8 6 4 2

Library of Congress Cataloging-in-Publication Data
Brown, Ruth, 1928–
Miss Rhythm : the autobiography of Ruth Brown, rhythm and blues
legend / Ruth Brown with Andrew Yule.
p.   cm.
ISBN 1-55611-486-9
1. Brown, Ruth, 1928–   2. Singers—United States—Biography.
I. Yule, Andrew.   II. Title.
ML420.B819A3   1996
782.42′1643′092—dc20   95-26363
[B]   CIP
                                                                         MN

This book is printed on acid-free paper.
∞
Printed in the United States of America

I dedicate this book to all the dear friends who've shared my journey and stood by me through good times and bad, to my fine sons and my grandchild, to my wonderful brothers and sisters, to my dad who gave me the priceless legacy of the voice, to my mama who taught me how a butterfly isn't born a butterfly, it has to work and endure to become one. Last but not least, loving thanks go to Howell, my attorney, and Andrew, my writing partner. Lord have mercy, exactly a decade apart, I finally found me the right man at the right time!

—RUTH BROWN,
Las Vegas, Nevada
November, 1995

To me, as for many others, Ruth has always been a legend, a truly remarkable, one-of-a-kind performer. Now the rest of the world is catching up. With a Tony, a Grammy and induction into the Rock and Roll Hall of Fame, most artists would rest content. Not Ruth, who to this day continues to extend the boundaries of her art. And her work for the Rhythm and Blues Foundation, which owes its very existence to her efforts, continues to benefit hundreds of pioneer artists who would otherwise have been denied their just rewards from the record industry. The cream always rises to the top—and Ruth, you are the cream.

—ANDREW YULE,
Kilmarnock, Scotland
November, 1995

PREVIOUS BOOKS BY ANDREW YULE

FAST FADE
David Puttnam, Columbia Pictures and the Battle for Hollywood

PICTURE SHOWS
The Life and Films of Peter Bogdanovich

LOSING THE LIGHT
Terry Gilliam and the Munchausen Saga

LIFE ON THE WIRE
The Life and Art of Al Pacino

SEAN CONNERY
From 007 to Hollywood Icon

RICHARD LESTER AND THE BEATLES

CONTENTS

INTRODUCTION

IT TOOK SEVERAL YEARS after *Black and Blue* opened in 1984 at the Chatelet, presented by the Theatre Musical de Paris, for impressarios Claudio Segovia and Hector Orezzoli to assemble the backing necessary for their Broadway shot. This was despite our success in France—we were booked originally for six weeks in the 3,000–seat theater and ran for the full eight-month season—and even then the money men had their own ideas about recasting. They wanted three younger women to play the leads, a complete change of concept from the well-seasoned divas, myself among them, who had laid Paris at their feet in the musical re-creation of Cotton Club days. My Argentinian friends ridiculed the notion and I made their stand easier by my high profile in 1988. At last, after years of struggling to re-establish my career, it seemed I was getting someplace.

In January I took part in a documentary, *That Rhythm, Those Blues,* going on to attend the premieres in the fall at the Telluride, Aspen and Denver film festivals. It was Emmy-nominated, the Boston *Globe* describing it as "exquisite" and a "sweet vindication of survival."

"I can't recall the last time I saw a movie that seemed too *short,*" Joel Siegel wrote, "but George T. Nierenberg's *That Rhythm, Those Blues* could run two or three times longer and I would have been delighted." He was kind enough to add, "Listening to Ruth Brown talk about her high times and hard times, we're reminded that *all* experience, no matter how discouraging, can lead to strength and

1

wisdom." I hope he was right, but I cannot be the judge. Maybe you can, once you've read my story.

Early in '88 I also opened in what my late friend, the irrepressible Redd Foxx, would have referred to as two "real class joints," the Cinegrill in Los Angeles and Michael's Pub in New York. The success of these gigs led to a Showtime special recorded at the Bottom Line, as well as a new record deal at Fantasy. And *Hairspray,* the John Waters movie I had filmed the year before, opened, unleashing the outrageous Motormouth Maybelle on an unsuspecting public, neatly handing me a whole new generation of fans. Lord have mercy, I was the hot new kid in town all over again—at the ripe old age of sixty. Sophie Tucker, you were out by twenty years!

To cap all of this, the outcome of my twenty-year battle with Atlantic records was widely reported. Back in the fifties the label became known in the industry as "The House That Ruth Brown Built." I was their first major signing and brought them a succession of hits, starting with "Teardrops from My Eyes," all the way through to "Mama, He Treats Your Daughter Mean," "Oh, What a Dream" and "Lucky Lips." Despite the fact that my records continued to sell both in the States and all round the world, I'd received not a penny over the years since a $1,000 handout in the mid-sixties. Atlantic's co-founder, Ahmet Ertegun, on the other hand, sold his company to Warner/Seven Arts in '67, collecting $17 million just a few years after I bowed out. Rough justice? I thought so. And with the aid of a brilliant young lawyer named Howell Begle, I set out to prove it.

DURING THE PREVIEWS of *Black and Blue* I was working at a deadly pace. To trumpet the show I was squeezing in interviews right, left and center, both on television and in the press. After an appearance on Phil Donahue's TV show I took a call from People magazine regarding a spread. I agreed, but turned down their idea of a fancy rendezvous. "Come and see me where I live," I suggested. I doubt if any of them had seen the inside of a one-room apartment in darkest Harlem before, and there was hardly enough space to turn around when they arrived with a photographer in tow. They intended to feature my story to coincide with *Black and Blue*'s first night in December '88. It was not to be. As my late mama would have said, 'Man proposes, God disposes.'

With only a few weeks to go before our official opening I was rushing to make a matinee performance when I began to feel terribly ill. Instead of a dressing room at the Minskoff, I ended up, rapidly turning blue, being wheeled into the emergency room of a hospital.

I do not recall much about the next couple of days. When I came to I was in intensive care, hoses and pipes threading in and out every which way. The first clear image I remember is that of Valerie and Rashamella, two of the young chorus girls from the show, looking down at me. One was silently praying, the other speaking in tongues. I found out later they had arrived in the hospital after midnight and been directed to my room upstairs by a lady in a green dress. This baffled the hospital staff. Nobody was allowed to visit so late, and no member of the staff, dressed in green or any other color, should have been there directing visitors, and certainly not to someone still on the danger list.

Before too long it was conveyed to me that our money men had been highly skeptical when they'd taken the call from my doctor. Nothing less than documentary proof of my angina attack, it seemed, would satisfy them. And they were all for going ahead with my understudy and opening on schedule. Hector and Claudio would have none of it. *"Black and Blue* will open without you, Ruth, *over our dead bodies,"* they assured me. "We'll simply keep on previewing until you're fit again."

What can you say about two guys with that much faith in you? With the first night indefinitely postponed, other supporters rallied round. David Hinckley of the New York *Daily News* printed a photograph of me, all decked out in my "St. Louis Blues" costume from the show, standing there opening a set of stage curtains. "Hold the curtain 'til Ruth gets back!" his caption ran. My doctor waited a few weeks to tell me how close to the brink I'd been. None of the hospital staff, it emerged, had thought I was going to make it.

*   *   *

IT TAKES A LOT of nerve at the best of times to predict what will click on Broadway, but with our Paris success behind us there was room for more than merely cautious optimism. Nevertheless, I really felt for Hector and Claudio when I was finally discharged from hospital and *Black and Blue* had its opening night set at the Minskoff in January '89. Thank the good Lord, it was an unqualified triumph, with notices the next day as good as anything we could have written ourselves. And People magazine, bless them, held their spread and ran it to give *Black and Blue* maximum benefit.

As the run continued my first visitors in hospital, Valerie and Rashamella, dropped by my dressing room one night. I had an altar set up in there with a picture of my mother in the center, flanked by twin candles, a single fresh rose in front. Valerie took one look and immediately declared, "Oh hey, *that's* the lady in the green dress who showed us to your room that night!" Rashamella was right behind her. "That's her, all right," she agreed. "How come you got her picture in here?"

Think what you like, I simply refer all doubters to these two kids, about the least likely pair of mystics you'll ever meet, two of the sweetest and most down-to-earth girls ever. My sister Goldie is the member of my family who has spiritual lines stretching clear to heaven, so you can guess her reaction when I told her the story: "Ruth, surely you're not surprised. You must *know* Mama's lookin' out for you!"

Before long there was talk of award nominations for our show. The presentation of any accolade is no time for vengeful thoughts, but after my first humiliating experience on Broadway earlier in the eighties, fired from *Blues in the Night,* the Outer Circle Critics Award I won for Best Performance by a Leading Actress in a Musical was one in the eye for those behind the decision, as well as representing a new peak in my career. When Carol Channing made the presentation at Sardi's I would not have claimed the queen of England as my kin.

That made it one down and one to go—and yes, I *am* kidding—for I swear to you that never in my wildest dreams had I ever considered being put up for a Tony, let alone winning. Even after the nomination came through, I was so sure I wasn't going to win. How could it be? I had been a singer all my life and until the Outer Circle Award had never won anything outside of an Amateur Night at the Apollo as a teenager in the forties. There had been no gold record (at least none I'd been allowed to keep), no Grammy, nothing. So why all of a sudden should I get lucky twice on Broadway? What made me especially doubtful was their nomination of Linda Hopkins, another of the *Black and Blue* threesome. Two people from the same show? I thought that was a certain way to wipe both of us out.

My companion at the Tony Awards presentation in June '89 was my lawyer, Howell. After what he'd achieved tackling the might of Warner Communications Inc., I regarded him as nothing less than the biblical David crossed with the Pied Piper of Hamlin, if you can imagine a self-effacing version of that combination bearing a distinct resemblance to Dick Cavett. I resorted to a wheelchair before the ceremony, for my legs had been giving me terrible pain, the legacy of a car crash in the forties in which they had both been broken. The organizers were anxious to keep the contraption off-stage, and I wanted to be out front in any case. Having watched the Tonys before on television, I knew they panned the cameras over the nominees. I was determined that my brothers and sister at home would at least *see* me on such an occasion!

It was Tommy Tune they chose to announce the winner in my category. As he opened the envelope and began to enunciate the name, I swear I could feel time stand still. Until, that is, I heard "Ruth Brown" ricocheting in my head. I knew it was not my imagination when Howell let out a yell and almost leaped from his seat into my lap.

"Do you want any help getting up there?" he asked me.

"Oh no," I replied, "I'm gonna *walk* this one!"

I had nothing planned to say, and as I made my way down the aisle I racked my brains for something suitable. All of a sudden I remembered something from my Granny Delia's farm in North Carolina, where I had spent my summers in the thirties helping sharecrop her fields. On Sundays, when we sat down at the table as a family, she would open her Bible and read from the Scriptures.

Then she would ask each child to recite a Bible verse. I used the same one every time, 'Let the words of my mouth and the meditation of my heart be acceptable in Thy sight, O Lord. You are my strength and my Redeemer.' I did not intend to sock that to the audience, but the sentiment gave me the tranquility I needed to clear my thoughts.

I counted the steps leading to the stage. There were eight of them, and I am only thankful the cameras did not show the difficulty I had getting to the top. "Thank you, ladies and gentlemen," I began. "Thank you, *Black and Blue.* Thank you, Hector and Claudio, thank you, Linda Hopkins, Carrie Smith, Bunny Briggs, all the wonderful people that I have had the privilege of working with in this performance. And the reason I thank them is because they are all so very talented that they really gave me my work to do. You *had* to be good, because you were working with the *best.* I want to dedicate this award to my dear Mama, and to my first grandbaby, who's probably looking in from Los Angeles."

I had just one more thing to say, and I said it with a rueful nod to the side of the stage. I did not expect it to bring the house down, but that is what it darned near did.

"It has taken me forty-two years," I declared, "to climb those eight steps!"

MY LIFE HAS BEEN A ROLLER-COASTER RIDE through a dazzling kaleidoscope of events, touching and being touched by a host of unforgettable people. All the way from jazz greats Billie Holiday, Dinah Washington, Sarah Vaughan, Billy Eckstine, the Duke, the Count, Lester Young and Charlie Parker to rock legends Jackie Wilson, Little Richard, Clyde McPhatter, Sam Cooke, Brook Benton, from sports heroes Joe Louis, Muhammad Ali and his court jester, "the Great Bundini," to movie directors Robert Altman and John Waters, on to Washington leading lights Jesse Jackson, Mickey Leland, Lee Attwater and John Conyers, full circle to today's musical megastar, Bonnie Raitt. If they'se under a hundred, honey, I knows 'em! And I swear to you, for every famous name in there, you'll discover an equally enthralling unsung hero.

There have been nightmare moments along the way, moments I never thought I'd get through. More often, as I look back, it's been like a dream.

But oh, what a dream . . .

1

PEPPERMINT AND PICKLES

ONE OF THE EARLIEST things I remember Mama saying was that she always knew I was going to be somebody special, that sooner or later the whole world would look at me. Her reasoning was simple. I was born that way, plumb center stage, with a whole bunch of people staring. She was at home when I decided to take a peek at what the outside world had to offer, and five ladies, one of them the midwife, gathered to help and watch the birth. It was Miss Ethlyn Gale, one of my schoolteachers years later, who declared as I emerged, "My God, I never seen a baby being born before!" Mama was so embarrassed with all those spectators, and when she eventually saw *Gone with the Wind,* Butterfly McQueen's famous remark, "I don't know nuthin' 'bout birthin' babies" brought it all back. That's how Ruth Alston Weston arrived in this world, kickin' and screamin', on January 12, 1928.

The Weston family had been none too pleased about the developing relationship between my mama and dad, for they harbored great aspirations for their son Leonard. They had good reason, for when Martha Jane Alston entered his life in 1927, he was a leading light on the varsity team in the Tidewater town of Portsmouth, Virginia, the best baseball player in school, a star football player

My dear friend,
my mother,
my everything—
Martha Weston and
her baby Ruth.
(COURTESY
OF RUTH BROWN)

and track athlete. A wonderful baritone voice added to an unrivaled series of choices for the seventeen-year-old's future career.

Martha was a farmgirl from Macon, North Carolina, dispatched at sixteen to Portsmouth to live with her cousin so she could attend high school. She first met Leonard heading out to baseball practice as she was climbing the school stairs. She dropped her books, he picked them up, that started them talking. Next day he spotted her waiting for a bus and walked her home, establishing a routine. Leonard had long been a target of lovesick local girls, none of whom had possessed enough of that certain something to seriously detain him. Martha was different, a beautiful, light-skinned stranger in town with a sparkle in her eye that refused to quit, and whose lustrous, jet-black hair reached halfway down to her trim waist.

With me on the way Martha and Leonard were married and moved in with the Westons, William and Ruth, in London Street, deep in the heart of the town's black community. Dad left school and worked as a laborer to support his family, all his fancy career dreams pushed into the background. By day he unloaded freight on the docks, then often doubled up at nights with odd jobs. It was a case of whatever he could pick up, for the Wall Street crash and the depression that followed took their toll. All the years he was alive he never saw a paycheck over thirty-five dollars. Not much, considering he eventually had seven of us to keep alive, with one new arrival every couple of years or so until I had four brothers and two sisters living. We lost one brother, William, in infancy.

We lived with my grandparents until I was two, then moved to the first little place of our own in Lincoln Street, in the middle of a row of terraced houses. When Dad was unable to raise the rent money, he noticed that the house next door was empty, so one night we did a moonlight through the fence and moved in there instead. It was okay to do that in those days, wiping the slate clean and starting over. In many ways it was a simpler time all round. One more move took us to Nelson Street, again near the senior Westons.

Dad was just under six feet tall, slim-built but tight-packed and wiry, aggressive and loud when he felt the occasion demanded, and always ready to square up to anyone. I felt he was hard on me as a young girl, probably because he'd dearly wanted his first-born to be a male child. As a consequence I got the back of his hand for most things, some of which I deserved, some of which I didn't. I realize now I was a lot like him in many ways, not the least of which was the harboring of a burning youthful ambition. His remained unfulfilled, he chose another path instead and extinguished that youthful flame, for there's no doubt that in marrying Mama he missed his moment, the chance to develop either his sport or vocal talents. I believe he came to see in me what he might have achieved.

One of his weaknesses was a fondness for a nip. When I was still a toddler he fashioned a sled from a wooden crate with little sides to grip on to as he dragged me along. That way he could bring me right there in the tavern with him, where I could sit on the sidelines while he talked trash with his cronies and sank a few. His friends would often warn him, "If your Martha Jane finds you here with that baby—!"

After a year in a nursery run by Reverend Birchet and his missus came a move to my first grade school, housed in an old dun-colored hacienda building encircled by a high chicken-wire fence. This is where I was introduced to Tom Sawyer, Huckleberry Finn and a whole lot of Mark Twain in picture books, stories set in the deep South. We had little social functions that provided my first taste of performing, dressing up in costumes Granny Ruth—"Big Mama" —made. My favorite was a dress with a huge underskirt and matching big hat with streamers in yellow and black, still my favorite color combination. I was the same age as Shirley Temple and wore her style of hats. Every Easter, whenever the magazines showed the new stuff she was wearing, I'd try getting as close to that as possible. I never really noticed that Shirley was white, I just wanted those lovely soft curls, and with the aid of a curling iron on the stove mama did the best she could. My baby sister Delia, on the other hand, hated to see that iron being produced. She'd say, "I wish Shirley Temple would *die!*"

Across the street from the grade school was George Peabody, the elementary establishment I joined when I was six. Right on the corner was a little store run by Miss Cutler where everyone lined up at lunchtime to get what we called a three-center, a soda that looked like a miniature Coke. She also had root beer, great big cookies for a nickel, huge peppermint sticks and a barrelful of pickles. Impaling one of them on a peppermint and sucking away on the result was like paradise—we really thought we had caviar. Small treats like that made us happy as children.

I used to walk through the white district to Portsmouth docks every Friday—payday—to meet Dad from work. He'd hand me the little brown envelope containing his pay, first removing his cigarette and drinking money; the remainder I'd take home to Mama. She did domestic work for a white family—in between birthin' babies, that is—and we used to wait at home until she arrived back, bringing leftovers from their kitchen. The scraps were not only for us but for every dog on the block. If us kids were in the house alone we'd be a-rippin' and a-runnin', fighting like crazy, then we'd look out the window and see all these dogs lined up outside, their little tails a-waggin'. "Look at the dogs!" we'd say. "Mama's comin'!" Those dogs were never wrong, and in no time the bus would be drawing up and dropping her off at the corner.

Dad was active in the church choir and accompanied me at the piano when I made my first appearance in public, singing at our local place of worship, the Emmanuel AME (African Methodist Episcopal) Church. That was where most of my musical training took place, singing spirituals rather than gospel. Dad had me performing at weddings by the time I was six, a skinny little thing standing on the piano singing the likes of "Ave Maria" and "I Love You Truly" in my high soprano voice. Everything I learned musically came from him, although not the correct way, for I never learned to read music. I just sang 'round the house, at these tiny wedding gigs, and with the groups in church.

When I was ten I began touring neighboring churches with him and was introduced to an all-male glee club he sang with, the Hiram Simmons Group. Simmons was unknown in the larger world of music but a name to reckon with wherever gospels and spirituals were performed in the Tidewater area. The choral music he wrote, both hymns and spirituals, was truly beautiful. He composed anthems for male groups, for up to a hundred untrained voices, my father's prominent among them.

We had an upright piano at home handed down from my grandparents, and many times I remember Dad coming home so tired, but sitting down before we started supper and filling the house with music and love. That was when everything pleased him and he arrived home sober. When it didn't, and he wasn't, all of us had to look out, Mama included. Dad was the one who had to dole out any punishment, for Mama could never stay around for that. Her way was much worse, though. She'd sit down and talk everything through, making you feel so ashamed. I'd think, "Hey, Ma, just give me a spankin' and let me outta here!"

If my father is who I am musically, then my mother is my spiritual guru. She taught me survival: be humble if you ever get famous, and be careful how you treat people on the way up, because you're bound to meet them on the way down. She had a cliché for every occasion, but the reason they survive is because they've stood the test of time. "What you are is God's gift to you," she'd tell me, "what you make of yourself is your gift to God." Or "Nothing can happen to you today that you and God can't handle together." Then there was, "Ruthie, don't ever lie, or it's going to change every time you say it. Remember, the truth always stays the same." When we made a mistake Mama would never say, "I told you so." She would look us right in the eye instead and simply ask "Why?" Later in life, whenever I felt depressed, sure I'd made the wrong decisions, she'd say "No doubt you had your reasons. When you find out what they were, come and tell me and I'll understand."

Mama was the best listener I ever knew, and an anchor in times of trouble. Throughout my life, whenever I've felt down, I called her. She was always there to help and inspire, showing me how to take stumbling blocks and turn them into stepping stones, how to turn problems into challenges.

I never really saw her angry, not once—until the day of Daddy's funeral, that is, but that's another story and we'll get to it.

Growing up in our close-knit little community our parents protected us from the worst of the racial prejudice that was going 'round. We lived in a predominantly black settlement, ten blocks wide and ten blocks long, bounded by the train tracks beyond which lay the white area. In Soulville we had our own churches, schools and shopping. We had a Jewish family next door to us on Nelson; we played with their children on the street and back porches. Another white family lived directly across the way, and playing with their kids we never felt any different either. Of course there was segregation when you ventured into the heart of town, where Woodrow Wilson was the all-white school. It now has a black homecoming queen, unthinkable back then.

For grownups the differences were harder to bear. There was a baseball park across from us in Lincoln that housed an all-white team called the Portsmouth Swans. Dad, who could have batted circles 'round any of them, was relegated to the black division. Locations like the nearby beaches were strictly segregated too, with blacks confined to Ocean Breeze, an extension of the main Virginia Beach, and Buckroe, near Newport News. Although there was no danger involved when I walked through the white district each week to collect Dad's pay, I knew better than to loiter in case they thought I was "up to something."

Public transportation, where we were obliged to travel at the back end of buses, didn't bother us youngsters at all; it was just the way it was, as far as we were concerned. It was really only when I got into show business and began to travel, especially further down South, that racism and bigotry hit hard.

Seeing blacks in movies playing domestics didn't strike a sensitive chord with me either, for that was what my mama did. What did come over as demeaning was that slow-walkin', slow-talkin' shuffle that Stepin Fetchit and a few others made their specialty, and their dialect was completely alien to my ears. We had our own colored theaters, and Mama took us to the Capitol every Saturday to catch the latest episode of the serial before the main feature. The movie that really made an impression was the 1934 version of Fannie Hurst's *Imitation of Life,* with Annie, the black maid, played by Louise Beavers, trying to deal with her daughter Peola's desperate desire to pass for white. The whole thing just tore at Mama's emotions, taking her all the way back to her childhood in North Carolina and how she lost her daddy forever. She only gave me hints about this at first, for the hurt was too deep, and several years elapsed before I got the whole story.

I never visited the white district's Colonial moviehouse, although it had a side entrance to the upper gallery where blacks were allowed. Apart from any other consideration, the Capitol had something the Colonial could never offer: all-black movies! Yep, all through the Depression years, right through wartime, we enjoyed our own black heroes in westerns, dramas, musicals and gangster movies. Apart from turning a dollar the idea was to counter the black stereotypes we were fed in mainstream fare and show blacks in a variety of roles—heroic, responsible and romantic. Oh, the villains of these pieces were black too, of course—and how we booed as they foreclosed on that ranch!—but at least we were portrayed as human beings, not caricatures.

We got a kick out of those movies and maybe they did raise our aspirations somewhat. If Bill "Bojangles" Robinson could land on the silver screen, so might we! If Herb Jeffries, "the Bronze Buckaroo," could ride those trails and save the damsel in distress, there was a chance for us. The one unattainable goddess as we eased our way into the forties who combined stunning looks with a figure and a voice to match was Lena Horne. Well, we could dream; and that is, after all, what movies are all about! Ralph Cooper, who later became emcee at New York's Apollo, was the top black gangster in those movies of ours, as well as a gorgeous-looking guy. *Murder on Lenox Avenue?* I was there! *After Dark in Harlem?* Right there too!

Growing up in those days it was not possible to get into a fight and drag your bones home looking the worse for wear, let alone having come off second best. That was a complete no-no. If you had fought and lost you had another whippin' comin' to you from Dad when you got home. With me I'm sure a lot of that stemmed from my being the oldest child, but whatever it was, I was expected to look out for all of my younger sisters and brothers.

I had lots of girlfriends, but a select few were real close. One was Connie Lee Spencer, nicknamed Bunky, then there was Barbara Jean Sanford. Bunky's still around, Barbara Jean entered the forces and was buried with full military honors in Arlington just a few years back. I remember sitting with Bunky and Barbara Jean on Bunky's mama's stoop, swingin' our legs in the morning sunshine, gassin', gigglin' and gawpin' at the cars going by. Across the street from Bunky's was a grocery store, and after a while her granny gave us some money to go buy ourselves some candy.

One day as we looked down the road before crossing we saw an object hitting the ground with a squelch, then bounce a little. We ran towards it, thinking it was a ball, but skidded to a halt when we saw it was a lady's head swathed in a white gossamer scarf that was rapidly turning scarlet. I don't recall who moved first because we were in shock, our appetite for candy or any other form of nourishment well and truly evaporated. It turned out that the lady had been to a beautician to have her hair done, and on arriving home a row had started with her husband, a Chinaman who ran a restaurant. The argument must have been a lulu, for it ended when he sliced her head clean off with a machete and tossed it out the window. By the time our local undertakers, Reid's, had arrived to take the pieces away the three of us had recovered our nerve sufficiently to deliver a lusty chorus, as their wagon was being loaded, of "I Ain't Got No-bo-d-y-y-y."

Days of the week were set as certain food days in the Weston household. Thursday I especially looked forward to, that was baked bean day. Mama boiled a pea bean, we called it a navy bean, serving it with baked sweet potato, a pan of cornbread or some hot biscuits, with a pitcher of lemonade to wash it down. Dad made his own ice cream in a small bucket freezer for dessert. He also made fruit cakes every year. We never knew what liquor it was he poured in there but boy, were they good!

Fish, mostly flounder or croak, was served on Sunday mornings with old-fashioned grits and rolls baked in a turkey roaster. Apart from fish I grew up eating very little fried food. Instead there was lots of onions and gravy, my dad's favorite. As far as he was concerned you could smother the world in onions and gravy and it would be a paradise.

When we caught a cold we were given onions fried in olive oil with a piece of lemon, stick of cinnamon and lumps of ginger added. A cabbage leaf on our brow eased a fever—in fact, all we ever had in our medicine cabinet was Vaseline, baking soda and two laxatives, Three Sixes and Raymond pills (how we hated to see those little pink suckers coming!). With all that good food and simple but effective medical care we were a pretty healthy bunch. And Mama's was an open house as far as any stray kids on our block were concerned, a place they could always be assured of a decent meal. A cup of water in the soup to make it go 'round? No problem.

Granny Ruth was a strange lady altogether, a houseproud fanatic who kept her henpecked husband, "Big Papa" William, on the shortest lead ever. His capacity for shrugging off her frequent tongue-lashings was nothing short of amazing. Even though I'm sure we all thought his patience would snap sometime, none of us imagined in our wildest dreams the terrible consequences that would result when the worm did finally turn.

Despite her carrying on, Granny Ruth was an inspiration to me as I grew up, decked out in her nurses' aide uniform for her work in elderly folk's homes, and for quite a while I harbored ambitions to be a nurse. At school I joined the Cadet Corps where we dressed in little capes like forces' nurses. I thought it was wonderful until we took our first field trip to a local hospital and I caught sight of all that blood. When they told us that a nurse should never get too attached to patients, that did it for me. Whenever I see babies I just want to hug and love them; that detachment would have been impossible. It's the same with the elderly; I always want to sit down and talk with someone who's lived all these years and share their experiences. They may be blind in the eye, like my great-grandmother Emily Baker, but they remember and talk about great and small events from way back, weaving a magic in verse and lyric that opens gateways to the past.

My dad had that gift, the ability to keep us enthralled for hours on end with the yarns he spun. And then there were the songs he made up that had us in stitches, the most ridiculous yet the sweetest stuff. One of our favorites began: "In the barnyard one night, by the pale moonlight, the vegetables was havin' a stew . . ." It went on: "The sweet potato did a flop with Mr. Turnip Top," then there was some nonsense about "the baby yam goin' on the lam with a real keen lima bean." This had all of us whoopin' and screamin' with every line. This ritual was usually conducted on the stoop after supper while Mama did the dishes. When he ran out of inspiration he'd pick up his trusty harmonica and just play the thing while we tried to recall the odd line, in between laughing fit to bust.

I can still hear him singing songs of a more serious nature, like the beautiful "Trees" and one of Hiram Simmons's compositions, "There Is a Hill Far, Far Away," and he was known throughout the church community for his rendition of "His Eye Is on the Sparrow." There was another tune he kept mostly to himself, we'd just hear snatches of it when entering a room he was in alone. It took me close on half a century to track down "They Say" and listen to the lyrics properly. When I did I searched for the significance they may have had in my dad's life. Whatever else, wistful yearning was in there in spades.

Christmas was one time of the year we might all have been brought face to face with our poverty, but dad found ways to get around this, at least for some of us. Knowing it was impossible to buy us all individual gifts, he tended to try and ensure that the girls always got something, even if it only meant an old pair of the boys' roller skates painted with high gloss silver paint and presented as new. For me it was a case of anything with a pretty butterfly motif in there someplace, for I was crazy about butterflies. The story handed down to us kids was that if you caught a butterfly and bit its head off, you'd get a dress the same color. Ugh! I could never even think about doing that.

Another Christmas scam was the presenting of a fully operational model railway to the latest son. Originally purchased for Leonard, Dad spirited it away a few months later, took it to pieces, reassembled it on Christmas Eve and presented it to Benny. And so on. At this festive time Dad and I had a famous annual argument, if I may presume to call it that, that lasted for years. I bought the lights for our Christmas tree, he bought the tree, and we always fought over who was to dress the darn thing. Believe it or not, he didn't always win.

Somehow over the years Dad scraped up enough cash to buy a beat-up ole piece of car we immediately dubbed the Green Hornet. It was a big deal at weekends when we all piled in and dad drove us out to Suffolk then back alongside the train tracks, trying to beat that loco to Portsmouth, blasting his horn while the engineer responded with his whistle.

Dad seldom dressed up except on Sundays, when he'd appear in his finest. How he managed to turn up so fresh was a mystery, for every man in town took a good drink with his pals on Saturday nights. It was a ritual, their God-given right, the one night they really cut loose after the week's toil. It got to be hard sometimes when he came on mean to Mama after a little taste. He was getting up to something, that much was obvious, but what it was remained Mama's secret for years. I used to see that green car parked outside different addresses from time to time, and run home and "tell." Mama just listened, nodded and carried on with her sewing.

During the week Dad and Big Papa William worked on the docks together, loading the seaboard trains, and they were handed a privilege pass once a year for any journey they cared to undertake. That was how, chaperoned by Granny Ruth, I was able to attend the 1939 World's Fair in New York. Our route was by ferry from Norfolk, the city across the Elizabeth River from Portsmouth, crossing the horseshoe to Cape Charles, then by train to New York. I was bursting for my first sight of the city and as we approached the rock through which the Harlem Tunnel had been blasted I saw a billboard advertising the fair that featured a clown's head with dancing legs that actually moved. At that precise moment Granny declared, "When we come out the other end of that tunnel we'll be in New York." I can still feel the chill that tingled my spine.

We stayed in Harlem for two weeks with Granny's eldest son William, nicknamed Monk, and his wife Eva, and during that visit I became aware not only of the larger world of the metropolis but of the wider world beyond. Germany had invaded Poland, and I remember Uncle Monk jumping up and down with joy when President Roosevelt's election was announced. Monk took me on the elevated tracks of the subway all the way out to Coney Island, then on to Flushing Meadow where the fair was being held. There was so much to see, but what I remember best, apart from the teeming crowds and holding on to my uncle so tight, was our ride together on the Ferris wheel and visiting Heinz's House of 57 Flavors. I thought I had died and gone to heaven.

EMILY BAKER, my great-grandmother on Mama's side, was born into slavery. Although she died in 1935 at age eighty-six, several vivid images of her survive. She may have been blind, but those milky eyes of hers had a way of staring you out, and it was quite a relief when she wore a patch. She kept an old rocker by the open fireplace in her North Carolina farmhouse that would creak, creak, creak as she snoozed and dreamed her dreams. Then she'd come to with a start if someone entered the room. "All right, all right, I kin hear you!" she'd declare, as if it were the devil himself she was challenging. In cold weather she'd feel her way out to the bucket and dipper on the porch, then scurry back right quick to the fireplace where she'd hitch her skirts up over her backside until she felt the warmth return.

Of her three daughters, Delia, Cindy and Ella, my Granny Delia was half-Cherokee, with the copper skin and high cheekbones of an Indian. That her husband, Benjamin Alston, was even lighter—and would you believe fair hair and blue-gray eyes?—led to the great tragedy of Mama's life. One day he just took himself off and disappeared into the white race.

Mama was eleven years old at the time. On the day he vanished she arrived home from school to find him hitching his champion

On my first trip to New York City in 1939. (COURTESY OF RUTH BROWN)

white horse, the one she loved to ride bareback, to their best buggy. Everyone else was away working in the fields as she watched her daddy, dressed to the nines in his cutaway coat, the type preachers wore, and striped hickory pants normally reserved for weddings, polishing his saddle and fixing up for his journey. After a while he strode back to the house and emerged wearing his kept-for-special wide-brimmed hat. Calling her over, he solemnly handed over two oranges. Using his pet name for her he said, "Plunk, Daddy's got to go away for a little bit. But you'll be hearing from me—and I love you." As she took fearful note of the large leather bag he had stashed away he saw the concern in her eyes. Easing himself into the buggy he said, reassuringly, "Don't worry, Plunk, I'll come back and git you."

As she reluctantly opened the swinging gate that led from their yard to the open road, a fine drizzle began to fall. Perching herself upon the gate as it yawned back and forth, she watched as her father turned the buggy in the direction of Warrenton, the nearest town. He waved back several times before disappearing over the brow of the hill, when the steady clickety-clack of his horse's hooves echoed still. There was nothing to break the terrible silence thereafter besides Mama's own racking sobs.

We hear a lot about "dancing lights" people claim to see nowadays, usually on some consecrated site. Mama said she saw them as a child, lights dancin' in back of a nearby church that was an old slave

burial ground. A few days before her father left for good she swears
those lights danced all the way up to their farmhouse and got themselves tangled up in his buggy wheels.

All her life, until the day she died, each time Mama walked along
a street she examined every face, still searching for her long-lost
dad. Word filtered back that he'd married a white woman from
Camden, New Jersey, before settling for a while in Philadelphia and
working for the Winchester rifle people.

Benjamin was one of those people called "issues" in those days,
too white to be black and too black to be white, who could still lay
claim to being white without having too many questions asked. His
mother could have been a slavemaster's favorite, and it's possible
that his children—if he dared to have any with a white woman—
would be considered white also. There's certainly a few hops and
skips in my family, with Mama being so light and Dad so dark.
Goldie is the darker of my two sisters, Delia the lighter (born with
auburn hair and green eyes!) and my four brothers, Leonard, Benjamin, Leroy and Alvin, run the gamut. Benny is fair like Mama,
Leroy is dark, Alvin darker still, Leonard darkest of all. I take my
complexion from Granny Delia, although she had even more of
that bronzed Indian look.

I was twenty years old and far away from home when my baby
brother Alvin finally made it into this world. Mama had been pregnant without even knowing it, and when he started to come she
delivered him at home all by herself. At first she thought he must
be stillborn, since he made no cryin', and I guess she was still
reeling from the shock of having him at all. Wrapping him in newspaper, she went to clean herself up. Then she heard a muffled
whimper and ran back to find he was alive. When I took the call to
say I had a baby brother I said, "It's impossible! You've got to be
kiddin'!" When I reached home to check it out for myself Mama
had him in a shoebox that was perched on a chair near the pot-
bellied stove in our kitchen. The little fella weighed less than two
and a half pounds. (There must be something in those Weston
genes. He weighs a hundred times that now and is bigger than any
of us!)

My father's side of the family is, like my Mama's, decidedly topsy-
turvy, not to say downright upsettin'. My paternal great-grand-

mother was, it seems, the original pistol-packin' mama, a rum-run-ner who sported double pistols worn criss-cross style. Great-grandad was a fisherman on the Chesapeake, working all up and down that river when he wasn't helping his wife run guns and liquor. I'm named after their daughter-in-law, Granny Ruth.

My father was the second of four brothers born to William and Ruth. First was William ("Monk") and after Dad ("Barrel") came George ("Gee") then the baby, Stafford ("Jug"). The Westons had a wooden shed in their backyard in Portsmouth, Virginia, that housed trophies handed down from Lord-knows-when-an'-done for-got. It was, after all, an Englishman who originally founded the town of Portsmouth in 1752 on sixty-five acres of his plantation lands. Maybe that accounts for the military hat in that shed, to-gether with the sheathed sword, french horn, violin and countless old books of the period. Big Papa was always ready to pose to his heart's content in that old hat. Me? I was happy just to sit there and travel the world by poring over those old volumes.

Having all that ancestry is kind of eerie, and what I'm talking about is only now being acknowledged as an integral part of our black history. In the years following the abolition of slavery, for example, when blacks were trying to find their way north it was often tribes of Indians that took them in and mixed the bloodlines. What I do know is that I have an instinctive love of Indian costumes, but more than that I cannot say, for when all is said and done I honestly don't know exactly what I am. I suspect I'm not alone. When Alex Haley and I talked for the last time he promised to help trace my family line, but he died before he could.

2

"LOOK WHAT THE MAILMAN BRUNG!"

YOUNG AND SUPPOSEDLY INSENSITIVE as we kids were, there was one character in town whose situation touched all of us deeply. There was no sadder sight than the man who had watched his wife board the Elizabeth River ferry for a shopping trip to Norfolk, then spent the rest of his days awaiting her return, faithfully reporting back to the quayside every afternoon. Everyone knew his story, everyone knew she'd skipped, but that didn't stop him waving to every arriving ferry until his death.

When school closed early in June each year I was dispatched by train the very next day, along with my brothers, sisters and cousins, to Norlina. Our ultimate destination was Macon, North Carolina, to help Granny Delia sharecrop her fields. Our train would be met either by Granny herself or by her brother, our great-uncle Tom Scott, yet another who bore those distinctive Indian features. We had an hour or so on their long wagon before we arrived at their farm, usually around suppertime. After we'd all hopped off Granny would say, "Alright, take them shoes *off*. Don't *even* come down here with them shoes on." That was her rule: bare feet on the ground, touch that good red-clay soil. I used to defiantly hide my shoes and wear them whenever she wasn't looking. Mama said that was why I ended up with the smallest feet in the family. Benny did the same and came close, growing to just a size seven.

Granny's two-story wood-frame house had a kitchen in the yard that dated back to the slavery period when the folks who did the cooking were housed outside. Not that the main house was in any way luxurious—it wasn't, it was downright basic—but the separate kitchen had the unarguable benefit of isolating the cooking smells.

Helping Granny D and her brother work that farm each summer was her only boy, our uncle Jesse. He left his timberyard business in Portsmouth behind for a couple of months—I guess we had enough relatives to mind the store while he was gone—and sometimes he brought along his wife Annabelle, their son and two daughters, and sometimes he left them behind. I remember thinking, with the mixture of honesty, spite and innocence that kids have, that if she was my wife I'd *always* have left her behind. I'd never heard the term *ball-breaker* before, but if I had, I'd have hung that sign 'round Annabelle's neck from the first moment I clapped eyes on her, yappin' away at her browbeaten husband. And she was no oil painting even then, while Jesse was tall, very handsome, light in color with thick black, wavy hair. In spite of his good looks I never did care for him, although he was Mama's only brother and I knew she loved him dearly. He called her "Sis Janie," which was foreign to me right off, but I kept my feelings to myself. Granny's other daughter, our Aunt Emily, was bedridden with consumption and kept isolated in a room not much bigger than a storage cupboard. She had skin that was almost translucent and never did look as if she was long for this world.

Then there was Uncle Willie, 'cept he was no uncle at all but someone Granny had adopted from the county home. He suffered from a speech impediment and had an unsettling habit of laughing when there was nothing funny going on. The first time I saw him go into one of his fits I was sure he was dying. Later I became familiar with the first signs. "Ooooh, *laaaaawdy,*" he'd croon, his eyes cloud-searchin'. Then he'd flop to the ground and the kicking and convulsing would start. To put it plainly, Granny D had got him cheap; although she paid him a wage it was more than covered by the allowance she got for his care. She was a canny business-lady, for Willie was strong as a horse and that's what counted.

All of us children bedded down on the first floor, up a staircase
with an open railing that made chasing each other in packs, which
we indulged in whenever Granny wasn't around, mighty hazardous.
On the right was the boys' room, on the left the girls', and we
usually slept five or six abed, packed like sardines in these unfamil-
iar tick's-paradise creations from way-back-when, the mattresses so
high the younger kids had to use a chair to scramble up. When a
couple of us got to sleep downstairs on a palette in the parlor that
was a special treat, for we were next door to the holy of holies,
Granny's bedroom. That gave us a grownup feeling that lasted exactly until we got our next spankin'.

Being the eldest and a girl I had to be up at four in the morning,
light or dark. I'd milk the cows by the light of an oil lamp, leave the
milk to cool for a while, churn some butter, bring the eggs in then
prepare breakfast for everyone. This consisted of a big biscuit called
a hoecake, together with fatback skins—slab bacon fried good 'n'
crispy—and a tray of scrambled eggs. I'd pour the bacon fat on a
plate and add homemade molasses in the middle. There would be
hot black coffee for the adults with that, the strongest I ever tasted,
and for the kids a big glass of milk, either sweet or, my favorite,
buttermilk. "Eat, eat, git some meat on your bones," Granny would
urge, producing her tempting homemade jelly just when we
thought we couldn't swallow another bite. By 6:00 A.M. the wagon
was hitched up outside and everybody was ready for their day's toil
in the fields.

Apart from salt, which we had to buy, we were well-nigh self-
sufficient on that farm. We made our own soap, used sugar cane to
make molasses, fashioned effective brooms from straw. We filled
our mattresses with what we called tick straw, wheat stalks cut into
short lengths that had a nasty habit of poking through the sacking
covers and jabbing right into you. Every now and then we were
forced to lift those mattresses off and attend to the box frame underneath, lighting a candle to burn off the ticks that had congregated there for the specific purpose of biting you half to death.
Granny used to say we had nothing to complain about unless we
woke up one morning and found the ticks carrying our beds outside. At least our pillows were comfortable, stuffed as they were with
duck down and chicken feathers. We'd sew them up in the eve-

nings, working outside by lantern light when the sun had gone down.

Granny had an abundant variety of crops, everything from wheat, barley and corn to tobacco, cotton, cucumbers, string beans, apples, peaches, plums, pears, black-eyed peas and white Irish potatoes. Close by the house she raised chickens, guinea hens, ducks and hogs. My brother Leroy was charged with the job of bringing in the livestock at night and feeding the hogs. Their meal consisted of dry ears of corn, mixed leftover slops and water. One night on his way to their pen he stepped on a snake and spilled both the slops and water in his fright. Scared to go any further in case the snake had brought its family along, he threw the corn in the direction of the pen. He saw that some of it fell short, but figured who would ever know in that tall grass? Come the following year that corn had taken root and was sprouting in fine style alongside the pen. "Okay," said Granny, eyeing him as he shifted uncomfortably while she nodded at the growth, "it seems we got ourselves a reg'lar *field o' corn* over there—*and you know why!* Go get Doctor Green!" That last, dreaded instruction was our cue to run outside and cut our own switch, Doctor Green, fresh from the tree—and God help you if that doctor wasn't big and nasty enough. Poor Leroy had a nasty start to his summer that year.

Granny D was gruff and tough, lean and mean, spry and full of energy. Already in her mid-fifties when I was first entrusted to her not-so-tender mercies, she was a lady who seldom displayed visible signs of affection to anybody. "Don't be sittin' down," she'd growl, *"I'm* standin' an' *I'm* older than you." She was a real little spitfire and I guess I got some of that from her. Mama told me the last time her mother embraced her was the morning her husband Benjamin walked out for good. After that Mama said she became hard and cold, a real disciplinarian. When she declared that we had to leave for those fields at six she didn't mean five after, she meant six. Most times she had a stick in her mouth that she chewed like a pipe. The only times I saw her remove it was at the table when she'd spit it to one side, or when she fancied a pinch of snuff, or to bawl one of us out.

Her field attire consisted of long skirts, a series of loose, layered tops, and always a scarf 'round her head knotted under her chin, with a straw hat perched on top. I saw her once or twice at bedtime in a beautiful calico nightgown, and she had long, gorgeous straight black hair that reached down past her shoulders. In her later years she took to wearing some sort of skull cap, and although nothing was ever said I gathered she'd lost her hair.

One of the worst things about Granny D was that she didn't always punish you at the time for a misdemeanor but often chose to save it up and zap you just when you were convinced she'd forgotten all about it. When Doctor Green had been fetched it was, "Okay, pull them damn clothes up, I ain't beatin' on no clothes, they cost too much money." She'd grab you by your shirt if you tried to run, pulling it over your head and twisting it, spinning you round and round 'til you didn't know if it was day or night, turning you tail-side up. Benny got it for hurling a corn cob at me once, cutting me near my eye. After she tended to me—snuff mixed with spit rubbed in—believe me, she tended to him.

Her style in selecting our evening repast was really something to see. She'd be out there feeding the chickens, rubbing away at those corn kennels, crooning, "Whoo, chick, chick," then all of a sudden she'd spot the exact one she wanted for the pot. In the blink of an eye she'd pick it up, twist and yank its head off, throw it down and wait 'til it was done running around headless, blood spurtin' everywhere.

One of my young cousins, new to the farm, had worked her way up a row of cucumbers and proudly presented her basket to Granny D. Thinking they were cuter than the green variety, the child had gathered the big, yellowing hog cucumbers, the ones left too long, the type—Lord have mercy!—that the pickling factory would never accept. Granny D took one look at them and fetched her a backhander across the mouth. The rest of us were just glad it hadn't happened to us, but we reached the stage of mutiny a few days later over another incident.

For several weeks a series of stray dogs had been turning up at the farm, the adoption of one leading inevitably to the arrival of another. The birth of a litter of puppies brought the refuge to an end. "I can't feed all them damn dogs," Granny declared, "and there ain't nuthin' I can do with them." As she loaded the litter into a sack we began crying and protesting, for it was clear what she intended to do. We still couldn't believe it when she carted them up on the buggy, mewling and whining, and drove to the nearest lake. There she weighted the sack down and let it drop like a stone. It upsets me even now when I recall the bubbles that came up.

We Westons decided that was *it*. For several days we saved lumps of lava bread, biscuits and whatever meat and fruit we could. Leaving our cousins to fend for themselves we stole out from our beds late at night, the food for our freedom flight packed in 'kerchiefs and tied, hobo-style, to sticks we all carried. By the time we'd gotten about three miles down the road we'd eaten everything. After a rapid pow-wow we decided we had no alternative but to go back—it was either that or face starvation on the road.

EVERY LIVING SOUL over five years of age was put to one type of work or other in the fields, picking or chopping cotton, stripping corn-stalks—"strippin' fodder," we called it—and gathering tobacco leaves. If we were working on that corn, Granny insisted we wear hats on our heads and stockings to cover our bare arms—the boys too, and how they hated it!—saying, "If you don't keep that dust off it'll stop your body breathin'." We took her word for that.

We worked all morning long until we heard Al Buggs, Granny's landlord, ring his bell at noon. You could always tell when that thing was about to sound, for you'd be raking away in the morning with your hoe and when you looked 'round your shadow would be at your back. By noon it had moved right around and if you could touch the head of it with your hoe, it was time. Sometimes you'd hear an indignant, "The bell is late!" if the shadow said so. When it did ring out it sounded like a cold water fountain, and it was just as welcome.

During my second summer at the farm I was allowed back to the house an hour early to prepare lunch. To get there I learned to ride a mule bareback, and although it wasn't the most comfortable mode of transport, and my muling was a far cry from Mama's horse-manship, it served its purpose. The meal would be something like corn fritters or baked sweet potato, picked fresh and cooked in the hot ashes of the fireplace inside the house. When everything was ready I'd pack the food in twin buckets, cover them with plates, put two strips under each handle and hang them round the mule's neck. After dropping them off back at the work site I'd take myself off to find a spring, using an old squash gourd to fill the emptied buckets. Granny always said, "Don't bring the water if there ain't no gudgens." She was referring to the little water bugs swimming around in there that looked like mosquitoes. That was the way, she insisted, you could tell if the water was safe to drink; if it was good enough for them gudgens, it was good enough for us. Hallelujah!

Echoes carried for miles in those fields, so we hardly dared to speak or misbehave for fear the sound would reach Granny's ears. If she did hear any raucous noises coming from our direction, she'd call up like some kind of demented bird: "Kwaaaaah, *kwaaaaaaak!*" We knew we'd better quit it, or else.

I remember my brothers slippin' off one day from strippin' fodder in favor of skinny-dippin' buck naked in a nearby creek. In their excitement they clean forgot how their voices would be carrying. Sure enough, Granny heard the commotion and began marching in their direction. She moved like she was jogging, jiggling her arms, chewing one stick and brandishing another. Her faithful Rottweiler Zip walked in front to protect her from snakes, stopping to carve a bite out of one of the critters whenever necessary. (That dog had been bitten so often you'd have sworn he must be immune, but he did eventually die from a snakebite.) When the boys heard her approaching—Zip gave the game away—they grabbed their britches and ran like crazy, all three pursued by a giant hook snake they'd disturbed in their panic. (You can bet it wasn't half as scary as the thought of Granny D's retribution!)

Picking cotton was hard, hard labor, especially with Granny as the pacesetter. She'd take two rows of the stuff and pick two hundred pounds a day, which a whole team of us struggled to match. We were required to gather one hundred pounds at a time to take to the scale without being laughed at, and one hundred pounds is a whole lot of cotton. Being devious children, of course we had all kinds of sneaky things we got up to, like dropping a few rocks in there to boost the weight. My brothers and male cousins had an even better idea: they "relieved" themselves on it, which made the cotton swell up. As fast as we developed these schemes to make our lives easier, Granny was right there on top of us, figuring it all out.

Benny was Granny D's favorite, first, last and always. This might be regarded as surprising in that he was the lightest-skinned of any of us and carried his absent grandaddy's name, a combination that should have made him as appealing to her as deadly nightshade. Contradictions like that kept us guessing, but there was no call to wonder how she felt about her daughter Martha's choice of husband. She let it all out in the fields, talking trash that upset us, most of all my poor dark brother Leonard. "Yore mama ain't never had but one good-lookin' child," she'd spit, "an' that's Benny. Why'd she have to take up with that black-faced nigger?" Poor Leonard took this personally and used to blubber all over his cucumbers as Granny glared in his direction. She frequently addressed him as "black boy" and otherwise made it clear she couldn't stand him. If physical proof were required, he got that too in the form of a beating most every day. Even mama wasn't immune from granny's junk when she visited. "Didn't I ever teach you nothin'?" Granny would snarl. "I *tole* you not to go marryin' no coal-black nigger!" Meanwhile Benny was the one allowed to quit early so he could heat the stoves up for supper.

Outside of church my musical diet in North Carolina consisted of spontaneous whoopin', shoutin' and hollerin' in the fields. Great-uncle Scott would usually be the one to start, just when we were flagging, then Willie would join in, providing little sketches of the blues as they plowed up and down the rows with their single blades. There was as much plain hummin' as there was singin', and they had instruments like jew's harps, simple comb and paper and penny-whistle flutes that didn't even cost a penny, they were nothing but lengths of sugar cane with holes punched through. The blues don't have to come from anyplace but the heart and soul of man, they don't require fancy orchestration, and they sure didn't get any from us as the sounds traveled from field to field, apart maybe from the counterpoint fellow toilers contributed. I remember Willie's stammer magically disappearing as he sang anything that came to mind. One minute it was:

> *I miss my baby,*
> *Wonder do my baby miss me?*

The next he'd be singin' about his ole mule:

> *Come on Bessie, walk a little fast,*
> *Got to git up to the house,*
> *I'se gittin' huuuuuunnggry!*

Many times it made no sense; Scott and Willie were simply enter-taining themselves, along with the rest of us, in that blazing hot sun. But the music they made was soaking in just as surely as the sweat was pouring out.

There were three trees in Granny's yard: a pecan, a walnut and a mimosa. The pecan had been all but swallowed up by a bench positioned alongside since time immemorial, where we used ham-mers to crack open the walnuts. They were the prizes when we played one of our favorite games—guessing the color of the next car over the hill. (The boys bet on the make; we girls didn't know all that technical nonsense.) We'd hear one chugging along in the distance and one of us would say, "Red!" If it was blue it'd be, "Aw, shucks!" followed by, "Gimme a walnut!" When I asked how that mimosa got there Granny said it had hitched a ride from Japan, what did I think? "That mimosa's been there since I was a girl," Mama told me. "All the tiny hummingbirds come to that tree." And so they did, a whole choir of them hovering, sipping and beat-ing their angel wings.

We never got paid for all the work we did, although we did go home after the summer laden with provisions like whole hams and pickled goodies. Apart from that it was "in the family," and that was considered enough. Granny did give me a pair of shoes at the end of our stay one summer. I don't recall which summer that was, but I sure know which one it wasn't. How? I'll tell you.

We worked many long hours in the fields with that tobacco. Each leaf had to be inspected individually on both sides, and after strip-ping they had to be graded, tied, wrapped and hung on sticks in the barn to dry out. The final process was curing, and for this we took turns sitting up in the shed all night making sure the fire stayed low. We'd been fed so many ghost stories, tales of the nearby slave burial ground ("They'll rise up and chew out yore innards if you as much as blink") that there were powerful reasons not to nod off, but that's just what I did in the early hours one morning. My innards were still intact when I woke up—I guess those ghosts must have been occupied elsewhere that night—but worse than that, the fire had flared up and burned the tobacco.

I simply cannot explain to you the depth and intensity of Granny's anger. Naturally I got one heckuva beating, and every time she looked at me for the longest time she'd glower and snarl, "You *nasty, stinkin' scoundrel!"* and yak on about the debt I'd get her into. It was the first time I'd ever heard the term "peonage." It meant that in her mind I owed her, big time. Together with Uncle Jesse she loaded the tobacco on her wagon anyway and hauled it off to the auction bond. They bought it, but for a much reduced price, claiming it was ruined. It was not my finest hour.

Al Buggs, the white king of the hill, was a gentle, soft-spoken guy we always recognized coming a mile away in his trademark dungarees and an old straw hat, and he had a large family up there in that sprawling house of his. We didn't see too much of his sons and daughters—like us, they were sent away for the summer; unlike us, it was to summer camp. As for his wife, she hadn't put in an appearance for years. We knew she was poorly, "bothered with her nerves" or "high strung," as Mama put it.

Although Granny D and her two sisters each sharecropped nine acres of Buggs's land, he was real close with Delia. If there was some little item or other she needed, she'd go up to see Buggs and invariably come back with it. She glared at me when I called him "Uncle Al" once, and nearly snapped my head right off: "He ain't no kin o'yores! It's *Mister* Buggs!" Granny D was the first to have the house and fields handed over to her, ending her sharecropping days. If they were ever lovers, and there was plenty of speculation, it's a secret they both took to their graves.

MY YOUNGEST SISTER was born on Granny's farm and named Delia after her. Mama, heavily pregnant, had joined us in North Carolina that year. That was unusual, but the birth was due in the revival month of August and it seemed a fitting time to come back to her roots for a spell. At the time I was ten, and we still believed Granny's story that the postman delivered babies. The morning Delia May was born I was sitting in the yard with the rest of the kids, when suddenly we heard this "Waaaaaa!" Granny came out holding a little bundle aloft, declaring, "Look what the mailman brung!" Well, we took a peek and were not at all impressed. What *was* this strange carrot-topped creature with the funny eyes? Next morning my brothers lay in wait for that postie, armed with a pile of rocks. As they threw them in the poor man's direction they shouted, "You brung us this *real ugly* baby!" That was my sister Delia.

Buggs employed a handyman the following summer we knew simply as Oliphant. He was a burly individual who looked to have mixed antecedents of his own. Swarthy can be attractive, but not his brand, and even less appealing is a terrible case of flatulence. Wherever he was you could hear a steady "phut, phut, phut" as he motored along. His eyes and hands were forever wandering as well, and it got to a point where he started coming 'round Granny's place far more often than necessary. He'd brush past me in a way that made me figure, even at thirteen, that he had more on his mind than just delivering messages.

I was home preparing lunch one day and had just packed the potatoes under the ashes when I sensed the presence of someone else in the room. I spun around and there stood Oliphant with a slack, stupid grin on his face, rubbing his crotch. Panic took hold of me; I dropped the poker with a clatter in the grate and looked right, left and all around for the nearest escape route, but with a couple of strides he was on me before I had a chance to move, hands reaching under my clothes, calloused hands everywhere, fingers probing where nobody but myself had touched before. I twisted, managed to pull away and backed myself halfway into the fireplace. Why I didn't just pick up that poker again and let him have it I'll never know. Instead I kicked some potatoes out from under the ash, stooping down to grab one in each hand. Please don't ask me what I intended to do with these deadly weapons, for I don't have a ready answer.

As he grinned and phut-phut-phutted at the fight I was putting up, the sound of an automobile outside screeching to a halt wiped the smile from his face. Hitching up his pants and tucking away his thing, in a very loud voice he said, "Now be sure to tell yore granny that Mr. Buggs needs that stuff right away." Then he was out that door lickety-split, phut-phut-phutting as if his life depended upon it. I dropped the potatoes, adjusted my clothing and ran outside to see who had saved me from the fate worse than death my girlfriends back in Portsmouth had been yakkin' on about all spring. An elderly white couple were sitting there in a battered convertible, beyond which I could see Oliphant scampering across the fields. "Is this the Sproules' dwelling?" the old gentleman asked. I directed him there, then went back inside and resumed making lunch.

That evening Granny D actually showed concern when she saw me cooling the palms of my hands. "How'd you *do* that?" she asked. "I got careless handling those hot potatoes at lunchtime," I replied, "but it could have been worse." She gave me the longest look. "You should be more careful," she scolded, but her voice was gentle. "There's some ointment in the medicine cupboard that'll ease yore blisterin'." It did. And we never saw hide nor hair of Oliphant again.

GRANNY D'S MAIDEN NAME was Baker and the Bakers were close kin to the Powells. Uncle Ben Powell and his wife Elma lived close by, Aunt Cindy and Cousin Mirabelle too, all of them sharecropping. Cindy was a sweet lady, once you got adjusted to the way she looked —she had an enormous goiter at her throat that, big as it was, was almost completely covered by a full-grown beard. She walked with a stick like Granny's and lived with just a dog for company. The sisters would trade off whatever they needed between them, be it a hog or a tobacco slab. We didn't see too much of Aunt Ella, who lived in another part of the county.

One way or another we were all related, or so Granny made out when it suited her. When one of my brothers was caught making calf eyes at a girl she'd snap, "None o' that, now! Don't be lookin' at her, she's yore cousin!" Despite Granny D's protests there were a few non-relatives around as well, like the Shepherds and the Sproules, and we all pitched in with them when there was a crop to be harvested or chores needed to be done.

The place we all met once a week without fail was the Lovely Hill Baptist Church, in Macon. Although all of us Westons had been christened in Portsmouth's Methodist church, when we were in Macon we'd rise up early each Sunday, get washed, dressed and fed, collect the mule and be at that Baptist church for the rest of the day. That's where I got my first chance to testify, to work in the service of the Lord, when at Granny's insistence I spent seventeen days on the mourner's bench. That's where sinners sit in the rural churches down South, listening to the preacher until they feel the Holy Spirit enter their bodies. "Sit still 'til the spirit moves you," Granny D told us. When it did, and we could feel the Holy Spirit enter our bodies, we were ready to give our souls to Christ; our souls were converted to Jesus.

The first time every single one of us faked it—Goldie, Leroy, Benny, Leonard and me. We planned our moves the night before the ceremony, exactly when we were going to rise up. We'd already seen how the deacon and his elders danced when the spirit entered, and we had our own little jig well choreographed. There's no need to tell you that Granny D cottoned on to us in no time flat. "Okay, okay," she muttered after balefully studying our performances, her hands planted firmly on her hips. Then she picked us off one by one, giving us the father and mother of a lickin'. *"That's for hoppin' up and playin' with God! You don't* ever *do that!"* she yelled between smacks. It was back to the mourner's bench and start again from scratch. This time we stayed there until we really could feel something, even if it was just a sore butt from the beatin'.

Mama's sister Emily died in Granny D's house when I was five years old, and I have vivid memories of being just tall enough to stand looking over her bed while she lay by the window wasting away. In those days they had what they called a cooling board where they laid the body out straight in the house—not in boxes, they didn't do that until the night before the burial. I watched as Granny bathed her dead daughter's body and dressed her in fresh clothes, all the while with an expression on her face she silently dared anyone to define.

Everyone came to see her lying on that board and pay their last respects, even far-flung Aunt Ella making the trip to bid her niece farewell. Then we sat up all night 'round lanterns, chanting prayers while the shadows on the walls, like a ghostly second gathering, flickered and danced.

3

FORCES' SWEETHEART

THE RECORDS I HEARD over the radio as I grew to maturity were by people like the Andrews Sisters, Bing Crosby, Vaughn Monroe, Hank Williams, Red Foley, pop and country more than anything else. At that time the main stations did not play so-called race records by black artists. I got to hear them on a local station program called "The Mailbag," courtesy of a deejay named Jack Holmes. I listened every morning as I got ready for school—after Dad had left for work, that is. We'd never have dared turn it on while he was there—it was "the devil's music"—but as soon as he trotted out that door we switched the dial.

That's how I began to hear wonderful stuff by artists like the Ink Spots, the Charioteers and the great Buddy Johnson Band, featuring Arthur Prysock as an exciting new young singer. Hadda Brooks was the first vocalist I heard singing "Trust In Me;" another favorite was Una Mae Carlisle with "Walkin' by the River." There was one show that pleased both Dad and me, "Wings over Jordan," where I took in marvellous groups like the Southernaires and the Golden Gate Quartet.

The first time I had met Uncle Monk during that World's Fair trip, the war in Europe had just been kicking off. Our second meeting, during a visit he made to Portsmouth, coincided with the Japanese attack on Pearl Harbor and America's entry into the conflict. Monk was a real livewire and arrived in town with a novelty in the form of the first portable Victrola I had ever seen. He also brought several Billie Holiday records with him, my first chance to hear the amazing Lady Day. Dad, I am sure, was more than a little concerned that all this excitement might prove a corrupting influence on his daughter, for it was church music alone he felt I should be listening to. He put up with it, though, largely out of respect for Monk.

By this time, in any case, I had already started to sit up and take notice of vocalists and bands who visited the black clubs in our area, like the Big Track Diner across in Norfolk. Betty Roche appeared there, as did "Doc" Wheeler and Oran "Hot Lips" Page. I also caught Honey Brown from Detroit and Maude Thomas from Baltimore; to me these people were all stars of the first rank. I dearly wanted to discuss my developing interest in singing for a living, but I knew Dad would hit the roof if I did. I had to sneak out to see these shows, with Mama and my brothers and sisters covering for me.

There was one hot item that kept me on what Dad regarded as the right track—attached to the church, that is. Soon after graduating from the Flowers of Emmanuel, the little butter-ain't-gonna-melt angels who collected the money to keep the church decked out in fresh blossoms, I got my first crush when I hit the junior choir. The dreamy object of my affections, although I'm sure he never imagined it for one moment, was the tall, scholarly and outrageously handsome preacher man, the Reverend Charles E. Stewart. After seeing *Gone with the Wind* for the umpteenth time one of my cousins came out with the remark that she would sell her soul to the devil just to spend one night in Clark Gable's arms. I thought that was ridiculous, until I got a load of this awe-inspiring pastor! There was something so special about the way his black jacket draped over his fine, athletic frame, not to mention the way he filled out those hickory pants all the way down from his long danglin' watchchain to his black polished boots, even to the wire spectacles perched so cute on his nose. Dad was known around church as Big Weston, because of his muscular baritone voice rather than his stature, and Reverend Stewart used to turn round in the middle of the Sunday service—with me positioned in the choir directly behind his chair, singing my heart out to get his attention!—and say, in a voice that seemed to emanate from underground caverns and with a smile that would melt ice caps, "I *know* Little Weston is here this morning!" Ooh, my soul!

That wiry preacher-man apart—and do I got to tell you absolutely nothing ever happened?—there was a rebel streak in me that could not be denied for long. I was desperate to sing, and being surrounded by army and navy bases—Little Creek, Camp Fort Eustace, Camp Lee, Langley Field—there was no shortage of clubs around, and the demand for entertainment was then at its peak. There were also several United Service Organizations, USOs, and the local For Coloreds Only was a few blocks from my school, right where the train tracks crossed. When I heard one day they were looking for a server at the soda fountain, that was my cue. I got myself in there whisking up milk shakes, my devious way of getting my foot in the door.

My boss there was a gentleman named Lavoisier Lamar, transferred from the Harlem Y to direct operations. At first I didn't push things, just let it be, until one day my I. C. Norcum school class visited and a few of the amateur groups we had formed were invited to do their stuff on the main stage. As one-third of the Norcum Sweethearts I sang "Down in the Valley." Nervous as I was, I saw Mr. Lamar listening intently, and after we were through he came over to talk. "You've got quite a voice," he told me. "Have you ever thought of doing anything with it? Would you like to come on the show here?"

"I'd love to," I replied, "but my daddy would kill me."

He suggested that he would be prepared to take to my parents about it, but I was scared and put him off. Instead I told Dad that my hours at the USO had been extended, and I began singing with the band after my stint at the soda fountain. There was no pay involved, but I loved everything about it, especially the soldier boys' response. Little me, the forces' sweetheart! These boys just went wild. Dad's hours were from four P.M. to midnight at that time, so I was safe as long as I did a Cinderella. In theory at least.

One night when I was halfway through "Chattanooga Choo-Choo" he marched right in there—oh, Lord have mercy—and headed down the center aisle, a grim expression on his face. He didn't have to say anything, for I was caught red-handed; I had lied and said I was attending choir practice that night. There was just that look, like Granny D's when the entire Weston brood had faked being moved by the Spirit at the Lovely Hill Baptist Church. I was so embarrassed, but I knew the best thing was to get off that stage mighty quick. He began to slide his belt off as I did, and when I met him halfway down the aisle he growled, "It makes no sense to wait. You *did* it here, I'm gonna *whip* you here."

That was my first public whipping from Dad, in front of an incredulous audience of a twelve-piece band and two hundred raw recruits. *The forces' sweetheart!* And I got my second only a few weeks later. By then I had my first steady, a boy who lived across from the Capitol movie theater. We were in the back row necking when Dad found us. Was I too old to get a whippin' goin' on fifteen? Forget it!

My companion in the balcony was Alvin, a kid just a couple of years older than me. He hailed from Wilson, North Carolina, and young as he was, he could have been the original smooth-talkin' papa. He was an immaculate dresser and possessed keen, handsome features. He oozed charm and spoke with the dialect of a well-educated individual, with no trace of a Southern accent. I never inquired too closely into how he earned his living, although I heard tell he had connections with the guys running the policy numbers game, where a single penny could get you fifty dollars if your luck was in. He and his elder brother Robert lived with their Aunt Claudia, who was nice enough to let me stop by from time to time. That was when I could get away without Dad knowing, for he had a word to describe Alvin, or what he referred to as his "type." *Slick* was Dad's ultimate definition of disapproval, neatly caging Alvin in the box marked "Not worthy of my daughter's hand," or any other part of her, for that matter. It wasn't that he disliked Alvin personally, once the incident in the Capitol had faded from memory, but Alvin's being "slick" just counted him out.

My escape route when Dad wouldn't allow me to leave the house was a tree outside my bedroom window which I'd shinny up and down. This worked fine until Beauty, a stray mongrel we took in, refused to let me in one night and woke the whole house with his barking. Next day Dad sawed the branches off and that was the end of that.

Alvin and I went through what many youngsters experience before we really got our act together physically, doing everything else *but,* sending hot and cold running shivers through each other without actually consummating the act. One night it was different. It happened behind Our Lady of Victory, the local Catholic church, a regular lovers' rendezvous. We were standing there, smooching hot and heavy in the pitch dark. I had about twenty minutes before I had to show my face at home, for that was when the witchin' hour became the whippin' hour. Alvin was doing his level best, and I sure was ready. Just when all that graspin', pokin', clutchin' and squeezin' seemed to be headed no place, I gasped as something much thicker, longer, hotter and more insistent than his finger began its slide inside me. We'd made it, we'd hit it, vertical though we were.

I think I deserved at least an Oscar nomination, if not the award itself, for the sassy way I breezed in at home, with only a couple of minutes to spare, and coolly answered dad's "I hope you worked hard tonight" with a matter-of-fact "I sure did" before heading upstairs to bathe my poor bruised self.

During the eighteen months I hung out with Alvin I took up with another boy as well, a young serviceman from Baton Rouge, Louisiana, named Walter Laboeuf. Dad was most impressed with him, and naturally I kept it from Alvin that I had a marine with a big crush on me. Truth to tell, the feeling was mutual, for I had never seen anything as beautiful as Walter in my life (I'm not forgetting the pastor; but hey, Walter was *attainable!*) And if Walter was a killer in his khakis, you should have caught him in his dress blues. In the parlance of the day, he made my liver quiver! There was no problem with our spending time together, either, for I was right behind that soda counter after school and he would hang around the USO and make eyes at me for hours on end. Sometimes we'd play a game or two of ping-pong in the games room, although it was not too long before we got 'round to less innocent assignations of the horizontal variety.

He always turned up to watch when I rehearsed with the band in continuing defiance of my dad, and he regularly visited my home, for Mama loved Walter too. He was a tall son of a gun who loped rather than walked, and he had the most handsome baby face imaginable, about which Mama used to tease him. "How your mama 'low you to enlist?" she'd ask. "Why, you ain't nuthin' but a little bitty baby!'' He'd laugh, hold his head down shyly, and reply, ''Oh, I'm old enough, ma'am.'' *So* cute and with such becoming politeness!

It was a real proud time when I looked out my bedroom window and saw Walter heading towards our door, all spruced up and sexy in his uniform. It couldn't last, and it didn't, for all too soon he found himself shipped abroad. A few letters trickled through over a couple of months, then they stopped. I've never forgotten him, for Walter was a sight to behold, in or out of his uniform. And it was a romantic and sentimental time with young men going off to war and the radio churning out tunes like ''When the Lights go on Again (All Over the World)'' and the Andrews Sisters' ''Don't Sit Under the Apple Tree (With Anyone Else but Me).'' The favorite, though, for young black girls whose sweethearts had gone to fight for their country was ''Sweet Slumber 'Til Dawn ('Til the Last Star is Gone).'' That really hit us where we lived.

By this time, in the way that one thing leads to another, word had spread from the USO about my singing and I was beginning to pick up the occasional paid gig round those army bases. Soon a bunch of airmen from Langley Field air force base helped put some money together for a train ticket to New York for me to try my luck at the Apollo's Amateur Night. This was all the rage then, with families throughout the South tuning in to the once-a-week hourly broadcast each Wednesday evening.

Tiny Bradshaw led the band on my big night, and I sang ''It Could Happen to You,'' which I'd heard Mr. Crosby croon on the radio. I got a tremendous reception and the emcee, ''Doc'' Wheeler, had to run right after me yelling, ''Hey, come back, come back!'' I did, and was forced to sing the song again, which they told me was an Apollo first. I won the first prize of fifteen dollars, and the offer of a week's engagement. I grabbed the money but declined the booking, figuring that I had pushed my luck far enough. It was back to Virginia with my big secret, keener than ever to spread my wings.

With Walter's example set in Dad's mind, Alvin became a bigger no-no than ever before, and Dad kept on at me constantly that I should promise never to see him again. I wouldn't promise, and it caused quite a fuss at home. At that stage it was at the level of a family disagreement. If only it had stayed that way. Matters came to a terrible head one night—leaving one dead and another in prison, his life in ruins—as I was preparing to leave the house and meet Alvin at the USO. Dad had recently surprised us all by quitting the yards and starting work at Sam Solomon's hardware store. He arrived back unexpectedly early, and had obviously enjoyed a good few snorts on the way. He took one look at my snazzy outfit and said, "And just where d'you think you're going?" I started to say "Choir practice" and changed it to "Work" halfway through. He knew I was lying and growled, "Send word you ain't goin'."

"But—"

"Don't 'but' me," he cut in. "You ain't goin' an' that's that." I could see he was in no mood to be messed with so I went back upstairs and sat on my bed, moodily staring at the patterns the rain was painting on my window.

Unknown to me, Dad had reluctantly bitten the bullet and accepted my USO outings, having extracted a promise from Lamar that he would do everything in his power to discourage the relationship between me and Alvin. Meanwhile, all on his own, Alvin had gotten it into his head that Lamar was playing fast and loose with the female staff at the club and, probably because of the way he was being treated as a result of Dad's visit, with me in particular. That night when I didn't show, Alvin started asking Lamar's staff where I was. When Alvin started a commotion in the lobby, Lamar was sent for. His arrival on the scene was like showing a red rag to a bull. Alvin just flew at him, fists swinging. Lamar was taken completely by surprise at the ferociousness of the attack, having no idea of the pent-up passion behind it. Staggering back, he reached for the nearest weapon he could find. This happened to be a broken chair leg, and when Alvin rushed him again he brought it crashing on his head, felling him down the steps and on to the pavement outside. What nobody could have known was that, following an accident years earlier, Alvin had a steel plate implanted in his skull . . .

It was Goldie who ran through the glistening wet streets with the news—Goldie, my regular alibi, my faithful cover, who really did attend choir practice regularly and usually called in at the USO on her way back to accompany me home. Dad had dropped off to sleep by this time and here was my sister, terribly distressed, calling my name from the foot of the stairs. "What's the matter?" I yelled back, suddenly anxious; I'd been sitting there half in a dream, hoping to hear Alvin's whistle, his signal to slip out and meet him if the coast was clear. Instead, a nightmare was beginning. "Alvin's hurt real bad, Ruthie, real bad. He got into a fight with Mr. Lamar and they can't get him to wake up. I think maybe that poor boy's dead."

I screamed, rushed back into my room and began frantically pulling my shoes on. The noise woke Dad up and he was there before me on the landing when I came out. "Hold it, hold it, stop right there," he ordered, then came the self-same question he'd asked not half an hour earlier, "Where d'you think you're goin'?"

"Alvin's hurt, maybe dead," I wailed.

"Well, I don't give a damn. You git back in that room an' stay there."

There are times in every person's life, I'm sure, when a stitch gets dropped that can never be picked back up. "Well, I don't give a damn either," I shouted hysterically, and pushed past him down the stairs and out our front door.

With Goldie at my back we ran the four blocks over and seven across that took us to the USO. A crowd was standing in front of the familiar glass-paneled door, picked out in the club's floodlighting, while lights from the stationary ambulance blinked away. There was Alvin's body, blood streaming from his head, being loaded onto a stretcher and carried inside. I felt my arms being pinned behind my back as I tried to follow, then the ambulance was moving off, its siren shrieking in the night. All that remained of the struggle was a scarlet stain on the pavement that the rain was fast washing away. Goldie put her arms around my shoulders and squeezed as I dropped to my knees in that lashing rain, screaming and sobbing, and as she did, a train siren began to sound. I remember thinking at first that they were bringing Alvin back, that he was all right after all, that maybe none of this was really happening.

Alvin was dead on arrival at the Parkview hospital, killed by that one freak blow.

* * *

DESPITE THE STATE I WAS IN, Dad cussed me out when I got home. It was different next day when he was sober, but no matter how regretful he acted it fell a long way short, especially when I found out about his little talk with Mr. Lamar. There was no comfort for me at all in the days that followed, apart from Mama's shoulder to cry on. Alvin's brother and aunt turned their backs on me, refusing even to allow my school group to sing the lament at his funeral. Dad had the decency to accompany me there, but still it wasn't enough. He and I had crossed a line.

The whole episode had left me thunderstruck, and in the weeks ahead I was angry at everybody. That did nothing to help, and things got no better. Mr. Lamar was placed under arrest, and initially the charge was first-degree murder. They changed that to manslaughter just before his trial, where I had to take the witness stand. The newspapers were full of it, real nasty stuff about the alleged goings-on at the For Coloreds Only USO, how it had been common knowledge that Lamar carried on with all the girls in there—oh, and that was only the tip of a very large iceberg! A lot of it was inspired by our own sanctimonious church elders, who portrayed the place as nothing less than the devil's den. All they were doing, if they had only had the brains to realize it, was playing into the hands of the holier-than-thou white community, who eagerly seized this stick to beat us. I knew it was all nonsense, I had never seen the slightest evidence of what they were saying, and certainly Mr. Lamar had never been anything but a perfect gentleman to me. That righteous innuendo turned me off from my hometown; the whole place began to feel too small. Lamar's wife and children traveled down from New York to hear the verdict of ten years' imprisonment, with no chance for parole before a minimum of five years was served. The lady had to be helped out of the courtroom, her bewildered kids crying behind her as their father and breadwinner was led away.

The way Dad acted on the night of Alvin's death pulled the plug on my emotions. All of a sudden, barely sixteen years old, I became an adult. There was simply no question now that I was going to leave home and try to achieve my goal of singing professionally. I had discovered, working army bases, that my voice could earn me good money, that I could make as much from one or two nights' singing as my Dad could in a whole week. As I prepared for the inevitable break I kept myself going with local gigs in Norfolk, Newport News and Virginia Beach.

Dad's warning when I did take off fell on deaf ears, although I had no doubt whatsoever that he meant every word he said: "Once you leave, don't come crawlin' back here for nothin'. An' remember—you ain't leavin' here with my blessin'." Mama? Out of his sight, she gave me the tightest hug of my life. It was all I needed to know. And years later when she insisted on naming her premature, unexpected youngest son Alvin, those that had a mind to understood where she was at.

I may not have gone far initially, but leave I surely did, a lifetime of memories, it seemed, already stored deep inside me. It was 1945 and the times they were a-changin'. Not just for the young woman that skinny little Ruth Alston Weston had become, but for the rest of the world as well. A black ball-player, Jackie Robinson, was about to be signed to the Brooklyn Dodgers. World War II was ending, soldiers were coming home, peace was breaking out.

And I had broken out.

The butterfly had taken flight.

4

"THE GIRL IS DEAD"

MY FIRST JOB after leaving home was in Norfolk, precisely five minutes by ferry across the Elizabeth River from Portsmouth. It was at the same Percy Simon's Big Track Diner on Church Street where I'd caught so many visiting acts. I recall thinking that Dad would at least have approved of the address, if absolutely nothing else. Despite the harshness of our break I still loved him and realized that whatever he had done, no matter how misguided, had been for what he considered my own good. And I somehow knew that eventually I would be redeemed in his eyes. Meantime I was off working for the devil, although the ready answer for that was, "Why should he get all the good stuff?"

If Dinah Washington was well on her way to fame as the Queen of the Blues, I was surely Queen of the Paratroopers as I went on to tour forces' bases nonstop. I hit Camp Lejeune in Greensboro, North Carolina, Fort Bragg in Columbus, Georgia, and on to Fort Bennett in Hopkinsville, Kentucky, where the boys streamed down from Fort Knox.

After a few months of this I teamed up with Raleigh Randolph's band. That came about very simply: he and an unknown young comedian named Redd Foxx were on the same bill with me at the TWA Club in Newport News, close to home. Raleigh's singer flounced out one night and I was hired as her replacement. I worried for a couple of weeks that she might flounce back in, since she and Raleigh had had a thing going, but she never did. As for Redd, he was destined to play a key role in my life three decades later.

Back in Norfolk on an engagement with Raleigh, I met a young midshipman named Jimmy Earle Brown, at eighteen just a year older than I. He took to moseying on over nights whenever he could skip his depot, and to sitting in with the band. He was pretty fair on trumpet and did some vocalizing as well. In between numbers we sat and talked and traded experiences, until it got to the point where I watched anxiously for his arrival. He was an attractive devil, and he knew it. As I was still pretty slim back then, Jimmy's nickname for me was "Runt." I was far from offended; he could have called me anything he wanted and gotten away with it.

He must have lied about his age when he enlisted, for he got his discharge during our engagement, and next thing I knew he joined Raleigh's band. We were scheduled to travel to Savannah, Georgia, next, and in no time at all Jimmy and I were duetting both on stage and off. Leaving home was one thing, taking up so soon with another "slick" son of a gun quite another; I could just hear Dad coming out with that word as soon as he clapped eyes on Jimmy. And yes, I did still care what he thought. Hoping against hope it would keep him off the scent if he saw the band advertised, I conjured up our professional name of Brown and Brown. And to keep anybody else from talking, I began spreading it around that Jimmy and I were married. On stage we sang numbers like "If I Didn't Care," "Trust in Me" and others I'd heard on the radio or in juke joints. I sang one verse, Jimmy followed with the next. He was a real crowd-pleaser, reaching out to all those young girls in front of the stage, touching and stroking their hands, crashing down on his knees, legs splayed, as he reached the end of his solo. He reveled in the hysterical reaction he got, and Raleigh had no cause for complaint, for it meant steady business.

As the months flew past and word spread, Brown and Brown became a big feature attraction on the circuit. My ballads stirred up a storm, Jimmy's acrobatics pressed all the right buttons and Raleigh's band began to grab press attention. When we returned to Georgia, this time working Gus Hayes's Lincoln Inn, we shared the bill with another outfit led by "Hot Lips" Page. The trumpeter really took a liking to Jimmy and started giving him lessons on trumpet and saxophone, even sitting him down at the piano. Jimmy took to this like a duck to water, for he had music in his bones.

Listening to Raleigh talk I had visions of Brown and Brown heading for the bright lights of New York or Los Angeles. I was seizing this red-hot career chance with both hands, and there was no question I was in love and it was going to last forever. All this, and beyond Dad's reach. Raleigh soon punctured my pretty balloon with news of a change of plan. The band was returning to Norfolk! After all the publicity we had attracted I knew it was only a matter of time before Dad traced me and instantly realized I was closer to Jimmy Brown than merely doing the boogie on stage. And I also knew it would take him less than fifteen minutes to reach Norfolk and check us out. There had to be an answer.

After traveling back through North Carolina we hit Elizabeth City, just thirty-five miles from Portsmouth. To get married then all you had to do was have a blood test and hand your little piece of paper to the local justice of the peace. So that is what we did, because I knew Dad would be pacified if it was legal and aboveboard. He was still far from pleased when the time came for the great reunion and reconciliation—guess what, Jimmy was too slick! —but the deed was done. Or so I thought.

I don't recall how exactly, maybe I was just being a nosy wife, but Jimmy left his wallet behind one day and when I picked it up a piece of paper fell out. It was a newspaper cutting reporting another marriage of Jimmy's just six months before we'd met. I confronted him with it and he couldn't deny it. I told him that my Dad would kill him and ran home crying with my tale of woe. I hated to do it and it took a lot of pride-swallowing, but I really had no choice. Sure enough, Dad's exact words were *"I'll kill him!"* Right on cue. I begged him to calm down and tearfully pointed out that Jimmy's father didn't know about the "other one" either (Jimmy had volunteered that much). Dad got hold of his number and called him up. Mr. Brown was mortified, and it turned out that my husband was just as scared of his dad as I'd been of mine. Both fathers had Christian names in common, together with deep religious beliefs. Jimmy's dad and stepmother made the trip hotfoot to Portsmouth from their home in Topeka, Kansas, determined to sort the mess out.

Every town in the south had its own prominent black lawyer. Ours was a gentleman named Tom Reid; another "issue," incidentally, but one who had chosen to remain with his people. When he had our marriage annulled Jimmy turned round and pleaded that it was me he really loved, that we'd always be together no matter what a piece of paper said, that it was all over with that first marriage in any case, that it had been a terrible mistake. He cried— Lord knows he cried. We had our music, he would mend his ways, all that stuff. I listened, but it put a dreadful strain on what was left of our relationship. Off we went, with both dads promising to keep a close eye on how matters developed.

It was a new beginning in more ways than one, for Raleigh had left us behind and engaged a new team while we sorted out our difficulties. Jimmy's solution, which had a lot to commend it if we could bring it off, was to organize a band of his own, with me the star vocalist. That's how "Jimmy Brown and the Band of Atomic Swing, featuring Ruth Brown" came to be, and for a while we did just fine—when we got paid, that is, for we soon discovered that that did not happen automatically. Life on the road with that six-piece band had its fair share of ups and downs, thanks to a school of promoters who were nothing more than sharks.

As the summer of '47 approached, bookings became few and far between for the Band of Atomic Swing. That was my cue to suggest something so illogical, so outrageous, so all-fired *ridiculous,* that I have trouble to this day believing I did it. It took a whole lot of coaxing, but I got Jimmy to disband our group for a couple of months so the two of us could take off for the fields of North Carolina to help out Granny D. What had started it was Mama's telling me that she intended to go.

Our arrival coincided with a major crisis. It seemed that since I had last been on the farm Mama had persuaded Granny D to have her house wired up so she could enjoy the luxury of electric light and a refrigerator. All had gone fine until Granny got her first bill. "Have you *seen* this!" she yelled, hurling the offending notice at mama. "Git that damn stuff outta my house!" The bill was for seven dollars.

Once that was resolved Jimmy and I settled in to life on the farm. Before long even his callouses had callouses, but he put in a day's work, I'll say that for him, even though it was of the woodchoppin' variety. Close to the house, that is. Fieldwork was out, for he was petrified of those snakes.

It was a strange period in my life, one that provided a rare and welcome respite from the showbiz grind I'd gotten into, a kind of last hurrah for my childhood. Granny's reaction to Jimmy, a disdainful snort whenever their paths crossed, brought me down to earth with a resounding thud. "Another black-faced coon," I heard her mutter to Mama, who winced at the insult that she had endured for years and was now being passed on to me.

Lying there at nights with Jimmy gave me a real funny feeling, for we occupied the same bed I had shared as a kid with my sisters and cousins. Although we were both tuckered out from our labors, the farm sounds and smells exercised a powerful aphrodisiac effect. This delivered a challenge of its own, namely how to keep the sounds of our lovemaking from reaching Granny's ears. After the first couple of nights we gave up trying, and the constant wheezy protests of our ancient mattress did nothing to lessen her daily mutterings.

Back on the road again, Jimmy's eye for the ladies went into overdrive. He was the leader of the band and knew how to use his position, to the point where discretion no longer seemed to count. He was a plausible so-and-so, I will say that for him, but I should have known after our marriage deal that our time together was limited. It's the same old thing. Women look at the face, see the fine-looking guy and they'll swallow anything. I took the opportunity to bow out when an offer arrived to tour Virginia as a solo.

In Petersburg, sixty-five miles from home, I worked in a black neighborhood club run by a gentleman named Moe Barney. Moe really took a shine to me and asked one day if I'd like to go as far as Detroit, Michigan, where he'd heard there was an opening for a featured girl singer. He didn't need to ask twice and was as good as his word, calling Benny and Hymie Gassman, owners of the Frolic Showbar. Based on what Moe told them, they offered me the spot.

If there was a time in that frantic period when I could have changed my name back to Weston, that was it. I didn't, reasoning that I had already become established, in however small a way. Ruth Brown it would remain.

On the show with me at the Frolic that spring of '48 was Emile Jones, the black Pavarotti of his day. His big song was "If I Should Lose You," which he took to impressively operatic heights. Sporting flamboyant white tails, he exemplified the dressing-up we did on stage, for no matter how small your income as a performer, one thing you did was dress up grand, ready for that spotlight. In many ways it was a crucial part of your act, for it defined your attitude. Also on the bill was a very funny comedian, Lewis "My Man" Heywood, and another singer, Chubby Newsome, who did a number called "I'm a Hip-Shakin' Mama" that unfailingly brought the house down.

I was on stage one night when in walked bandleader Lucky Millinder, accompanied by guitarist Chico Alvarez of the Stan Kenton Orchestra. They were playing in the Paradise Theater, the prestige equivalent of New York's Apollo except that they brought in all the great acts, black and white regardless.

We performers really put it on when someone of importance is in the house, and Lucky had this reputation of having an ear for young talent and giving them a break. Sure enough, he offered me an audition the following morning. I was over the moon, especially when the Gassmans gave me their blessing.

Lucky lay sprawled in a chair in his hotel suite while his piano man hovered over the keys. I stood there in the middle of the room as one song after another was called out. Fortunately it was almost all ballads he wanted to hear, for my repertoire was loaded with them at the time. After I had finished at least ten numbers Lucky held his hand up like a traffic cop. "Whoa," he said. "You're hired." Just like that! We didn't talk about money, we didn't talk about anything, but I could have cared less. I just wanted to go with Lucky's big-name band and I was so elated. Benny and Hymie were pleased for me and even threw a small party in my honor the night I left. I could hardly believe my luck. I was joining a group with a bunch of hit records to its name. I really felt the big time was beckoning.

FOR OVER A MONTH I rode the bus with the Millinder band without getting to sing one note. Lucky chose to stick with his two regular singers, Bull Moose Jackson and Annisteen Allen, and left me out of it. That changed when we hit Washington, D.C., for our Fourth of July dance date, probably because I let it drop that I knew quite a few people there; a lot of my school contemporaries had enrolled at Howard University. Lucky had a couple of songs specially arranged for me, Lonnie Johnson's "Tomorrow Night" and Dinah Washington's "Evil Gal Blues," and I was so excited as we prepared to open at Turner's Arena.

I was resplendent in a brand-new navy-blue taffeta dress I had blown all my savings on, and after my first number the audience just went crazy. The second went equally well, and as I made to leave the stage after taking my bows, one of the band members asked if I'd mind getting a half-dozen Cokes from the refreshment stand. As I walked back with them in a cardboard box and crossed the front of the stage, Lucky turned and glared at me, his face like thunder. After the drinks had been dispensed he called me over. I had no idea what was coming, except maybe he wanted to tell me how pleased he was with my reception. That was not what he had in mind. "I hired you to sing," he snapped, "not to be a waitress." Then he looked me up and down contemptuously and said, "On the other hand, you can't sing either. You're fired!"

I just stared at him like a rabbit hypnotized by a snake, then crumpled in disbelief as he turned on his heel and marched off. Shattered though I was, I still thought he had to be joking.

Cecilia's Stage Door was a watering hole where all the entertainers in town congregated after hours. Its side entrance faced the stage door of the city's number-one theater, the Howard, situated in the black hub. When the dance was over I piled into the bus with the rest of the band to have a meal there, and as we alighted it was announced that we had an hour and a half before our departure. My head was spinning, but I thought that even if Lucky were serious about firing me, he would never ditch me right there and then. That was until I saw him waiting in the doorway with a scowl on his face as we left Cecilia's. "You still around? I said you're fired!" he barked. So saying, he turned and told the band valet to take my bags off the bus. I managed to stammer, "Well, I know I don't have much money coming . . ." He looked me straight in the eye and replied, "You don't have *anythin'* comin'. As long as you've been ridin' this bus I've been payin' your hotel bills and feedin' you. You don't have *any* money comin'. Matter of fact, you owe *me!*"

I was in a complete state of shock as I watched the bus pull away, leaving me standing on the street corner. Annisteen had slipped me ten dollars before she got on the bus, but apart from that I had only four dollars of my own and change.

I was over two hundred miles from home, out of a job, informed by one of the top bandleaders in the business that I couldn't sing, ashamed to call home, and without so much as a coat on my back. Although Dad and I had reached some sort of understanding since, his words came back to me with greater force than ever before: "Once you leave, don't come crawlin' back here for nuthin'." The big time had beckoned, all right—then it turned round and bopped me right in the eye.

I was beginning to think in terms of the nearest bus shelter when a young man walked out of Cecilia's and did a double take as he passed. "Ruth Weston?" he asked. His face was familiar. "Newport News?" he prompted me. I was so sunk in my misery I had failed to recognize Tommy Mosely, a Virginia boy who'd won a talent contest singing "Two Loves Have I" and had gone off ahead of me to make his way professionally. He was working in a club in Washington and when I explained what had happened he took off his coat and draped it around my shoulders. "I don't have a pocketful of money right now," he told me, "but I've got a room nearby. I'll bunk with one of our band and you can have my place until you decide what you're gonna do."

"I don't want to go home," I said. "In fact, I *can't* go home. Maybe you know some place I could get a job around here?"

"There's a lady who's been very kind to me," he replied. "I'll take you over to her place tomorrow if you like. Her name is Blanche Calloway."

That was my introduction to the woman who became my best friend, my manager, my mentor, my second mother . . . everything. Blanche, a sister of the legendary Cab, had been way ahead of her time, the first female African-American bandleader. Rumor was she'd given it up to push Cab instead. She was a gorgeous lady, tall, graceful and statuesque, and full of religious wisdom. She agreed to let me sing in her club, the Crystal Caverns, that very night as a guest. I did just one number, the Vaughn Monroe hit, "Maybe You'll Be There," and the response both from the audience and from Blanche went some way to rebuilding the confidence Lucky Millinder had all but demolished.

"Hey, you're good," she told me. "Unfortunately, my show is loaded right now, but I'll let you work here long enough to pay your way home." She gave me a job singing for thirty dollars a week, then took me to a house where she was rooming and introduced me to her landlady, Miss Bessie, who found me a room at Bessie's Boarding House for Ladies for seven dollars a week. Even before Blanche decided to keep me on, she was handing out good advice to me on everything from how to dress to relating to an audience. She had a tremendous store of showbiz knowledge she was willing and able to share. One of the first things she insisted upon was the stripping away of all the extraneous beads and jewelry I'd been weighing myself down with. It was hard to swallow that I'd been overdressing like crazy, presenting myself like a dish of fish, but I realized that I was lucky enough to be on the receiving end of priceless advice from someone with impeccable taste.

Before too long I had gathered such a following at the Crystal Caverns that Blanche had a kitty set up for me on the piano. In this way I was able to double my salary as customers put a dollar or two at a time in there. One night, halfway through my set, I felt a buzz of excitement sweeping through the club as a group of people made their way inside. As I took my bow at the end of my number I heard the musicians behind me whispering the names of the three famous personalities seated out front—deejay Willis Conover, "the Voice of America"; Sonny Til, lead singer of the Orioles; and the one, the only Duke Ellington. As soon as I heard this I asked the band to accompany me on "It's Too Soon to Know," the Orioles' current hit. Towards the end of the number I saw Conover push back his chair, mutter something to his companions, then head for the back of the club. The first question on my mind was, "Why is he walking out?" the second (I was still smarting from the Millinder mauling), "Was it that bad?" Then I watched as he stopped at the phone booth next to the cloakroom, picked up the receiver and dialed my future . . .

After my spot Conover came backstage with Blanche. He looked at me appreciatively and asked if I had any aspirations to record. "You bet," the two of us choroused. He told us he knew Ahmet Ertegun and Herb Abramson of Atlantic Records, a fledgling company that was struggling to establish itself, and that his call was to Abramson at his home. Ertegun, it seemed, was the son of the Turkish ambassador to the United States, Abramson was an ex-dentist with some experience at National Records, and they were in partnership with a Washington-based friend of Ertegun's, Dr. Vahdi Sabit.

Next thing I knew, Blacky Sales, Atlantic's promotion man and talent scout, dropped by the Crystal Caverns to check me out, followed by Abramson and finally Ertegun. By this time I had asked Blanche to act as my manager, and I listened to her advice and signed with Atlantic.

To keep the ball rolling Blanche called Frank Schiffman at the Apollo. I had the talent show win to my credit, but this was something quite different, Blanche persuading him that I was good enough to take the stage as a professional artist. His first question, reasonable enough, was whether I had cut any records. He took Blanche's word that I was signed to Atlantic and booked me on a bill supporting one of my idols, Billie Holiday. Finally, I remember thinking, I was on my way. Since meeting Blanche, nothing but good things had been happening.

Three days before the Apollo opening Blanche and I received a wire saying that the date had been changed, Miss Holiday having decreed that no other female singer be allowed to share her bill. My disappointment was minimized when Schiffman merely switched the date from the week of October 22, 1948 to the following week, appearing with Dizzy Gillespie and his Orchestra.

In the meantime, none other than the long-lost and mainly unlamented Jimmy Earle Brown showed up, supposedly to pick up where we left off. His Band of Atomic Swing had blown sky-high, he said, and he needed a breather before attempting another foray with the Earls of Rhythm. With nobody else in prospect I took another look at that fine brown frame of his and thought, what the heck. Our "marriage" certainly hadn't been cooked up in heaven, but we had enjoyed more than a few tasty moments.

When it came time to head for New York and the Apollo date,

Jimmy made it clear he expected to tag along. This immediately blew our budget, for Blanche and I had planned to travel by bus. With Jimmy to contend with, she decided to make the trip in her powder-blue convertible. Her barman Tommy Tombleson and his girlfriend would share the driving, with Blanche navigating in the front seat and me and Jimmy cozy in the back. Well, that was the theory.

I'm not psychic, but I have always felt that somewhere deep down in my spiritual self there's been a special someone looking out for me. If only I had paid attention to the signs along the way. The night we left, that trunk flat refused to close with Jimmy's suitcase in there. We'd take it out, it would close; put it back in, no. Was I being told something? I ignored it and stored the darn thing on the back seat between us. In taking up again with Jimmy that old female self-esteem trap had been sprung. There was that empty feeling of being an incomplete woman unless there was a man around. I paid for that many times, perhaps never more so than on that trip.

SINCE WE HAD to be in New York for three P.M. rehearsals, we left Washington at three A.M. that Thursday morning. I'd been working the night before and nodded off as soon as we left, my head resting not romantically on Jimmy but on his trunk. The next thing I heard, just outside Philadelphia, was a screeching of tires and Blanche screaming, "Oh, my God!" The deafening silence that followed our collision with a tree trunk seemed to last for an eternity, until I became aware of voices outside the car of people who had stopped to help, together with the wailing of sirens. Jimmy, with just a few light bruises, scrambled out and began calling, "Runt? Runt?"

Tommy had been at the wheel and had cracked ribs from the steering wheel smashing into his chest; his girlfriend was badly concussed. As for poor Blanche, she had gone through the windshield and had blood from the gashes in her face pouring on to her pride and joy, the long black monkey fur she sported. I heard her say, "I don't want no doctors, just call my brother." She was a Christian Scientist, and cut face or not, she would allow no treatment.

As for myself, my legs had been broken and bent back under me.

The left leg was worse; it had folded up like an accordion, the femur cracked in three places. I was paralyzed with the shock and pain, totally unable to move or speak. At one point someone in a uniform, I think it was a policeman, flashed a torch around the inside of the car. "Get the rest of them out," he ordered. "Forget the girl in the back—she's dead." Well, I just let that news sink in.

The sirens began to shriek again as the ambulance took off with everyone else inside, leaving me behind. Just when I'd begun to think they had given up on the possibility that I might have survived, they tried to pull me out by the legs. Later they said they knew I was a singer the moment they heard my voice, for I let out a scream that could be heard several counties away. I've never managed it before or since, but I soared way over high C on that occasion.

That's how I ended up at Chester Hospital, Pennsylvania, on the day of my professional debut at the Apollo. Blanche was in the bed alongside mine for a month or so before she was allowed out. She continued to refuse treatment and although she had a large, livid scar for a while, it healed up completely all by itself through time. Lying in bed she'd talk about spiritual matters and faithfully recite the Lord's Prayer every night and day. She had a practitioner who dropped in regularly and she never once lost her wonderful serenity.

When she was gone the staff and my fellow patients, led by a wonderful blonde nurse, Mrs. Annie Gross, did their level best to keep my spirits up as the weeks stretched into months. When Thanksgiving came around it was particularly hard, being the family person I am. I got through it, with everybody calling up and sending cards. Outside those from the family and a few close friends, one that I really appreciated was a beautiful "Get Well Soon" from a friend of Blanche's, none other than the timeless Lena Horne. I was so touched that she'd taken the time to make such a thoughtful gesture, for compared to her I was a nobody in the business.

Now Christmas itself was round the corner and I really didn't know how I was going to cope with that. As early as the first week of December, seasonal decorations began to make an appearance, with little Santas draped round the window to my left where

Blanche's bed had been. That sinking feeling grew when carol singers started visiting the wards. Apart from missing my family like
crazy, I had had not a single visit or word of any kind from Jimmy
Brown, although I'd heard he had been in and out of the Crystal
Caverns, struttin' his stuff.

When Christmas Day dawned we were wakened as usual at six
A.M., washed and given breakfast. I was still in traction, but I
watched as everything sort of began to come alive on this special
morning. Mama had sent me a nice gown which Mrs. Gross dressed
me in, and I lay there looking towards that window and the Santas.
It had begun to snow gently outside and I could see snowflakes
clinging. The loneliness I felt was settling into an ache when I suddenly heard this incredibly beautiful, impossibly rich voice singing
"Silent Night." Well nobody, but *nobody*, sang like that except my
dad . . .

Without telling me, my parents had ridden a Trailway bus
through the night to be with their delinquent daughter on Christmas Day. I started to cry like a baby when the two of them came
bursting through the door, laden down with gifts from all the family. After we'd kissed and embraced, Dad handed me a package and
said, "Here, String Bean"—my heart leapt, he hadn't called me
that since I was in junior high—"this is for you." He had brought
me a pair of red velvet bedroom shoes. I pointed to my leg, still in
traction, and said, "But Daddy—" I couldn't even get out of bed,
let alone put shoes on! Many years before James Brown made the
line famous, Dad replied, quick as a flash, "Put them on the good
foot!" I did, and Mama and I cried and cried, for we were a family
again, together again at last.

The Christmas I had dreaded turned out so wonderfully, even
taking into account the letter from Jimmy that arrived next day. His
timing really was superb: "Dear Ruth," it began, "I'm young and
you may never walk again, and I gotta move on . . ."

Lord have mercy, that James Earle Brown surely was a grade-A
honeydrippin' heartbreaker!

5

AHMET, HERB AND ME

I STAYED IN CHESTER HOSPITAL, mostly in traction, for close on eleven months. It was a considerable setback, for not only had Dizzy and the Apollo management been stood up, but Atlantic Records as well. Ahmet Ertegun brought to the hospital a contract for me to sign in my hospital bed on January 12, 1949, because they had never gotten around to that. We were on first-name terms from the start, and I could tell from the way he talked that he and Herb Abramson were as enthusiastic as I was about getting started. During the visit he handed me a book on how to sight-read, a pitch pipe and a large tablet to scribble down any lyrics that came to mind.

I have no idea what the total bill for my stay amounted to, for I was extremely naive about such matters. Without taking any legal advice I allowed an insurance adjuster to talk me into signing away most of what I could have claimed. Atlantic paid the final bill, less what the insurance did cough up, so by the time I joined Atlantic I was already in their debt. The little company was having a hard time, although by the time I arrived they had graduated from a humble suite at the Hotel Jefferson to a scarcely less modest walk-up office at 301 West 54th Street, with a roster that boasted Sticks McGhee, Tiny Grimes and Ivory Joe Hunter.

On April 6, still on crutches and wearing a leg brace, I hobbled into the Apex Studio at the tail end of a John "Texas Johnny" Brown session, with Amos Milburn sitting hunched over the piano.

59

I sang "Rain Is a Bringdown," a tune I'd doodled in the hospital, just to give Ahmet and Herb an idea of how my voice came over on disc. Then Herb began to talk material, mentioning "So Long," the bluesy ballad we all knew from Little Miss Cornshuck's version. We talked a little bit about the tempo and treatment, and Herb said he'd have an arrangement worked out by the time we were set to record at WOR the following month. We recorded the song with Eddie Condon's orchestra on May 25, and after listening to the playback Ahmet and Herb decided the track was strong enough for my first A-side. "It's Raining" formed the B-side.

Within a few weeks of its release "So Long" was selling well, climbing to number six on Billboard's R-and-B chart. It was only the company's second hit after Sticks McGhee's "Drinkin' Wine, Spo-dee-o-dee," and everybody at Atlantic was thrilled to see the company's name back on the charts. Me too, believe it! This time they were determined it would be no one-hit wonder.

After four of my follow-up releases to "So Long" went nowhere, however, it was time for a reappraisal. The problem on Atlantic's side was they couldn't figure out what to do with me. I was recorded with the Delta Rhythm Boys, singing spirituals, even flirting with Yiddish songs in English. *"Too* darn versatile," I heard Herb mutter more than once. The problem I posed, in turn, was my resistance to singing anything but my first love, ballads. I wanted to tell stories in songs, to explore emotions, to the lush sounds of velvety string accompaniments I'd always conjured up when dreaming of record-ing. A solution had to be found; meanwhile I was working regularly, and for decent money, although I was hampered by the legacy of that car crash.

On my discharge from the hospital I'd been fitted with a metal brace on my left leg, a real medieval torture device consisting of two heavy bars and a strap that laced and fastened across the knee. Before undertaking any movement I had to remember to click a button into place to secure the contraption, otherwise my knee would bend, blowing the whole object of the exercise. I always re-moved it before going onstage; the last thing I wanted to hear as I struggled to get established was: "Oh, she's a cripple!"

The darn thing weighed a ton and I reached the limit one night when I was leaving Blanche's house in Philadelphia. I forgot to click

An early Atlantic publicity shot.
(COURTESY OF RUTH BROWN)

the vital button and took a header down a flight of stone steps. The combination of hurt and embarrassment caused me to discard the brace completely. It's a decision I made against everyone's advice, and one I've had cause to regret over the years.

DURING MUCH OF '49 I stayed at Monk and Eva's at 153rd Street in Harlem. Monk was a real music lover, like everyone on Dad's side, so I heard a lot of good stuff during my stay with them, both in their house and at the nearby Apollo. Every night was party night at Monk's, the men playing poker and digging hot music, the ladies playing bridge and swapping hot gossip. I heard all of Lucky Millinder's new stuff as it came out, as if I needed reminding, and new records by artists such as Billie, Ella, Sarah and Dinah. It got to where Granny Ruth came to feel I was having *too* good a time there, and at her insistence I moved to her sister Annie's place on West 115th Street, where Annie lived with her husband, John Guess. They were much straighter-laced than Monk and Eva; I could practically hear the Westons' collective sigh of relief that I was led away from temptation. It didn't last long—as soon as steady money began rolling in I checked into the Hotel Theresa, just walking distance from the Apollo.

WHENEVER I THOUGHT OF AHMET in those days I always thought of Herb, for they were working so closely together as a team that when you saw one you usually saw the other. Both were natty dressers; Ahmet's hairline was already way into recession and he was sporting his distinctive black-rimmed glasses, Herb was tall and suave, every inch the man-about-town. We used to visit all the leading clubs in Harlem, together with Herb's wife Miriam, the company comptroller and even then a real piece of work. They'd call and ask me along to a whole variety of restaurants, where I had my first taste of "ethnic" food. They took me to a Thai restaurant, a Chinese, a Japanese, a Spanish, a Mexican—and of course a Turkish!—a new one every week until I felt I had tasted the world. Our relationship was such that I could pick up the phone any time day or night and say, "This is Ruth. Let me speak to Ahmet," and be put straight through. Herb had a vast knowledge of music and musicians, their lifestyles and histories. Whenever I visited his home I marveled at the huge collection of records he had. Playing through them was an education in itself and enabled me to catch up on the work of the early blues pioneers, Bessie Smith and Ma Rainey in particular. Of the two men Ahmet was undoubtedly the more forceful; Herb was softer, more erratic and ready to bend. Much as I loved and respected Ahmet, I felt closer to Herb.

The house writer that broke the dry spell after "So Long" was Rudolph "Rudy" Toombs. The song Rudy composed especially for me, "Teardrops from My Eyes," took me to the top of the R-and-B chart in October 1950. And there it stayed for eleven solid weeks, with a total chart run of twenty-six weeks. One-hit wonder? Not me, baby! The disc also became a tiny piece of history, being Atlantic's first record made available on seven-inch 45–rpm vinyl as well as the standard ten-inch 78–rpm shellac.

Rudy was my good friend, a man who was simply bursting with life, as effervescent as any of his songs. The things he did for me were different rhythmically from what I was into, but I finally had to give in to the fact that Ahmet, Herb and their team were a step

On stage in 1949 with Billy Ford and his band in Philadelphia. I was still singing ballads and my leg braces were hidden under the Salvation Army dress. (COURTESY OF RUTH BROWN)

ahead of the accepted sound of the day. Taking a deep breath, I went along with it. Although I had no right of veto in my contract, that did not stop me from fighting if I wasn't happy with what came up. On most issues we reached common ground, with Ahmet and Herb resigned to my singing the occasional ballad, if only for a B-side. Although Herb was the man in charge of my sessions, many of the decisions regarding material were made by Ahmet and arranger Jesse Stone, whose remarkable body of compositions ranged from "Smack Dab in the Middle" all the way to "Shake, Rattle and Roll." He was the man behind so many of the great things that came out of Atlantic, together, of course, with the engineering wizard, Tom Dowd. Tommy had impeccable intuition and was a fixture in the control booth with Ahmet and Herb.

A couple of times during early morning sessions, with sunshine streaming through the windows, I remember protesting it was the

Recording at Atlantic in 1953. (Courtesy of B.J. Jones)

wrong time of day to capture a blue mood. "Ruth, just sing like you've got tears in your eyes," Herb would direct me. Another time it would be, "Give me that million-dollar squeal." There were occasions when my throat felt sore, or what I used to call "rusty." "I *like* your sound when it's like that," Herb would enthuse. "It has an earthy quality, a sexiness." *"Down,* boy!" I'd kid him.

THERE WAS SOMETHING about performing near home that really brought out the firebrand in me. I was singing in a hall in Newport News soon after "Teardrops" began hitting, resplendent in a beautiful new red chiffon dress, when a woman lurched towards the stage, armed with a large paper cup of beer. "Sing 'Teardrops,' " she cried. I mouthed, "Later" and continued singing "So Long." "Sing 'Teardrops' right now!" she insisted. As calmly as I could I finished the song, waited for the applause to die down, and listened as the band struck up our next number. When she discovered it wasn't "Teardrops"—we were naturally saving that for the grand finale—she screamed, "Hey, don't get cute with me, bitch! I know you're from over there in Portsmouth!" That was her cue to hurl the entire contents of her cup over my brand-new dress: "Ya hear me talkin' to ya, bitch?" she said. I lifted the dress clear over my head, tossed it to one side and leaped straight off the stage, landing right on her.

My brother Leonard had watched all this from the side and dove in after me, trying desperately to separate us as we rolled over and over on the floor. "What in the world are you *doin'?"* he shouted.

Somehow he extracted me from the skin and hair that was flying, got me standing and held my hands behind me as I struggled to get loose and finish what that creature had started. She had ideas of her own and began making for me, brandishing a nasty-looking knife. By the grace of God someone saw where she was at and grabbed her as she lunged, then dragged her away while she was screaming her lungs out. Jerking my arms free, I turned on Leonard. "I could have been cut open!" I yelled at him. "Why'd you hold me back like that?" I began beating up on him, but he wouldn't fight back. There was no satisfaction in that, and neither was there any way that concert was getting restarted. "Oh, just get my damn things," I told him, "let's get out of here."

On the journey home our car was loaded and I simply could not be silenced, mad as I was at Leonard. The adrenalin was still pumping as we crossed the James River bridge. "Ain't no reason to hold me like that!" I fumed. "I could have been killed! Pull the damn car over and you get out!" He did, and I tried to bop him in the mouth as he ducked and weaved. We all fell into hysterics when it came time to relate the story, but at the time it was serious stuff.

Soon I felt like the Queen of the One-Nighters, with dates stretching through the Litchman Theater chain from New York to Washington, Baltimore, Richmond, and near home again (no fisticuffs this time!) at the Booker T in Norfolk. One-night dance dates followed into the Carolinas and all the way down to Georgia, Alabama and Tennessee, bringing me face to face with all those racial problems, rubbing my nose in them. We did close on seventy one-nighters on the trot, spending most days riding the tour bus. When we hit Atlanta we set up camp and made excursions to neighboring towns like Columbus and Augusta, and in Atlanta itself there were lots of clubs to work.

On stage I took to wearing multicolored petticoats and accordion-pleated skirts, featuring all the colors of the rainbow, and from the brighter end of the spectrum: peacock blue, surprise pink, sunshine yellow, orange and lavender. Apart from fellow performers, you had the audiences to compete with, who came along dressed to the nines. Our dates were once-in-a-lifetime-style affairs, a big night out, with posters up months before we arrived. In the South it was even trickier; you had to watch in case a member of the audience was wearing the same dress as you and took offense.

I finally got to the Apollo a year and half after the original date had been set up, and during one show Dad gave me a real surprise, diving out of the audience and hot-footing it down the aisle. When he reached the band he began conducting, just like he had back at the Emmanuel AME! Bless him, he had ridden the bus from Virginia just to see the show. Nipsey Russell, our emcee, rose to the occasion: "You'll just have to forgive him," he said to the audience, "this is his daughter up here!"

Dad had always wanted a white suit and matching Panama hat, and soon after his Apollo caper when I was home visiting I got him the whole outfit. The last we saw of him that particular Friday evening he was struttin' his stuff with the guys on the street corner, looking like the dog who owned the boneyard. I tell you, he did not come home for three days after that, and he wasn't the only beneficiary on that trip home. I was only too happy to spread some of the cash around that had come my way. I bought presents for everyone and took my baby sister Delia to the biggest department store in Portsmouth, the Famous, treating her first to a beautiful cotillion, later to her first pair of high heels and nylon stockings.

There was a downside to that otherwise joyous trip. The rest of my family had never felt too much affection towards Granny Ruth. She had been good to me, though, and I had always been ready to take her side in any discussion—until the shocking news that coincided with my dad's disappearance that weekend. It was hard at first to take it in. Granny had committed "Big Papa" William to the mental asylum in Petersburg.

He had, it seemed, turned on her after years of being the archetypal meek, henpecked husband, and her response had been to use her contacts in the medical field to have him certified insane. Incredibly, it was a done deed, with no court of appeal. I had seen for myself, on the most horrific school trip ever, the bedlam that reigned at Petersburg, with violent patients shackled in chains, all in one state or another of misery. The news cast a terrible blight on my visit, and I left home with a heavy heart.

An early ad for Atlantic, featuring my first hits. (COURTESY OF RUTH BROWN)

*   *   *

WITH THE CONTINUING SUCCESS of "Teardrops" and that change of style for me I began to land some bigger theater engagements. Mama came to stay with me for the week in Philly, where I played the Earle Theater on a bill headed by Frankie "Mr. Rhythm" Laine. He took in the audience reaction to my song, the handclapping and dancing in the aisles, and introduced me next day by saying, "I think I'll call her *Miss* Rhythm." I decided to adopt the title. It seemed only fair since Frankie's wife, the delightful Nan Grey, seemed to have adopted my mother.

Taking Delia out on the road with me during her summer break from school seemed like a good idea at the time. Now I'm not so sure! Certainly it gave her an early education in the facts of life, although I guess I underestimated the effect on a thirteen-year-old of traveling with a bunch of hard-drinkin', hard-livin' and hard-lovin' musicians. Not that she ever got involved personally, for even if she'd been inclined, I was the strictest chaperone in history. Still it was inevitable that she would overhear some of the jive they laid down, sitting in adjoining booths in diners or even at opposite ends of buses. Delia ended up a genuinely baffled kid, unable to understand that all them friendly brothers and uncles who were so sweet and kind to her by day were the same guys who picked up a willing chick by night, took her to a hotel and played "pass the parcel" with her, each doin' the wild thing. *And* talking about it next morning!

SOME PEOPLE to this day call Atlantic "The House that Ruth Brown Built," and even if this is an exaggeration, few would deny that I contributed a solid portion of the foundation as well as quite a few of the actual bricks. No doubt the cement was the matchless team at the company, Ahmet, Herb, Jesse and Tommy, together with the incredible mix of outstanding musical talent they employed and nurtured.

The stellar bunch of Atlantic sidemen apart, those who knew me best entertained no doubts as to my favorite accompanist. How come? Real easy. During 1950 I became inseparable, both personally and professionally, from a tenor sax killer-diller.

Name of Willis "Gator Tail" Jackson.

6

LIGHTHOUSE KEEPING

IN THE FIFTIES there were five theaters forming a circuit that all the name black acts toured. If you could get through them, you had it made. First was the Apollo, then the Regal in Baltimore, the Howard in Washington, the Regal in Chicago and finally the Hippodrome in Richmond, Virginia.

After my long-delayed appearance at the Apollo I moved on to Chicago's Regal. While rehearsing there with the band, I noticed out of the corner of my eye their tenor-sax man taking in the view. I glanced back just long enough to note that he was tall and a fine-looking guy. Sashaying by me on his way offstage he said, "Miss Brown? My name is Willis Jackson, but they call me Gator." After a second's pause he added, "But you can call me later!"

Over the course of the week's engagement I continued the habit drummed into me by Blanche of standing in the wings while the act before mine did its stuff, just in case something went wrong and I had to go on early. I was wearing a yellow gown I had bought in a local thrift shop that had two bands of black velvet and a bow on the shoulder, and as I stood there I couldn't help noticing that tenor-sax man focusing on me again. When I blushingly acknowledged his look, he gave me a little wave. Cootie Williams, the bandleader, saw what he was at and told me years later I should have stopped it right there and then. Maybe I should have, but if I had I'd have missed the love of my life.

We were all staying in the same digs, a small hotel across the

Publicity shot, 1951.
(COURTESY OF B.J. JONES)

street from the theater. We did double shows, a matinee and evening performance daily. Constant invitations from Willis to lunch or dinner followed each show, and we ended up eating at an extremely humble joint called the Chili Bowl. "Is this as good as it gets?" I cracked. We talked music and our careers, about all our hopes and dreams, and I think we both felt like two kids on the threshold of limitless opportunities.

With several well-received instrumentals for the Apollo label under his belt, Willis's immediate ambition was to quit Cootie's band and go out on his own. "It's about time *you* had your own group," he told me. Naturally he meant with *him* leading it! That's how we got started, because I took his advice. My records were really working for me, the demand was there and it was the logical next step. First I introduced Willis to Atlantic, where he was eagerly snapped up.

Rudy Toombs was responsible for the next smash I enjoyed. His original title was "5–10–15 Minutes (Of Your Love)" until Herb coolly informed him that "minutes" was no longer enough now that we were in the era of Billy Ward and the Dominoes' *Sixty-Minute Man*. Presto, it became "5–10–15 Hours (Of Your Love)." The song followed "Daddy, Daddy" into the R-and-B chart in '52 and lodged at number one for seven weeks. Ruth Brown? Hotter than a pistol!

Soon Willis and I had become an institution—at Atlantic, where he accompanied me on several records; around town, where we went everywhere together; and on the road. You can hear that bootin', dirty sax behind me on tracks from "I Know" and "5–10–15 Hours" to "Have a Good Time" and "Daddy, Daddy." You want pretty? Listen to the man define yearning on "Be Anything (But Be Mine)."

As they had with Jimmy Brown, people assumed we were married, and neither one of us did anything to discourage the notion. Initially we did what is known as "lighthouse keeping," moving in together in someone else's house, in this case bandleader Luis Russell's. We occupied just one room there, but it was real cozy and a start. That's where I discovered it was Willis's Floridian roots that gave him his nickname, and he lived up to it with stuffed leather alligators scattered throughout our tiny quarters. They were mostly expensive items, gifts from ex-ladyfriends. That should have given me a clue.

I had paid no attention to such mundane but all-important matters as transportation, leaving them all to my booking agency, Ben Bart's Universal Attractions, and I paid their price, which was steep. They had several mini-buses they called suburbans, made to hold up to twelve people, which they allowed you to rent to take your musicians and the rest of your entourage on the road. You were provided with a driver, and a sign on the side saying who you were. If our group of eight or ten made $1,000 a night, a lot of money back then, $350 came right off the top for the suburban and driver. We practically lived in that darn thing when we were on the road and I had to pay for everything—wages, accommodation, meals—and still hope to clear something at the end of it all for the kitty. As with the Band of Atomic Swing there were many times when the promoters ran off with the ticket money, leaving us high and dry. We had no clauses in our contracts saying we had to be paid before we performed, or even at the intermission, so we were wide open to

On tour in 1951 with Willis "Gator" Jackson, Thelma Manley, Leonard Weston (my eldest brother) and Ray Jones (Blanche Calloway's husband). (COURTESY OF RUTH BROWN)

such abuse. When it happened it was considered just too bad, and I had to make it up to everybody.

On the road Universal subcontracted our services to local agents. You worked through them and there was no way you could go around them; even in those days these guys had a stranglehold on the business. I met them all, and while none were standoffish, you immediately knew who they were when they walked into a room. People in the towns where we took up residence knew them too, and you could get a lot of things done just by mentioning their names—and no questions asked. The Weinbergs, father and son, used to book us for all the extensive tours. They controlled all of Virginia, clear through North Carolina all the way to Louisiana. From there we'd be picked up in Georgia and subcontracted again to one of the two famous black promoters in Atlanta, Henry Winn or B. B. Beamon. In Texas the black kingpins were Don Robey and Howard Lewis, who both worked out of Dallas.

With Willis around and my stock still rising, the money situation improved to the point where I felt confident enough to invest in a Cadillac for each of us. Although that may sound over the top, we were immediately able to stop paying Universal's exhorbitant rate for their suburbans and dispense with their driver. Apart from any-thing else, I felt entitled to what I saw as the trappings of success, our little "toys." Willis was with me, conducting the band behind me, warming my bed at night. And I was deeply in love with him. There was a little gesture of his that really touched my heart. Every time I entered a room where he was playing, he'd lead into "Can't Help Loving That Man of Mine," the lovely tune from *Showboat.* How could I *help* loving that man?

THELMA MANLEY FIRST CAME into my life at the Renaissance Ballroom, sitting through two shows before introducing herself backstage as a Virginia girl from Newport News—oh, and I ought to give her a job! She was a fresh, attractive slip of a girl, even younger than she claimed to be, and when I took her on as my dresser I had to report to her parents regularly. She virtually grew up on the road with me and we spent close on a decade together.

Dave Crew was in his mid-thirties when I met him in Washington, D.C., working for a car dealer cum deejay named Hal Jackson. Dave sold us those first cars and eventually became my road manager and a trusted friend of both me and my parents. If you can picture Roy Glen, who played the fight manager in the movie *Carmen Jones,* as well as Sidney Poitier's father in *Guess Who's Coming to Dinner,* you've got Dave. My entourage was complete, once Chickie Horne entered the picture.

When the one, the only Jimmy "Chickie" Horne and I first met, he was working his drag act at Newport News under the name of Hazelle Horne. The next time our paths crossed was at the Lido in New York. As well as having a terrific act, it soon transpired that Chickie was an expert beautician, and before too long I asked him to tour with me. We continued for years, off and on, with the under-standing that if he landed another gig we parted company for a while, and sometimes, while touring with me, he might earn extra money performing. He used to call me his big sister. Chickie is someone who has seen me at my lowest ebb as well as during the high times. In his stately progression from "Hazelle Horne" to "Miss Effie Throckbottom" he managed to acquire at least a half dozen of my cast-off dresses.

All four of us took to dressing alike when it came to little accoutrements. When I bought myself a cap, I bought four more; five if one of my family was around. Willis, of course, would have no truck with any of that. He had his own ideas on how to dress, and they did not include caps, believe it. He wore those "Mr. B" shirts with wide, flaring collars and had a nervous habit of continually adjusting his tie. That was in keeping, I guess, with his general appearance—as immaculate as good grooming and fine clothes could make him, with every processed hair exactly in place. Silk suits? Sure! Willis would buy himself clothes if he didn't eat. If he wore a hat on his head it simply had to be suede velour. A *cap?* Are you *crazy?*

Each member of my team had to go through a baptism of fire. Dave's came in several terrifying episodes down South, Thelma's in her date with Charlie "Bird" Parker. Chickie's came soon after joining me, when a real bruiser appeared backstage. I took in the start of it as I sat in front of my dressing room mirror. The bruiser said: "I wanna see Ruth Brown!"

"Hold on, please," Chickie said in his most refined voice, "I'll see if it's convenient for Miss Brown at this time."

"Wha-a-a-t? Git outta my way, *faggot!*"

That did it for me. Next thing Chickie knew I was out of that chair and had pushed him aside like a toy. I found myself addressing the visitor's belly button, for the guy must have been all of six feet, six inches tall, and put together like a brick outhouse. That did not detain me one single moment from saying my piece: "Don't you *ever*, nigger, call anyone in my group names. Especially one who's only doin' his job—keeping undesirables out."

The guy's jaw dropped. "Wha-a-a-t?" he managed.

"You heard. Now *scram!*" God bless him, he did, and when the door was shut Chickie and I had to gag ourselves to keep from laughing out loud.

"Did I hear you right?" Chickie asked when we'd recovered. "Did you call that child a *nigger?* And you're tellin' *him* not to call names?"

"That's different," I explained, in best big-sister fashion. "We'se family!"

More often than not one of my family was around on those fifties tours. Leonard was first, followed by every other brother and sister,

Thelma Manley, Blanche Calloway, Dave Crew, me and Jack Mitchell—backstage at the Apollo. (COURTESY OF RUTH BROWN)

Mama too. Goldie came out only for a very short spell, unable to bear being separated from Bobby Robinson, the childhood sweetheart who became her husband. Delia met her first husband on the road with me, bandleader Paul "Hucklebuck" Williams' son, Earl. Leonard entertained ambitions to be a singer for a while, spurred by winning first prize at an amateur show at the Paradise in Detroit. He modestly maintains he would never have stayed the course as a vocalist, that he was too much of a copyist, but I say that's how a lot of top artists begin until they find their own style. Apart from a fine voice he was quite a looker, and a positive menace to society on the road, where it was a case of lock up your daughters or take the consequences! Maybe, looking back now, Leonard didn't really want success enough. Not only had I wanted it desperately, I had *needed* it, and that makes a difference. So had taking to heart Mama's talks on turning stumbling blocks into stepping stones.

* * *

CAUGHT UP in the euphoria of having a contract to sign at all, I had taken no advice beyond a quick word with Blanche before signing with Atlantic. Ahmet had a great pitch that settled any questions: "Only Bing Crosby gets five percent at Decca." Ruth Brown on the same percentage as Der Bingle? Sure sounded good to me, although I knew I was starting at the bottom as far as advances were concerned—I'm sure Bing had long since worked his way past sixty-nine dollars a side. I also understood that I was responsible for certain production costs, but how big a deal could they be if I sold enough records?

Strangely enough, despite my continuing chart success, I had to ask every time I needed cash. Any real money I made came from touring, and I was always out there promoting the records. Back then any record by a black artist needed every ounce of help it could get. The expression "R-and-B chart" was another way in the late forties and early fifties to list "race and black" as well as "rhythm and blues" records. And the reason so few discs by black artists crossed over to Billboard's mainstream chart was simple: it was compiled from white-owned radio station playlists featuring music by white artists, with our list confined to stations catering to blacks. As Jerry Wexler, Herb's successor at Atlantic, put it when asked if it was difficult to get R-and-B records played on general-audience stations in the early fifties, *"Difficult* would have been easy. It was *impossible."*

It very gradually became less so, of course, as R-and-B artists broke through the barriers by the sheer strength and quality of their music. But it took time, and throughout my biggest hit-making period I was forced to stand by as white singers like Georgia Gibbs and Patti Page duplicated my records note for note and were able to plug them on top television shows like *The Ed Sullivan Show,* to which I had no access.

Chuck Willis wrote "Oh, What a Dream" especially for me, and it was my favorite song, but it was Patti Page, with an identical arrangement, who got to sing it on national television. Even topical stuff like my "Mambo Baby" had a Georgia Gibbs duplicate rushed out. My labelmate and good friend LaVern Baker, who joined At-

1951. (COURTESY OF B.J. JONES)

lantic in '53, suffered the same fate on her original of "Tweedle Dee"—another note-for-note copy by Her Nibs Miss Gibbs. There was no pretense, either, that they were anything but duplicates. Mercury actually called up Tommy Dowd on the day they were cutting "Tweedle Dee" and said, "Look, we've got the same arrangement, musicians and tempo, we might as well have the same sound engineer too."

It was tough enough coming up with hit sounds, therefore doubly galling to see them stolen from under our noses. Few seemed to stop and question the morality of this, least of all the publishers, to whom it was a case of the more the merrier. LaVern for one did, protesting to her congressman over her treatment at Mercury's hands, but then as now, there was no copyright protection on arrangements.

I was denied sales abroad as well, although I knew nothing of this at the time. "Abroad," as far as the feedback from Atlantic's accounting department was concerned, could have been the moon. Having made number three on Billboard's R-and-B chart in the States, and actually crossing over to their pop charts as well, reaching number twenty-five, my version of "Lucky Lips" was ignored in Britain. The number itself hit there years later in a 1963 version by Cliff Richard. Naturally the lyrics were suitably amended for him,

1952. (Courtesy of B.J. Jones)

for "When I was just a little girl my curls were long and silky" sounded pretty ridiculous even for me. Cliff took the tune to number four on the British charts, well into his unprecedented run of over one hundred chart entries that continues—and deservedly so —to this day. Why he's not bigger in the U.S. I'll never know.

IT WAS BECAUSE of Willis that I couldn't relate to "Mama, He Treats Your Daughter Mean" when it was first presented to me at Atlantic. Maybe it reminded me of a past relationship I wanted to forget, maybe I felt that singing it would put a jinx on us. I had to be coaxed into it by Herb, who upped the tempo from the slow ballad it had been. The tune had been written by two friends of mine, Herb Lance and Johnny Wallace (brother to a young fighter named Coley, who played the champion in *The Joe Louis Story*). There was a lot of joking around the night we recorded it, for everyone present knew I was less than keen. And Willis was absent, off doing a session of his own. "Does *your man* treat you mean, Ruthie?" drummer Connie Kay inquired, mock-anxiety written all over his teasin' face. "Anybody here seen Gator?" trumpeter Taft Jordan chimed in. I tell you, spitfires can be a target themselves sometimes.

During the first playback Herb and the others all looked at me expectantly. Although I still didn't like it, there was something so

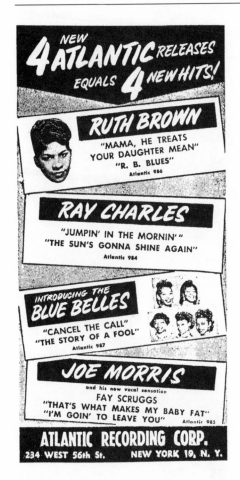

Still on top with the release of two new tracks.
(COURTESY OF RUTH BROWN)

comical about their concern that I had to smile and relax into the second take. This time we hit it just right. I can't put my finger on what was so special about that record, for the rhythm pattern was similar to a lot of stuff that was out there, but boy, did it take a trick. I was never so wrong about any piece of material in my life.

Whenever I did the number in a club I worked with a tambourine covered with fluorescent paint. The audience always knew "Mama" was coming when I lifted it over my head, it was a sure signal and they just went wild. Once in Charleston, South Carolina, I had to repeat "Mama" eight times before they'd let me off the stage. In Nashville, Tennessee, the mikes went down and I sang the number without them. The audience knew I was doing it to prevent a riot

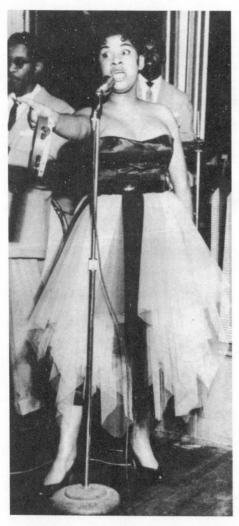

On tour with Charles Brown,
belting out "Mama, He Treats
Your Daughter Mean,"
complete with tambourine—and
pregnant with Ronnie. 1954.
(COURTESY OF RUTH BROWN)

and joined in, singing along with me. In Kansas City I did the same
thing when Jackie Wilson failed to turn up, singing it over and over.
On that occasion, I have to say, I overstayed my welcome.

What happened was that Jackie, Bo Diddley, Paul Williams and I
had played Atlanta together. Leaving Jackie behind—he'd met
someone he wanted to spend the night with—the rest of us drove
through the night to the next stop, the Auditorium in Kansas City.
Jackie had promised he would catch up, telling us to start the show

without him, he'd be there in time for his spot. There was no sign of him as Paul started the show, and when Bo followed him he did an extended act. He had to, for every time he left the stage Paul would say, "Get back on and do another encore, Jackie ain't showed yet!"

Eventually it was my turn to trawl through every song in my repertoire, saving "Mama" for the finale. "Still no sign of Jackie. Keep goin'!" was the frantic message from Paul. As I was about to hit that tambourine for the eighth time, someone in the front of the huge crowd yelled out, "Don't you sing that, not another damn time! Where's Jackie?" As the words echoed all over a bottle whistled past my head, a sure sign they meant business.

In those days Bo was transporting his musicians in a hearse. We had all driven our cars inside the auditorium and as we ran from the stage, hoping to escape the crowd's wrath, I realized there was little chance of making it to my buggy, it being the farthest away. Bottles were flying everywhere as Bo and his maraca player, Jerome, grabbed me and pulled me into the back of their hearse, where they slammed the door shut. We lay there flat on our stomachs until the crowd was brought under control.

Jackie? He ain't showed yet, and I've never returned to Kansas City since.

Savannah Churchill and me backstage in 1956. (COURTESY OF RUTH BROWN)

7

WITH MR. B AND THE COUNT

WILLIS AND I WERE together every day, and it was magical for quite a while. He was a real casanova and could charm you like a snake. He had the most soulful eyes and would look straight at you as he said the nicest things, like how pretty you looked, your dress was gorgeous, what a show you had put on. The first professional picture of his that he gave to me was signed, "To Shorty, with the big brown eyes, eyes I'll be looking in 'til the day I die, Gator." We'd dress in similar colors when we ventured out on the town and I took pride in people nodding and saying, "That's Ruth Brown's fella."

Having just that one relationship was important, for it demonstrated to my folks at home that I wasn't running wild out there in the world of show business, that one man was enough for me. In the beginning when we traveled down South and did those hard gigs, playing barns, suffering insults, he was by my side and that made it easier to bear.

He took me once on vacation to Paradise Farms in Cuttybackville, a resort frequented by blacks owned and run by a lady known as Sally Walker. It was a whole new scene for us, a wonderful romantic interlude in the sweet fresh air, far away from city streets and smoky clubs. We shared a trailer in the grounds, took night rides in a buggy, went fishing and horseriding. I had to be helped on my chosen steed, with my legs and all, but once I was up there I became a regular Calamity Jane, nothing and nobody could budge me.

Back in the city we took ourselves along to Birdland and thrilled to the sound of Charlie Parker. We were enjoying our success, and in Willis I had a partner who knew how to help me flaunt it. We enjoyed good food in the smartest restaurants, visited lots of movies together for yet another shared experience in the dark, shopped, danced, laughed and loved together. Willis was an entertainer to his heart who lived for his music and, for a while, Ruth Brown. My parents liked him too; when Willis was at his best there was nothing to dislike. Maybe it was too wonderful to last, maybe we're allocated only so much complete happiness in life, our allowance, then it's gone. Slowly but surely the magic began to slip through our fingers like grains of sand.

IN THE SPRING OF '53 I was invited to tour on a bill with Billy Eckstine and the Count Basie Orchestra, one of several we'd do together. I'd first seen "Mr. B" perform at Birdland, but we'd never met until the tour. He was a wonderful character, the most handsome man— light-skinned (even Granny D would have approved), green-eyed, a dream. He was also the fastest and most witty guy you could ever hope to meet. Of course he was well respected among musicians, since he was one himself, and as such was no slouch at pointing out mistakes. He could be sharp of tongue while doing it, somehow without ever losing his tremendous warmth.

I'm one of the few people who know how Billy got to meet his second wife, for it happened on our tour, in Memphis, Tennessee. Carol Drake Falconer was a well-known black model and aspiring actress. She appeared in the Clark Gable movie *Band of Angels,* playing the black slave who worked in Gable's house and loved him. When word got around in Memphis that Carol was in the audience, Basie and the entire band, aware how smitten he was, bet Eckstine that he couldn't take her home. They lost that bet in spectacular fashion and the marriage lasted until 1977, seven children later.

Billy could charm the ladies like few men I've ever seen, and he had women around who loved him for years. One was the singer

Chickie Horne, me,
Carol Drake
Falconer (The
Future Mrs. B),
Thelma Manley,
Mr. B.
(Courtesy of Ruth Brown)

Fran Warren. Another was the French actress Denise Darcel, who got to be a real problem. She was crazy about Billy, worshipped the ground he walked on, and she'd be forever showing up, whether he wanted her to or not. This went on for years and was one of the reasons Billy never got anywhere in Hollywood, a repeat of the blackballing that affected Sammy Davis, Jr. after his affair with Kim Novak. Sinatra arrived to save Sammy's movie career, but there was no such savior on hand for Billy, "the Sepia Sinatra." (In turn, the fiercely proud Billy turned down the one big role he was offered, the lead in *Carmen Jones* that later went to Harry Belafonte. "Too many 'dems' and 'dats'," he said.)

BILLY AND I broke in a comedy duet on the very first night of the tour, in Roanoke, Virginia. It was the Willie Mabon tune currently high on the charts, "I Don't Know," and it never failed to bring the house down. I'd kick off with, "I'm dead sick an' tired of the things you do, Good-time papa, gonna *poison* you." Billy would interject, *"What?"* Then we'd hum together in harmony, "You shouldn't say that!" It was a natural showstopper, and I still had the all-conquering "Mama" up my sleeve for later. It was firmly lodged at number one on Billboard's R-and-B chart and would be voted the top R-and-B record of '53 by readers of Down Beat.

It was a constant source of wonder to Eckstine that I felt Willis was required on the tour, since my regular musicians were cooling their heels at home and the well-oiled machine that was the Basie orchestra was at my disposal. The answer, of course, was that I simply needed him around. "You got *him* givin' the downbeat with Eddie Davis and Bill Basie around? Are you serious?" Eckstine would ask with a wicked gleam in his eye. "Shut up, you *dog*," I'd plead if I saw Willis come anywhere near earshot.

Our bill also included George Shearing, the blind English pianist who was hitting with "Lullaby of Birdland," together with my fellow Atlantic artists, the Clovers. Up until we reached Atlanta, Bill Basie had been introducing the acts. For Atlanta Eckstine decided we needed a helping of comedy between the routines, a suggestion of finesse rather than Bill's clipped two-word intros, someone to get us on and off with a flourish and a smile. I recommended Nipsey Russell, who stuck to good clean jokes and had become a fixture at the Baby Grand in Harlem. The proprietors agreed to release him and he joined us as soon as he could get on a plane. He was just as terrific as before, quick-witted, with an incredible vocabulary, someone who rhymed everything and always had a charming way of getting you onstage. He was to become one of my best and most loyal friends.

The devil in Eckstine came out on that tour, and everybody felt it, from Basie and his musicians—among them Gus Johnson, Joe Newman, Marshall Royal and Eddie Davis—to singers Bixie Crawford and Joe Williams. Me and my happy band of Willis, Thelma and Chickie were regarded as guests rather than victims, I'm glad to say. There was a water cooler at the back of our bus held in place by a steel band, which Eckstine and his cohorts kept full of gin, the band's liquid of choice, rather than water, and they had a unique method of insuring it was faithfully filled up at every stop. Gus Johnson would run up and down the hotel corridors at night with his camera, snapping away through the transom windows of each room, attempting to catch his fellow musicians in compromising positions. The next day Eckstine and Basie would take their positions at the front of the bus, behind the driver. As soon as the city limits were reached, a blue-painted basketball would be propelled down the aisle from the back. It was the signal Eckstine had been waiting for, the signal that someone had been photographed in bed with a "bear" (shall we say, a less than attractive woman) and they were about to be tried for the "offense." Naturally, Eckstine was the judge. As he took up his position in the stairwell he'd say, with that devastating smile of his, "Okay, court is in session." The defendant had a choice of pleading his case, with no idea how damning the photographic evidence against him might be, or he could prevent the evidence from being produced by agreeing to top up the gin supply.

"Today," Eckstine would intone, "the jury calls upon—"

Most guys would jump up at this point, yelling something like, "Okay, okay, I'm guilty. I'll pay! Just don't pull the pics, for God's sake."

We soon discovered that nobody in the group was exempt, and we'd already heard that not even the fairer sex had been spared in the past. When Bixie first arrived the rest of the band had considered her snooty, looking as she did down her pretty little nose at their fun and games. Sure enough they soon caught her with the male equivalent of a "bear." At first, knowing they couldn't possibly have the usual photographic evidence (it seems she had hung a blanket over the transom—resourceful girl, Bixie, you gotta give her that!), she tried to bluff it out and refused to acknowledge her guilt. *"Okay,"* Eckstine said, relishing every syllable. "We got this *tape recording* we made of the whole proceedin's . . ." It turned out they had set her up with somebody. She had to beg them to turn it off. *And* she had to pay up.

In the early hours of the morning a week or so into the tour Willis and I heard a furtive *tap, tap* at our hotel door. "Who is it?" we chorused. "B," came the reply. "Come on out, we're going for the big one." Soon Eckstine had the entire busload assembled in bathrobes outside in the hallway, except for two key personnel. One was Marshall Royal, who just five minutes earlier had been preserved on film for all eternity, soaking in a bath with not one but two bearish members of the opposite sex. The other was Bill Basie himself. "He's got someone in there with him," Mr. B whispered. Up to Basie's door he went, and knocked. The only response was a single *beee-ing* from the bedsprings inside. "I know you're in there, Basie," B. said. "Open the door!" This time there was a whole frantic series of *beee-ings,* followed by an agonized, "B, get away, you can't do that!" We stood there, convulsed.

"Basie, open the damn door!" B insisted. Now there was a positive symphony of springs. "Ain't no use you tryin' to get her out the window," he warned, "we got that covered." No response. B tried again: "Basie, open the—*awright,* I'm gonna start countin' . . . !" We all joined in as he did: "One . . . two . . . three . . . four . . . five . . . six—" Feet could be heard scrabbling desperately across the floor inside. "Get the hell away from there!" we heard Basie yell. "—seven . . . eight . . . nine—" (By this time I should tell you that Basie and B, the closest buddies in musical history, were addressing each other by a series of totally unprintable pet names they apparently reserved for occasions such as this.)

At the count of ten Eckstine put his shoulder to the door and pushed. It flew open, he took in the scene, then in a split second he spread his arms wide so us innocent lambs couldn't see. "Oh, boy," we heard him breathe. "When you come to that bus this mornin', Basie, you'd better bring a *case* of gin." As he slammed the door shut we could still hear Basie inside, cussin' and layin' B out like there was no tomorrow.

When Basie made to board the bus after breakfast Eckstine was awaiting him on the stairwell, arms folded. "Where's the gin?" B said, but Basie was in no mood. "Don't mess with me now, you sonofabitch." We all sat there as the bus took off, demurely waiting for the city limits to be reached. Then down the aisle that blue ball rolled, followed by B taking up his usual position. "Court is in session!" he declared, savoring every word, as well as Bill Basie's obvious discomfort. "Today, ladies and gentlemen of the jury, we have before us an internationally known personality. The world knows only one side of this man, but we are going to make the world aware of the *bear* that shared his room last night!"

"Awright, *awright,"* Basie butted in, "that's enough. I'll pay up. When we get to the next city I'll buy the goddamn gin, okay? And leave it at that. *Okay?"*

I'm not saying that Basie had something on his mind, but he bought four of the biggest bottles of gin I've ever seen and filled that cooler to overflowing. We were left wondering on two counts: how Basie had smuggled his visitor out, and who she might have been. The favorite among betting men on that tour was a young singer who certainly had been in town that night. Whoever it was, B and Basie kept that hot little item entirely to themselves.

The unfortunate side to all this was Willis's having gotten a load of Mr. B's bathrobe. "Shorty, did you see that?" he asked after we'd made our way back to our room.

"See what?" I replied.

"Billy's bathrobe," he answered. "I've never seen anything like it. I believe it was pure cashmere."

"Really?" I said, pretending it had gone in one ear and out the other, but taking a weary mental note that the item had gone straight to the top of Willis's wish list of what the well-dressed man was wearing. I ain't cheap, but I wasn't about to break the news when I asked Billy and it turned out to be vicuna, the world's most expensive fiber. Besides, Willis was thrilled from here to Harlem with the cashmere beauty I bought him, and at least the color was the same as Mr. B's.

WHEN OUR TOUR took us to Alexandria, Louisiana, I began singing a new song of mine, "Love Contest." Halfway through, a woman staggered to the front of the stage, very drunk, and passed out as she leaned there at my feet. Whether inspired by the lyrics of my song or not, quick as a flash two young bucks came up behind and started coming on to her. Billy took all this in from the wings and for a week after that, every time we met he'd say, "My, my, Ruth Brown—the girl who can make them do their thing in the auditorium!"

In New Orleans we played a hall that normally had whites upstairs in a place known as the "spectators' balcony," with seats for blacks in the stalls. They had sold out this particular night, and with the balcony seats overflowing they gave the stall seats to the whites as well, pushing the blacks behind the stage. When Billy walked on and saw what had happened he told Bill and the band to turn their chairs around to face the blacks. How he got away with it I'll never know, but he did. I had already come close to being arrested earlier in the evening while innocently booty-buttin' to the music with the band's white drummer. We had traveled thousands of miles together on the bus and it never even occurred to us that we were breaking the law. We soon discovered that segregation was strictly enforced there, however, when a cop saw us dancing together and snatched me away. Luckily, Fats Domino's musical director Dave Bartholomew was around; he sped to the rescue, slipping the cop something to get him to overlook the incident.

For some strange reason known only to the bookers, maybe not even to them, we found ourselves appearing at the Grand Ole Opry in Nashville, Tennessee. This time it was George Shearing's turn to hit trouble. George had two black musicians with him, conga drummer Amando Pereira and bass player John Simmons. When the curtain rose and the crowd took in that combination of white and black faces, it was too much for them. They began to boo. "Stop the music," George instructed his fellow musicians. As the noise from both the group and the audience died he announced that he'd like to say a few words before continuing with the musical program he'd planned. "There are people who feel sorry for me," he declared. "I've often been pitied for being blind. But it's on occasions like these I feel grateful for at least part of my inability to see. Just imagine if you could become color-blind, wouldn't that be a wonderful thing? Maybe then you could use the rest of your senses properly and see through to the hearts of men, where we're all the same color. These fellows with me are here because of their God-given ability, because they're the best there is. The color of their skin is immaterial to me. Just for tonight, won't you share that with me?"

George's speech, which certainly brought tears to my eyes, was greeted at first with a stunned, disbelieving silence. Can you imagine some of those rednecks chowing down on what George had just delivered? Well, I'm here to tell you that they did. George gave the downbeat and went straight into "Lullaby." He had to reprise it twice before they'd let him off the stage.

At the end of that truly wonderful string of engagements Billy handed me an envelope. "There's a bonus in there," he said. "Go buy yourself a gift." It was the first thousand-dollar bill I'd ever seen in my life.

Yes, that was some tour. Thelma acquired two nicknames: "Flook," which Willis contributed (for no particular reason) and

Happy as can be on
the Mr. B tour.
(COURTESY OF RUTH BROWN)

"Jane Russell," coined by Joe Williams (for two very particular reasons. I tell you, that slip of a girl was bustin' out all over!). Chickie?
He was not that much older than Thelma and was as slim as she,
but those young stage-door Johnnys beat a path to that child's door
until he had his own faithful retinue of camp followers. As for Willis, he became restless on that tour. He was not the star, which he
certainly could be in the right setting, because he was one heck of a
player, and this caused more than a few tense moments. Thelma
and I were chatting away one day in my dressing room as she ironed
the outfits I intended to wear that night. Willis walked in, looking
tight-lipped, and said, "Flook, take a walk."

"But I got these dresses to finish—"

"Do them later. Please, Flook."

When Thelma left it all poured out. He was the spare man on the
team. One member of the band had made a slighting reference to
his contribution. Thelma and Chickie had more responsibility than

he did. He felt like a fish out of water. He should never have agreed to do the tour in the first place. He was taking money under false pretenses. I let him talk as long as he wanted, then gently reminded him how much he meant to me. And the tour was only for eight weeks, then we'd be back in the city and he'd be pounding the beat he knew best, bigger and sassier than ever. I talked, coaxed and cajoled until I got him out of that downer, but it was a close-run thing.

MY NEXT TOUR immediately following B and Basie, was with heavy-weight champ Joe Louis. Willis was okay on this trip, with a proper role to play and more company, I guess, of his own speed. My entourage included brother Benny, and we had Lester "Prez" Young, the Buddy Johnson Orchestra and the Clovers completing the bill. As with the last tour, the fun and games on display all but eclipsed the musical highlights. And there were plenty of those.

Joe's friend and partner, a skinny little guy named Leonard Reed, was light enough to pass for white. As our bus drove through the outskirts of Dallas, Texas, heading for Green Acres, the black hotel where we always stayed, all of us were fast asleep. All except Leonard. He had the driver stop at a white hotel on the way, and alighted, quiet as a mouse, with his suitcase and golf clubs.

When we drew in alongside Green Acres, Joe looked around: "Where's L-Leonard?" After the driver explained where he'd been dropped off, Joe turned to me. "That s-s-sonofabitch!" he exploded. "I should have kn-kn-known what he'd be at. Well, he ain't g-g-gettin' away with it! Ruth, see that lady on the s-s-sidewalk walking those three kids? Give her this fifty-dollar bill an' tell her Joe Louis wants a w-w-word with her."

We drove straight back to Leonard's hotel, complete with the mama and her children. "Okay, R-R-Ruth," said Joe, "now go do what you gotta do."

In I trooped to that hotel, straight up to reception, trailing the three borrowed black kids with me. I have to say it felt scary being stared at the way I was, but what the heck, I was in there and there was no backing out. Quieting my brood the best I could, I ad-

Miss Rhythm 93

dressed the gentleman behind the front desk: "I'd like to speak to my husband, please."

"Does he work here?" the man asked. "What is it he does?"

"Oh, no, sir," I replied. "He don't work here. He be *stayin'* here."

"That's impossible."

" 'T'aint neither. Why, I do believe he checked in not one hour ago."

"What? You must be mistaken."

"Mistake ain't on my side, mister."

"What's his name?"

"Why, Mr. Leonard Reed."

Everyone on that bus was craning their neck to see how I was doing. They didn't have long to wait, for poor Leonard was bundled out of his room and hustled out the front door so fast it's a wonder he didn't get a nosebleed. "P-p-pass for white, willya, ya skunk," Joe admonished as his buddy clambered aboard. "You ought n-never do that stuff!" And he wasn't through with Leonard yet. "Just watch what h-h-happens tonight," he told the rest of us. "The k-k-key word'll be *duckin'.* Just wait!"

JOE'S ACT BEGAN with his bounding into the ring they set up on stage, and that entrance alone, even the act of pulling the rope up, was enough to stop the show in its tracks. These folks were seeing their black hero, the supreme champ of champs, in the flesh. Boy, did they let him know how they felt! After the ovation died down Leonard was due on as Joe's sparring partner, expertly avoiding the blows Joe threw at him. His line after five minutes of this duckin' and weavin' was, "I'm a duckin' little sucker!" That night, as he got the word *duckin'* out, Joe landed him the smartest clip on the chin you ever saw, sending him flying halfway across the ring, knocked out cold. Buddy Johnson was laughing so hard he took a tumble off the bandstand, while the rest of his orchestra fell over, helpless, as what remained of Leonard got carted off to the dressing room. As he was being revived with ice water Joe arrived to press his point home: "I t-t-told you, don't *do* that!"

Joe, Leonard confided, had a crush on me. I was too naive to believe that, and was just thrilled to be in the presence of the champion of maybe every black person alive. Leonard also told me I was the only woman who made the champ take back the gifts he offered. He plied me with a beautiful set of luggage halfway through the tour, and it was Dave Crew who warned me against accepting it: "If you do, he'll take it as a sign . . ." They all knew what Joe was at, what acceptance of the gifts would mean, and Joe couldn't get over it when the set was returned. "Ain't n-n-nobody ever returned a gift of mine before . . ." he spluttered, shaking his great head in wonderment.

"Yep, you made a big mistake this time," Leonard informed him, undisguised glee drippin' like chocolate sauce from an ice cream cone.

On our bus the band members took to hiding their booze and stashes in Joe's golf bag, knowing it was safe, since Joe's valet always handled it. That was until the day Joe grabbed it himself and was off the bus and into the hotel before any of them. When he set it down in the lobby it toppled over, emptying out an unexpected variety of goodies, not least Prez's beloved Johnnie Walker Red. Joe stormed out and dumped all the stuff down the nearest drain. "D-don't *do* that stuff!" he admonished one and all.

THE LESSON I'D TAKEN AWAY from my first tour with Eckstine and Basie was well learned. When a second was set up at the end of summer I encouraged Willis to stay behind and attend to his own career. Atlantic immediately booked him for several backing sessions and talked about him laying down some tracks of his own. Together with some club gigs and radio work he also lined up, I left behind me a happier Willis than he'd been at the end of that first go-round.

While preparing to leave I heard some devastating news from home. It came in a call from Goldie: "Ruth, Mama's left home."

"What?"

"Mama's left home and taken Alvin and Delia with her. She phoned Blanche this morning in Philadelphia and she'll be staying with her for a while."

"But why?"

"Oh, Dad's been real mean to her lately, arrivin' home drunk at all hours an' beatin' up on her if she as much as opens her mouth."

My insides were churning as I listened, my emotions flung every which way. There was concern for Mama, of course, but—

"What about Dad? How's he going to manage? There's hardly anyone left with Mama gone."

"Ruth, there's *nobody* left, we're all outta there. We don't know. We can't talk to him in the state he's in, either drunk or sober. Oh, Ruth"—I could hear my sister begin to cry—"I don't know what's goin' to happen."

The tour was due in Norfolk on August 29, ten days after my sister's call. It was a date I'll never forget. I stayed on the bus as it drove through Portsmouth to guide the band to the Plaza Hotel in Norfolk, where they were booked for the night. I was standing in the foyer with them when I saw Goldie appear through the revolving doors, a grim expression clouding her face. "You gotta come right away, Ruth," she said, "our dad's dyin'."

Her husband and baby son were outside in their car and we rushed out to join them. *Dad dyin'?* Dear God, he was only forty-two years old! It was impossible.

Mama's departure had led to the last, fatal bender. Leroy had discovered Dad slumped over the dining table in our front room and had somehow managed to load him on his bike and wheel him over to Granny Ruth's. By the time we got there he'd been dead a half-hour. That was when I discovered what they're talking about when they say, "The show must go on," for I had to perform that same night in Norfolk. It was tough, really tough, maybe the toughest thing I've ever had to do, and I knew I had Richmond to face the following evening before I could return for the funeral. In Norfolk I had Basie on one side and Mr. B on the other when I broke down and began weeping in the middle of a number. Mr. B grabbed the mike and said, "We can't keep this a secret. You have to know what this girl is goin' through. Her father just died."

That got me through, but the headline in the local paper next day really did it to me:

"RUTH BROWN SINGS THE BLUES WHILE FATHER LIES DEAD."

Sensitive, huh? The old hometown had struck again.

8

THE "GREAT" BUNDINI

A LOT OF PEOPLE turned up for my father's wake only because it was for "Ruth Brown's daddy." As I stood at the top of our stairs the night before the funeral I overheard one lady say to her companion, "My goodness, can you believe this is where she grew up? There's not even a bathroom inside the house!" I was stung, and vowed right there to build Mama a little house of her own as soon as I could.

Next thing I knew there was a commotion downstairs. I discovered Dad's baby brother Jug, drunk as a cootie bird, violently shaking the coffin. "Get up, get up," he was calling out, "you can't be dead, you just can't!" Then he spun on my mother: "You'd better never marry again!" Poor Jug, he was already halfway down the slippery slope Dad had gotten himself onto. We knew Dad had had a problem with drink, but we were still shocked to see a combination of cirrhosis of the liver and high blood pressure listed as the cause of death. Because of this the insurance people refused to honor the little health policy he'd taken out.

I finally got to see Mama's anger at the graveside. We lingered there for a spell in silent contemplation, all of us thinking our own thoughts, I am sure, the family on one side of the open grave, the rest of the mourners on the other. Suddenly a heavily veiled figure detached itself from the crowd opposite. Gazing down at Dad's grave, she began crying, moaning and calling out his name.

As if it were in slow motion, I watched my mother lift up her veil.

96

She'd heard rumors of this woman, but they had never met face to face, let alone across an open grave. Mama's face was like something carved from granite, and when she stepped forward we all thought she was about to leap across to tackle the intruder. While my brothers held her back I went over and dealt with the woman. For once in my life I had no need to resort to my fists, for the words that poured out of my mouth were enough. That she could do this to my mother—! My hair had been sprayed red a few days earlier to match the dresses I intended to wear on tour, and I had been unable to wash all of it out. Dressed all in black, I was probably looking like the very devil, and certainly delivered the kind of fire and brimstone I'll bet that woman remembers to this day, if she's been spared.

The house I chose for mama was in Cedar Grove Acres, a new development on the outskirts of town. Being only the second home to be built there, it caused a great deal of curiosity, with sightseers by the bushel-load crowding round at weekends. That died away as the estate filled up and matured, leaving Mama in a beautiful house with a garden of her own on the edge of a forest. Compared to anything she had ever known, it was a well deserved paradise.

THE NEXT TOUR Willis and I undertook together was memorable, but for a far different reason than our previous Eckstine/Basie gig. One of the dates was a one-nighter in Miami, Willis's home patch. We booked ourselves into the plush Sir John Hotel, where all the black acts stayed. Before the show began he pointed out his mom and dad as they moved into their balcony seats, accompanied by a young woman whose presence he neglected to acknowledge. When the band break came I waited eagerly to be introduced to my future in-laws. Unfortunately, Willis seemed to have done a disappearing act. Instead, his friend, the bass player Ivan "Loco" Rolls sidled over to me. "Wanna go have a drink?" he asked. "Gator asked me to look out for you 'til he got back."

"Why? Where is he?" I asked.

"Well, he's gone to organize a car to get his parents home."

I felt like I had been punched in the stomach. Loco looked decidedly uncomfortable as I gulped and stammered, "I-Isn't he even going to *introduce* me?"

"I guess he'll be gettin' 'round to that tomorrow."

That's how the scam was pulled. When Willis called to say he was spending the night with his folks, I just left it. Next day, after an early breakfast on my own in the hotel room, a woman arrived to clean up. Before I knew what was happening she began to talk about Willis. "I hear he's doin' so well, really gittin' well-established," she gushed. Then she dropped her bombshell: "Me and his missus went to school together. One of his boys is the same age as mine."

"Hold it right there," I told her, that pain returning in the pit of my stomach. "You must be mistaken"—trying desperately to sound nonchalant and probably failing miserably—"he ain't married."

"What are you talking about?" she replied. " 'Course he is! I should know, hometown boy like that! Why, most everyone 'round here knows them. Willis and Leona. Real nice people."

I tried my best to act cool, though my insides were in a terrible turmoil. "Oh, I didn't know that," I managed. "I haven't been with the tour long enough to know everybody's personal business, anyway."

I cried my eyes out the minute she left. "Eyes I'll be looking in 'til the day I die"? I felt a distinct sense of *déjà vu*. First Jimmy Brown, now Willis. If this was a joke, it was a mighty cruel one. When he showed up at lunchtime I laid straight into him. He had all his explanations ready: "Last time I saw her, we were on the verge of breakin' up, and I'm just doin' what I have to do. It's only for the sake of the boys, and she's a friend of Mom's. And I didn't want to tell you in case I lost you."

Well, *good Lord!* I sensed he was lying. No, let me take another, more honest run at that—I *knew* he was lying! I just couldn't bring myself to admit it, that's all. He went further, going on to explain that it was all down to legalities. Oh, and another thing, she was mentally ill, liable to be confined at any moment. Then Mom would be left to look after the kids, arrangements would have to be made, it was a real tough, tricky situation.

Fool that I am, I asked Loco about the whole situation, neatly overlooking the fact that he and Willis had been best friends from school and there was no way he was going to contradict anything that was laid down. "Yes, it's true," he assured me, shaking that lyin' head of his as if giving in to some deeply felt sorrow, "she's not well, really not well 't all."

I had bought that dream way back when Willis and I first met. How could I just abandon it? I often think geography affects how we feel, and certainly the farther I got from Miami the better I felt. And for a while Willis was on his best behavior, contrite, polite, charming and disarming. When I suggested he should find us an apartment of our own and give up lighthousing, he agreed immediately and promised to start looking as soon as we hit New York. He did too, and found us a nice place on 163rd and St. Nicholas.

Just as we were settling in, another bombshell went off under my feet. Ace baseball catcher Roy Campanella was in the process of divorcing his wife, and before I could say, "That chair would look better in the corner," Willis's picture was splashed all over the newspapers; he'd been cited as co-respondent. Soon after that it transpired that a doctor's wife in Washington, D.C., had been seeing him off and on for years. And it seemed he had a white woman in Canada crazy about him. I kept patching and patching, clinging to the dream, but in my heart I knew it was ending.

He took me to an after-hours spot in Harlem one night called Welles's to have some supper. I felt terribly upset, we had argued back and forth since our show ended and I could not face the food that arrived. That started another fight. Willis got to his feet and stomped out, leaving me sitting there on my own. Naturally, he took our car with him. I began to realize he was using any excuse to disappear when he had something or someone else lined up. On the bandstand, meanwhile, he had taken to doing just what he had to do. There would be no conversation afterwards, except for the verbal abuse that initiated the next fight. In one of our more conciliatory periods I went out and bought him a beautiful cashmere overcoat. That was the day I heard one of the band whisper, "Oh, yeah, he's just pimpin' off Ruth." The remark tore at my heart. If it wasn't true, it was terribly unkind. If it was true, how could I live with it?

It was an incident at the Apollo that brought the full hopelessness of my situation home to me. I was up on the catwalk one afternoon

when I looked down and saw Willis smooching behind the curtain
with one of the chorus girls. I'm not proud of the fact that I lost
control—and reached inside my handbag for the gun I kept there.
The gun? Relax, it was one I'd bought back in Denver that only shot
blanks, but it felt great in my hand as I shinnied down there after
Willis, yelling blue murder. And it certainly had the desired effect.
You should have seen that Gator run! Once Thanksgiving, Christmas and the holiday season were over, I knew that the start of '54
would see me making some difficult choices.

AFTER REHEARSING for the holiday show I was set to do at the Apollo
with Sugar Ray Robinson in his tap mode, I made for the Palm Cafe
for a bite. Willis was out of town on some business of his own and
had chosen not to discuss its nature with me, but since a few calls to
Washington had been sneaked before departing I had a pretty fair
idea it was not musical chairs he had on his mind. Ralph Cooper,
my hero from the black movies of the thirties, was the deejay at the
Palm, with a guy named Bob Royal as the maitre d', and between
the two of them they never failed to cheer me up whenever I felt
blue.

A couple of friends from the Apollo were seated at a booth near
mine and invited me over. With them was a tall stranger—he
looked tall even sitting down—and there was a twinkle in his eye as
his companions introduced him as "the Great Bundini."

"Pleased to meet you," I said, then added sassily, "Did I get that
right—the *Great* Bundini?" The twinkle never faltered, but what
threw me was the stream of unknown dialect that poured like a
torrent from his mouth. "How's that again?" I asked when he was
through. While Bundini flashed a mighty expanse of brilliant white
teeth, my friends explained that he was new in town, having just
arrived from Africa. And—get this—he was a black prince and
didn't speak a word of English. I remember thinking how he must
have stopped over from the banana boat en route to Harlem to
outfit himself in the snazziest black silk suit I'd ever seen. I could
feel his eyes boring into mine, and there was charisma oozing from
every pore. Before I excused myself he let go another exotic out-

burst. "He says he really likes you, Ruth, and hopes he'll meet you again soon," one of my acquaintances helpfully interpreted.

One week later the phone rang in my dressing room, and when I picked it up a man's voice came over loud and clear: "Ruth, can I buy you dinner tonight?"

"Who is this?"

"Drew Brown."

"I'm sorry, I don't know any—"

"Also known as 'the Great Bundini.' "

"Huh?"

"Sorry, Ruth, that black prince stuff wasn't my idea. But my professional name *is* 'the Great Bundini.' "

I was intrigued enough to accept the invitation. My friends had really taken me for a ride and must have split their sides after I'd left their company that night, but I prided myself on being a good sport, and besides, with Willis hardly around, and the two of us not talking when he was, I was in need of congenial company.

Drew Brown provided that in spades. With all that nonsense about royal birth, foreign extraction and hambone tongues out of the way, he proved a wonderful escort, kind, considerate, extremely charming and very, very attractive. I could see heads, both male and female, turning as we entered the Palm, and it suddenly felt good again to be out on the town with such a companion. It still took several more dates, and a major fight with Willis, before I finally felt ready to melt into his arms, as the saying goes.

The night it happened began with my dining alone, this time at Frank's Steakhouse. "If you were my woman," I heard this voice say, "you'd never be on your own." As soon as I asked Drew to sit down I knew that this was the night it was going to happen. He ordered wine, we talked, he suggested, I resisted, he pressed and before I knew what was happening we were strolling in the direction of his place. I had heard by this time that he was in the fight game in some capacity or other, also that he was somehow attached, but felt neither the need nor the inclination to pursue the details, for with a man like Drew it was clear in any case he would be here today, gone tomorrow. In the past I had gone for romance, first, last and always—and fallen flat on my butt every time. Maybe it was time for a different approach, or at the very least a break from all that emotional wear and tear.

We spent the next two days and nights together in each other's arms before returning, as I knew we must, to the real world. We laid absolutely no claims on each other, and I certainly had no regrets. What I did not know was that I had seen only one side of Drew, that alcohol allowed his other side to escape. Our next meeting, just over a month later, was a world removed from the idyll we'd shared.

By this time matters had reached such a pitch with Willis that cohabitation had become next to impossible, and I had moved in to the Hotel Theresa. I was busy dressing there one morning when a knock came on the door. Thinking it was room service, I quickly threw on a robe and cried, "It's open." It was Drew, "the Great Bundini," except he wasn't looking so great. In fact, he looked to have been up half the night. This was neither the black prince he'd started out as nor the romantic, chivalrous knight I'd gotten to know. More like the black dragon!

"Gimme a kiss, Ruth," he slurred, lurching toward me.

"Are you kidding?" I asked. "Drew, get out and get yourself cleaned up."

"Can't do that," he replied, "not 'til I get my kiss." *Kiss?* By this time he was tearing away at my robe. I struggled, he pushed, and we both collapsed on the floor, his bulk pinning me there. I was scared, and my legs were hurting.

"Let me up, Drew," I shouted. "Get off me and let me up!"

"Jus' a li'l kiss, that's all," he insisted, tearing at my brassiere as we struggled. He was hot to trot, I was anything but, and I felt hurt and insulted that he had assumed, even drunk, I'd be available whenever he called. And if he thought for one fraction of a second I could be taken by force, he was about to discover different. In our fall the telephone had tumbled to the floor. I grabbed the receiver with my one free hand, lifted it as high as I could and brought it crashing down on the side of his head. As he slumped across me, groaning, I saw over his shoulder the crowd that had gathered at the door he had so thoughtfully left open. Inevitably, someone had contacted the gentlemen of the press. With our names splashed all over the newspapers, I charged Drew with attempted rape, and he charged me with assault with a deadly weapon.

After weeks of huffing and puffing, each of us dropped the whole thing. Drew was contrite and we agreed to remain friends, but we certainly didn't fall over each other to set up any future dates. Amazingly enough, we did get together again on and off during the next couple of years, but to all intents and purposes our "tingum" (the phrase Chickie used for two people who go bump in the night on a very temporary basis) was over. Except for one small but decidedly vital detail. Although I became temporarily reconciled with Willis, I left him behind in New York and embarked on a ninety-day tour with blues singer and pianist Charles Brown in the spring of '54. We'd never worked together before, and he and I became good friends. Our identical surnames promoted considerable speculation along the lines of were we married, related or what. Willis's absence fuelled this, and it was encouraged by our promoters on the basis that it sold a few more tickets. When Roy Brown was later added to the bill, interest was piqued even further.

Charles was and remains something else. Back then he was a rival of Little Richard's in the outrageous stakes, except on stage, where his presentation was sophistication personified. He was handsome as all get-out, and the women just went crazy for him. He traveled all over, even down South, in a powder blue Fleetwood, his immaculate suit topped by a mink cape and matching tie. Invariably his pedigree Doberman would be crouched beside him in the front passenger seat while his grandfather, a full-blooded Cherokee Indian, sat bolt upright in the back. What those redneck sheriffs made of all this I cannot imagine, but certainly Charles sailed through it all and survived in his own splendid style, broken hearts trailing in his wake.

During that tour there was a news flash that Tiny Bradshaw had died. That hit both of us hard, for we liked and admired Tiny, my accompanist at the Apollo's amateur hour. With Charles's agreement I stopped the band, we bowed our heads and I announced, "Folks, we've just heard that one of the great musicians of all time has passed. We'd like to ask for a moment of silence as a token of respect." The gesture was widely reported in the papers next day, and around mid-morning I accepted a long-distance collect call—from none other than Tiny! "Ruth, honey," he said, "don't bury me 'fore I'm dead!" The reports of his death had, it appeared,

With my first born and a genuine shellac. (Courtesy of Ruth Brown)

been greatly exaggerrated. Charles, Tiny and I laughed for years over that one.

I felt unwell from the beginning of that tour and by the time we reached Chattanooga, Tennessee, I was really sick. Charles persuaded me to visit a doctor, and it came as a terrible shock when fibroid tumors were diagnosed. I decided to obtain a second opinion and took a two-day break to visit my own physician, Dr. Wylie Martin, in New York. There are shocks and shocks, I was about to discover. "Take a look at these x-rays, Ruth," he told me. "That's no tumor, that's a baby."

I was completely floored, especially since after the auto accident specialists had advised me that my chances of ever becoming pregnant were minimal due to the altered position of my pelvic bones.

Back on tour I was able to hide my condition for a while with fuller skirts, until one date where I was so sick with pain I had to cry off. They rushed in the singer who was neck and neck with me in the polls at the time as my replacement. Unfortunately, they forgot to tell the audience until the announcement was made: "Ladies and gentlemen, the Queen of the Blues, Miss Dinah Washington . . ." One voice immediately yelled out from the front, "I don't give a damn *what* she's Queen of. I paid to see Ruth Brown!"

Happy moments with young Ronnie and Willis. (COURTESY OF RUTH BROWN)

The booing that followed was just the lull before the storm. Did you ever see Marlene Dietrich and James Stewart in *Destry Rides Again?* Do you recall the famous barroom fight? As Charles described the scene at that concert later, multiply that twenty-fold, and you begin to get the picture.

In Dallas a couple of nights later I watched Willis on the Ed Sullivan television show, showcased with Bo Diddley and WWRL-NY's deejay, Tommy "Dr. Jive" Smalls, in a feature on Harlem and black music. Afterwards I picked up the phone to congratulate him on what everyone agreed had been a showstopping performance. On impulse I added, "By the way, I got some surprise news. I'm expecting a child."

His response was immediate, so fast there was no time for any words of explanation I might have cared to offer: "It's not mine! Let's face it, Shorty, you've been down the road awhile. Ain't no tellin'."

Despite his bluster, Willis was winging it; he had no way of knowing. I did. Drew Brown was the father of my baby. And the news from that quarter was that his wife was also pregnant.

When I returned to New York I called Mama to come up from Virginia to take care of me. Willis stayed around most of the time in our apartment, but we were no longer speaking to each other.

Ronnie, Willis and me.
(Courtesy of Ruth Brown)

When he announced he was taking a trip to Canada to visit his white girlfriend, there was very little I in my situation could say to prevent it.

When I went into labor, Willis refused even to give me a lift to Mount Eden Hospital. "Get a cab," he suggested. I did, and after a tense couple of hours I was cradling my newborn son in my arms. I named him Ronald David after my piano player, Ronald Lee Anderson, and my road manager Dave Crew. I'd called them both and they hurried along to the hospital, which is more than either of the two leading lights in my life did. Okay, I had no reason to expect Drew, for I hadn't even contacted him after hearing about his other forthcoming happy event, but I was shattered by the callousness Willis displayed.

Assuming that the two of us were still together, and married into the bargain, the press announced the birth of Ronald David *Jackson,* for as far as they were concerned it was, "Ooh, Gator and Ruth got a baby!" What confirmed it was Willis's reaction when the press arrived on our doorstep the day I got home. He got to pose with his "son" and get his mug in the paper. He was pictured holding a saxophone to Ronnie's lips, with the caption, "Like father, like son. You're never too young to start!" Just to cap it all, Ronnie had been born with a cute junior version of Willis's hairstyle—the "Quo Vadis," complete with bangs. Lord have mercy! I was just grateful Ronnie had a name, and as he grew up there was never any reason to say other than Willis was his daddy, for the only person in our family who knew that the two of us had never actually tied the knot was Mama.

Four weeks later, in February '55, I felt able to go back to work. First I took mama home to Virginia, then I flew to California and hired a lawyer. He produced a legal document, sent a trunk into the apartment Willis and I shared in New York and pulled my furniture out.

I never went back there. That dream—and it *had* been a dream, for Lord knows I loved that man dearly—was over.

Memo to Allan Arkush: Allan, you'd better make sure whoever plays me in your movie is *gorgeous!* (COURTESY OF B.J. JONES)

9

OH, WHAT A DREAM

CHUCK WILLIS WAS a very soft-spoken, unassuming, humble guy, just bubbling over with talent. He had a style all of his own, which included being something of a hypochondriac. He had a little makeup bag that he carried with him everywhere containing all the pills known to mankind. And while others such as Charles Brown, Bill Doggett and Paul Williams reacted to the approach of baldness with toupees (God love them, their first few models were like helmets) Chuck's answer was a swamilike turban, with black shoe polish to darken what still showed. (Outrageous to the last and not to be outdone, Charles took to wearing a bejeweled beret on top of his "helmet." Vanity, thy name is not exclusively woman.)

Chuck and I were discussing material at Atlantic one day in the spring of '54. "When are you going to write a song for me?" I asked him, half-joking. "Are you kidding?" he replied. "Do you really want a song from me?"

"Of course I do. I've never been more serious about anything." I was simply staggered at his modesty. "Well," he said, "I may have something that could be perfect for you. It's not finished yet, but I'll show it to you when it is."

A few weeks later he produced a set of lyrics written out on yellow legal pad paper, and proceeded to hum the tune for me. In view of what I was going through with Willis, "Oh, What a Dream" was a killer title, but I fell in love right away with the wonderful slow, bluesy mood he'd created in his combination of words and music.

109

All we needed was for Jesse Stone to come up with an arrangement to match, and we were home free—well, almost. The record was barely on the streets when the inevitable happened. You guessed it, a Patti Page duplicate on Mercury.

Atlantic mounted one of its strongest counteroffenses, determined not to have this particular rug pulled from under them. Bolstered by my version having been picked out as a Billboard "Spotlight," an expensive advertising campaign was mounted in the trade papers that had the spunk and sheer *chutzpah* of the Atlantic boys written all over it. "Oh, What a Hit!" it trumpeted. "Because it has the Style . . . Because it has the Feeling . . . *Because it can't be duplicated . . .* BECAUSE IT'S THE ORIGINAL!" The result of all this huffing and puffing? Patti Page made Billboard's mainstream Top Forty; I settled as usual for the upper reaches of the R-and-B chart. It would be nice to report that my original had crossed over to the white chart. Instead, the reverse happened. "The Singing Rage" crossed over to the black R-and-B list!

Later that same year I hit again with the topical "Mambo Baby." Mercury, not to be outdone, hit back with a Georgia Gibbs duplicate. (Didn't they have *any* original ideas of their own over there?) Same result, the bulk of the sales creamed off. Never mind, the tunes kept the name of Ruth Brown hot, hot, hot in the same year that Atlantic, with its black originals, was declared the "most-covered label" in the U.S.

Personally I think "most-covered" was a misnomer; I would have termed it "most-*duplicated,*" for my gripe would never be with legitimate covers, or subsequent versions like Cliff Richard's, but with bare-faced duplicates, with no artistic merit whatsoever. Everybody in the business accepted covers as fair game. There were umpteen versions of songs like "Hey, There," "Stranger in Paradise" and "Around the World," and you chose your favorite version based not only on the singer, but on the different treatments and arrangements on offer. I covered several songs myself, like "Be Anything (But Be Mine)," originated by Winnie Brown with the Lionel Hampton Orchestra, and Larry Darnell's "I'll Get Along Somehow," but they were never by any stretch of the imagination mere duplicates. We *contributed* to the songs.

Atlantic label-mates in the mid-fifties. (COURTESY OF RUTH BROWN)

*   *   *

MAMA CAME UP from Virginia to look after Ronnie in those first few
months, and she brought with her my baby brother Alvin. Young as
he was, Alvin really took to the funky life of the theater. I introduced him to Clyde McPhatter backstage at the Apollo and Dinah
Washington rehearsing with Quincy Jones in the theater's basement, and he was doing backflips with excitement. The only thing
that threw him a little bit on this, his first trip to the Big Apple, was
being the only black child in Central Park.

After being so close to Blanche for so long it came as quite a
shock when she announced I should sign with George Treadwell
for personal management. She would still be around, she emphasized, but I needed more full-time attention than she was able to
give. In fact, this was Blanche's prelude to announcing her retirement. George was an ex-trumpeter with Mr. B's short-lived forties
orchestra, married at the time to Billy's ex-vocalist Sarah Vaughan,
and managing both her and the Drifters. My association with him
was fairly brief, a bit like his marriage to Sarah. When they broke up
he married again, and after his death it was Faye Treadwell who
inherited the Drifters' name. I never knew what George's qualifications were as a trumpeter, but he certainly possessed the gift of the
gab and liked the finer things in life. He was what you'd call a pretty
boy and in many ways he reminded me of Clyde McPhatter; there
was a manly side but a softer, feminine side as well. Tall, a bit flashy
(Dad would have trotted out "slick"), with a pencil-thin mustache
and always impeccably groomed, George, bless him, was a real black
Dorian Gray who never lived long enough to complete the role he
was playing. Although I didn't get to know Sarah very well in those
days—I did later, I'm thankful to say—I could see that her relationship with George was one more example of a female diva experi-
encing the problem of having a man walk in her shadow.

Blanche's subsequent announcement that she was packing it all
in and moving to Florida really threw me, for with George I'd never
enjoyed anything like the feeling of closeness that the two of us had
shared. Although she kept it a secret, she had been diagnosed with
cancer, and true to her religious beliefs had spurned any suggestion of treatment. We kept in touch, although it eventually boiled

down to a card at Christmas, and I heard she did some deejay work down there, as well as dabbling in politics.

Her departure left me feeling like a ship without a sail.

ALTHOUGH THERE WERE some great times on tour, we also had some hair-raising experiences, and these continued after I said goodbye to Blanche. Especially down South, where I was well warned by Dave Crew and others to keep my mouth shut in case it landed me in trouble. It was good advice. I remember thinking during the civil rights march on Washington and those sit-downs in the street that I could never have taken part personally, much as my spirit, hopes and prayers were with the participants. If someone had turned a water hose on me, I would have retaliated. I would have fought back, I would have been killed, they would have had to bury me. If there was one piece of advice from the Bible even Mama could never get me to swallow, it was, "Turn the other cheek."

In the beginning we relied on the agency's white "suburban" driver, usually someone of Italian extraction. He was the one who carried our shopping lists into stores in Southern states, where they refused to serve blacks. It was either that or do without, although sometimes we were allowed to use the back door, out of sight of delicate white sensibilities. We didn't find so much of that in North Carolina, but we had to look out in Alabama, Mississippi, Georgia and Florida.

As far as visiting a restaurant was concerned and actually sitting down to eat, we had first to cross those train tracks and find the local Soulville. What we did in every town was to trace someone who ran a little tourist house or had a place with chalets in the grounds that they could make available. We did lots of cooking in hotels, "our way"—that is, using electric irons, wrapping hamburgers in foil and cooking first on one side, then turning them over. Or we used radiators, or sometimes tiny stoves, opening a window to disperse the cooking smells.

We learned the art of survival, and every now and then we got lucky, finding a place where the lady of the house would cook for us and feed everyone off big trestle tables. Mama was like that—she'd feed a whole busload without batting an eye. When I called to say we were on the way she'd cook up a big ole pot of peas and heaps of fried chicken. You found a seat wherever you could, loaded your paper plate and tucked in.

Embarrassing situations abounded on these Southern tours, and we would often feel dejected by the time we hit our destinations. More often than not we just had to stop by the roadside to relieve ourselves, for there was seldom any question of using restaurant or gas station facilities. Once when I had the audacity to visit the ladies' room in a restaurant in Alabama, they broke the lock, hauled me out of there, half-undressed, and dragged me off to jail. "All it said was Ladies Only," I protested to the judge. "You knew damn well it meant *white* ladies," he replied. "Now git yore black ass back in that cell 'til they arrive to pay yore fine."

Often the "stages" of the venues we played would be just the back of tobacco trucks, a couple of logs under the wheels to stop them moving. And some of the barns we visited had no washing or changing facilities. We simply put up a blanket and applied our makeup by the headlights of our bus, using witch hazel and alcohol to wash ourselves.

It was the folks who came to see us perform who made it all worthwhile. Sometimes they would bring along fried chicken and biscuits and we'd be invited to join their table and eat. I still run across people who tell me they were in the audience when I played such and such a place, and they tell me what a great time they had. In Toronto a couple of years back I met a man who'd caught one of my shows in Texas back in the fifties. He opened up his wallet right there and showed me the yellowing piece of paper where I'd signed my autograph. Those were the kinds of things that kept us going, together with the fact that at least we knew we'd be moving on next day, unlike the poor souls who'd come to see us. Often the local landowners were the promoters of these dances or shows, and it was a whole different thing to see folks lining up to sign the book for admission instead of paying cash, knowing it would be duly deducted from their pay at the end of the week.

There was a convoy of us—Charles Brown, Roy Brown, Larry Darnell and myself—driving through Atlanta one time, all in our individual Cadillacs, when we were stopped by the police. They said they had a report that a truck used to transport cars had been stolen, and guess what, our Caddies exactly fitted the description of the missing load. Even though we all had thousands of miles on our odometers they persisted with the whole ridiculous charade. Hey, why not? Look at the enjoyment it gave them!

Charles, Larry and I had all our papers in order, but we all had to get out of our cars and dig them out. As I was handed mine back I looked over to where Larry stood and watched as the cop "accidentally" dropped his documents on the road. When Larry bent down to retrieve them, the cop trampled them with one boot and gave him a swift, savage kick on the side with the other.

While this was going on, Roy was in trouble of his own. He'd gotten his car from Universal Attractions and the papers identified the company as the owner, not Roy. They hauled him off to jail and impounded his car. B. B. Beamon was contacted and got him out, but it cost plenty.

One local policeman took his pistol to me in Knoxville, Tennessee, during my last visit there, and it caused quite a riot. The venue was Chillowee Park, where I had performed several times in the past and had always been directed to a particular room upstairs to dress. On this occasion it turned out changes had been made, unbeknownst to me. I climbed the stairs as usual and innocently opened the door to what I assumed was the dressing room. Instead, there was some kind of card game going on, and this cop immediately leapt to his feet, pulled his gun, and roughly pushed me back, yelling, "I'm gonna kill you, you black bitch!"

I was scared but belligerent enough to reply, "Well, I *beg* your pardon, I'm sure!" before he started in again. The hall we were playing was big enough so we could open the door at the back and drive our cars right in and park behind the stage. I had left the top of my powder-blue Caddy down and parked it there, and it seemed this had not gone unnoticed, based on the cop's next outburst: "Who do you think you are, anyhow, comin' here in yore fancy cars like you own the goddamn place? Iffen you don't move right now I'll blow you right back where you came from!" Now I really was scared, for he was prodding my midriff with the pistol to emphasize his every word, and pushing me back near a steep set of stairs. Even if he was bluffing and I only fell, I dreaded to think what it might do to my legs.

All of a sudden there was a noise like a cattle stampede, and when I looked around there were my friends, led by Dave Crew, Charles and Roy Brown and Amos Milburn, rushing up the stairs to my rescue. The last I saw of the cop he was being carried aloft as I was bundled down those stairs. I jumped straight into my car, reversed out of there like a crazy thing, and drove back to my digs.

That caused another fuss, for people had paid good money for their tickets and demanded my return. It was either that or they were going to wreck the joint. I was staying at Fred Logan's house at the time, Fred being one of the good guys who opened his place up for black entertainers, and was still shaking from the experience when the chief of police arrived. This was the nearest I ever got to a white apology down South, but I told him I could not possibly return, I was too shattered. Next to arrive were the Weinbergs—*both* of them (a fairly rare sight, let me tell you). They took their turn at coaxing me to return. "I won't," I protested, "I'll *die* before I do." (Chickie's subsequent send-up of this scene had the entire unit in hysterics. "I'll *die* before I do!" he declared in a high-flown contralto, flailing his arms in a grand theatrical gesture before half-covering his face with one palm, fingers spread wide. No matter how grim the situation, there was always Chickie, or *a* Chickie, to enable us to see the funny side.)

I did return when I had cooled off, only because I didn't want to let those ticketholders down. At the end of the show I thanked them for coming, but added that they would never see me in their city again. And they never have.

In another incident in the same friendly state we were stopped by three members of the Highway Patrol, me in my Caddy, the band in a green Dodge station wagon with MISS RHYTHM emblazoned on the side. This time they claimed we were speeding. It was a lie, but we had these confounded New York number plates they hated down South, and that was enough. "An' just where d'you think yore goin'?" they asked Dave. He tried his best to tell them in his matter-of-fact way, even producing our itinerary, but still it wasn't good enough. They demanded that he open up the back of the wagon where the band's instruments were stored. "Well, lookey-here what we got. These look mighty like stolen goods," was their immediate verdict. I watched Dave protest in his low-key manner as I sat in my car fuming, for I just knew his words were wasted. I could sense what was coming, and come it did: "If you're musicians like you claim, line up yore boys on the side of the road there, and let's hear the critters play."

Having little choice, they did, all except Lee Anderson, our piano player. One of the cops sashayed over to him, one hand ominously on his pistol: "What do you do, *boy?* Why ain't *you* playin'?"

Lee spread out his arms helplessly. "I play piano, man," he tried to explain, "and there ain't no piano here. We don't travel with one."

"Well, you better play *somethin'*, boy, an' fast, iffen you don't want to spend the night enjoyin' our hospitality." Galvanized by this threat, Lee turned around, leaned over the front end of the Dodge and—I'll never forget it if I live to be a thousand—mimed playing piano on the hood of that car.

All the while Dave was busy imploring me to stay put, but by the time Lee was plunking out Lord-knows-what on that station wagon I could contain myself no longer. The moment I hit the road one of the patrol fixed on me: "I s'pose you're another pianist?" I told him what I did, at the same time aware of Dave watching me in an effort to force me to keep my head. "Miss *Rhythm?*" the patrolman echoed mockingly as I pointed to the sign on the Dodge. This was one tremendous source of amusement to the three of them, but I still ended up singing by the roadside while the cops stood there listening, fondling their guns, sneering at us and laughing fit to bust while passing traffic slowed down to watch the spectacle.

I swear Dave had me positively hypnotized during that incident, staring me out as I endured that ordeal, willing me to keep my big mouth shut. His reward came later that evening when he whispered in my ear, "You did good today, Ruth."

"Go to hell," I replied.

We were stopped another time for doing thirty-five miles an hour in a thirty-mile-an-hour zone, something silly like that, and we really wondered what was going on when they began herding us into a deep wood, pushing and shoving. It turned out, thank the Lord, that the local judge simply had a cottage in there. After paying our fines we were left to find our own way back out. When you did get arrested, like that time, or the time I invaded the sanctity of the white ladies' room, they didn't usually detain you any longer than it took to get your fine paid. To do that it was quite common to haul you off to the judge's house to have it set, rather than put him to the inconvenience of visiting the jailhouse.

My brother Leonard had a terrible experience in Waycross, Georgia. He'd driven me into town and decided to stay behind when I left for rehearsal. Cruising along the main drag, he was pulled over by two cops who proceeded to verbally abuse him. One, short, fat and bald and smelling of alcohol, got violently angry as Leonard refused to rise to his bait that he was driving a stolen car, or that he was involved in some kind of drug or liquor-peddling. The cop pulled his gun on Leonard and spun him around, running his hands up and down his body—in search of a weapon, was his story —while his partner combed the car. Waycross clearly wasn't ready for a black man behind the wheel of a blue Caddy, let alone one with New York license plates. Leonard found himself handcuffed and under arrest; my car was impounded. The arresting officer's naked hatred careered out of control when he and Leonard were alone in the escalator on the way to the cells. Reeking of booze, he again ordered him to turn round. "Don't *look* at me, nigger!" he screamed, drawing his pistol and pressing it to the back of my brother's head. "Don't even *breathe!*" I don't know if you've ever had a cop pull a gun and point it at you, but it's a hell of a thing.

Leonard was flung into a cell, where he eventually managed to get word to me. I went to pieces at the news and contacted the NAACP, the local branch of the musicians' union, anybody and everybody I could think of in my panic, short of the FBI. This was happening to my brother! The police refused to let me speak to Leonard, but allowed me to leave food I'd brought, which I later heard they just dropped through the door hatch. Before I could get him out the following day the captain in charge asked Leonard to sign what he laughingly called a "gentleman's agreement" admitting that the arrest was perfectly legitimate, since they had "found" number slips in the trunk of my vehicle. The charge was preposterous—a stranger in town for a day muscling in on the local numbers racket?—but I was ready to do anything to get him out of there. Not Leonard. "I'm not signing anything, sis," he told me, and I could tell from his expression there was no point in arguing. The captain sensed this too and crumpled up his little "confession" as he pointed his finger at the door: "Why don't you just git outta here?" He did not have to ask twice, and I was never so proud of my brother.

Leroy was next in line for this kind of treatment. He was driving with me from Cleveland to Virginia, approaching Salisbury, North Carolina, when he nearly fell asleep at the wheel. He plowed into the side of the road, struck the curb and careered for the longest time along the grass verge. A mail box was demolished in the process, which probably slowed us down a little and lessened the impact as we connected with a small tree. I was in the back with Thelma and Chickie, and although we were shaken, we'd recovered by the time an ambulance was called to take care of Leroy and his badly busted knee. The last I saw of my brother he was being loaded on a stretcher while we hitched a lift to the nearest digs. No sooner had we left than the local cops arrived on the scene and demanded to know what was going on. "There's been an accident," the attendants explained. Pointing to Leroy, stretched out in the ambulance, helpless and moaning piteously, they added, "There's the driver. He's going to the hospital."

"No, he ain't," one of the cops announced. "He ain't goin' to no hospital. He's goin' to *jail.*"

"Why? He's hurt bad and needs treatment for that knee right away."

"Too bad. That was the mayor's mailbox he willfully destroyed."

At the jailhouse Leroy was refused medical help and spent the night on the floor of his cell in absolute agony. It was only by hailing a passing stranger on the street through the bars of his cell window in the morning that he was able to get word to me. As with Leonard, I panicked at first before making all the calls. I'll tell you why. We hear a lot today about unexplained deaths, often alleged suicides, during incarceration, and I dreaded this happening to any kin of mine in the South that existed back then. Thank God, I got him out safely and rushed him to a hospital, but it took a fortune in taxi fares, bribes, fine payments and car repair bills before we were able to resume our journey.

One afternoon back in Memphis I returned to my hotel room to find Thelma slumped in a chair, looking half dead. "What on earth's the matter?" I asked. "Oh, I'm okay now," my girl replied, "but, please God, never let me go through that again."

She had been out walking after lunch, on the other side of town, when she'd suddenly been taken ill with acute stomach cramps and urgently needed to find a rest room. No matter where she tried, she was turned away. "No Negroes allowed, strict rule of the house, no 'ceptions" was the polite turn-down, "Haul yore black ass outta here" the not-so-polite. Half-fainting, she attempted to hail a taxi. Several had drawn up alongside—Thelma looks pale enough from a distance—then taken off again when they saw she was black. In desperation, she discovered the existence of a black cab service, Tiger Flower Taxis. She called them, and the forty minutes she had to wait on that burning sidewalk, close to collapsing, but determined not to let herself down on the sidewalk in front of them white folks, she really thought her time had come.

The next night Dave was driving along, heading further South, when we spotted an unearthly glow in the distance over the brow of the hill. A mile further on we came within a hundred yards of a burning cross and a score of white-hooded KKK figures parading in front of it. I felt seized by a terrible rage. Worse, a *helpless* rage. If this is where we're at, I suddenly thought, I want no part of it. I was about to say, "To hell with all this! Turn around, Dave, point the car north, and *go!*" Instead I merely said, "Step on it, Dave," although I could tell by the look on his face it was hardly necessary.

They really had thought of everything to prevent being contaminated by us black folks. When ordering a take-out burger at the back door of the poorest restaurant there was often just a slit in the wall where you placed your order. That way you never even saw the person who served you. More importantly, I guess, they never had to see you, let alone touch your black skin.

"What you want?"

"Four hamburgers."

"Three dollars." That was the nearest we got to intimacy. After a wait the food would be pushed through the hole, good and greasy, the transaction consummated.

When Dave, a great family man, pillar of the black community and all-around solid citizen, went to collect a few Cokes from the ice bucket outside a gas station, a sawn-off attendant, looking for all the world as if he had just dragged his butt from a bowl of primordial soup, pounced on him: "Git yore hands outta there, *boy! I* do the gittin' roun' here!"

Add separate black and white water fountains, curtains in railroad dining cars to separate the races, signs everywhere with crudely painted hands pointing the way For Coloreds, and a thousand more of the so-called civilized indignities, insults and affronts we had to suffer. For a long time there was a particularly demeaning sight at Atlanta airport. They had an old black gent there, looking like Uncle Remus brought to life, sitting on a bale of cotton and crooning as he rang his little bell, "Come to the restaurant, massa, come to the restaurant." I don't see that now, which I guess is progress.

Audiences apart, first and foremost for us on those difficult but economically essential tours was the music. That was the compensation. Most good R-and-B musicians were not professionally trained, and the way we played in these often dangerous circumstances, well, there has to be a different kind of attitude when you look down and observe the segregated curtain or clothesline down the center of an auditorium or dancehall, with blacks and whites being dared to bump each other. As soon as the line dropped they did it, mind, until someone in charge noticed. Then the band would be cut until the line was back up. Anybody can sing or play our music now, but in those days people like us had their faces ground in the dirt. The local people just waited for the music to come, and for those of us who brought it to their neighborhood—the Charles Browns, the Clovers, the Drifters, the Clyde McPhatters, the Coasters, the Jackie Wilsons, the Sam Cookes, the Fats Dominos, the Little Richards. All these people, all these groups, with their great backing musicians, they're the ones who suffered every sling and arrow the South had to offer in those days. It was for the sake of the music that we did it. And maybe we helped the progress along a little.

One final compensation lay in the camaraderie among artists on these tours. We told jokes, played games, laughed, cheated, shot the bull and made love. That last was inevitable, for we were all flung in at the deep end of the adrenalin tank, and for up to ninety days at a time. There was travel together, hanging out together, performing together. And sometimes there was love together. It seldom got to the point of "Let's get married," it was just being natural and keeping your business within your business, but these "tingums" could be hot stuff while they lasted. Of course there were also jealousies, but I swear the main competitiveness between us lay in the threads we hung on our poor tired bodies when showtime came around. There were plenty of brushes and polish to keep us looking spruce on board whatever transport we had, but whether I was in the company of LaVern Baker, Mary Wells, Shirley Alston and her Shirelles, Zola Taylor of the Platters or Buddy Johnson's l'il singin' sister Ella, it was no-holds-barred on the dress front.

Even in the worst of situations, and the segregationist South came mighty close, it was possible to take comfort from little things. I saw a cartoon once in a newspaper down there that surprised me. It showed two adult males, one black and one white. The black man had his Afro hairstyle and open sandals, the white man had his Klan uniform on, and coming out of their mouths were all kinds of racial epithets.

At the same time each of them had a small boy by the hand, except that the two of them had pulled around and one was saying to the other, "Hey, I'll meet you at the ballpark just as soon as they get through with all this stupidity."

For me that said it all. Out of the mouths of babes!

10

ROCK CHILDREN

LITTLE RICHARD? Let me tell you about Little Richard, for there's so much misconception. Onstage he is showbiz personified, flashy, glitzy, the essence of camp, completely over the top. Offstage he's a decent, down-to-earth guy, with none of that showbiz phoniness about him whatsoever. On one memorable occasion the two of us shared a bill with Jerry Lee Lewis, where it truly was a battle to the death between their dueling pianos. Those keys were hit with everything they had to give that night, with toes, ears, noses, temples, crotches and butts, with Richard shaking his wig fit to send it spinning into orbit. When he visited Virginia after our tour, Mama presented herself backstage as Ruth Brown's mother—she was doing stuff like that by this time, not shy at all—and invited him back for a meal. Off they went, and the two of them talked for hours. Mama loved that, and she loved Little Richard too.

"When I first came along I never heard any rock 'n' roll," he once told Rolling Stone. 'I only heard Elmore James, Sonny Boy Williamson, Ruth Brown and Roy Brown. And this thing you hear me do—"Lucille-*uh*"—I got that from Ruth Brown. I used to like the way she'd sing "Mama-*uh*, He Treats Your Daughter Mean.' I put it all together." I guess he was referring to what Herb called my "million-dollar squeal!"

I first heard about a young man by the name of Sam Cooke from my brother Benny, who'd caught an appearance of his with the Soul Stirrers gospel group during a tour of Southern churches.

"They've got this kid who can sing up a storm, but with the clean-est, purest voice you ever heard," is how Benny put it during my second tour with Billy and Basie. I met Sam just a week or so later in Houston, where promoter Don Robey had booked Mr. B and my-self into the only hotel that would accept black entertainers. The Soul Stirrers and another gospel troup, the Pilgrim Travelers, were in there at the same time, together with a whole bunch of other artists, among them Johnny Ace (Don Robey's young star on his Duke record label), veteran Willie Mae Thornton and Little Rich-ard and his Upsetters.

When we all got together that night and sallied forth for some-thing to eat, Sam introduced himself. We broke off for a spell from the rest of the company as he let his hair down and discussed the dilemma facing him. He felt pulled in the direction of R and B, blues and secular music in general, but was scared of abandoning his roots. "I want to be real sure of exactly what it is I want to do," he told me. "It's easy to get out there—I've had offers—but a lot harder to get back in."

"I know," I replied, "they'll say the devil's got you. Sam, I know the feeling."

After the meal we all ended up on the steps around the side of the hotel—Sam, Willie Mae, Billy, Little Richard, Johnny, the guitar man from the Pilgrim Travelers, and myself. Oh Lord, how I wish I'd had a tape recorder with me, for the sounds that reverberated through that Texas night were something else entirely. As soon as the guitar man sounded his first chord Sam began singing the hymn all of us had agreed was the first we'd learned, "Jesus Loves Me (This I Know)." Little Richard came in at the halfway stage, calling and responding to Sam like some demented angel. We all had our moments of glory on numbers that tumbled out one after the other, pairing up as the spirit dictated, soloing where there was space and humming in the mellow background on "Mary, Don't You Weep," "Take My Hand, Precious Lord," "The Old Rugged Cross" and "Abide with Me." Let nobody claim we were found wanting during those few hours in the sight of the Lord. My father, who had recently passed away, could not have had a finer memorial service, for there was everything he would have wished—true dig-nity, devotion and fervor, whether expressed in sacred or secular terms. Sam was a sweetheart, a hunk all wrapped in white, a darling, and we often turned up at each other's gigs after that. The last time I saw him before his tragic death was at a club in Miami, the Harlem Square, where he made his wonderful live recording.

That same venue was also where I last saw a completely different kettle of fish, Little Willie John, laying on the floor dead drunk behind the bar, singing his heart out. I had first been introduced to young Willie through Paul Williams. They both came from Detroit and Willie's dad had asked Paul to keep an eye on his teenage son on the road. Young Delia was out with me at the time, and the same age as Willie, and she developed quite a crush. His dad joined him on the road for a while as the hits began with "All Around the World." By the time "Fever" came along, though, the erstwhile sweet young kid had begun to cop an attitude. What caused the change I do not know, maybe it was the booze he discovered, maybe success had gone to his head. Delia saw him as a very talented, hot-tempered kid who made a lot of money too quickly and couldn't handle it, a country bumpkin unable to shake off his poverty-stricken roots. Whatever it was, he became extremely arrogant and every word that spilled out of his mouth was a cuss word. This was particularly offensive to me—I can't take it, I don't do it, I won't tolerate it, get out of my way!

He got on the wrong side of Little Richard during an Apollo gig we did together and got brained with a straightening comb for his pains. Due to follow me on stage a couple of nights later, he missed his cue, and when I bumped into him after the show I said, "Now Willie, you gotta do better than that. You can't maintain a star position unless you act like one." Well, that boy backed up, stood on his hind legs and said, "Bitch, you don't tell me *nothin'!*"

They tell me I smashed him clear through the swinging doors at the back of the Apollo stage, knocking out two of his front teeth in the process. He landed in the anteroom where the stagehands and artists played checkers. I ran right through there, grabbed him by his collar and lifted him to his feet. "Don't you *ever* speak to me like that again," I said. "Respect my presence, that's all I ask."

After I tossed him back down like a rag doll, Frank Schiffman arrived backstage. "Oh my God, Ruth, you knocked out Little Wil-

Joe Williams, me and B.B. King, all skinny-minnies back then, with Miss Ebony in the 1950's.
(COURTESY OF RUTH BROWN)

lie!'' he declared. ''I'm surprised at you. You were always such a lady!''

''That's why,'' I replied. ''I couldn't take this boy's jive.''

Compared to Wynonie ''Mr. Blues'' Harris, of course, Little Willie was a mere junior apprentice. There were codes of conduct on those buses we traveled on, codes that were normally well observed. Not by Wynonie, though. Normally the men would wait until the girls were out of earshot before launching into their raunchiest stories. We'd hear these deep guffaws and say, ''Uh-oh, there they go!'' Wynonie, on the other hand, had a mouth that would freeze a sailor in his tracks, his every second word a kiss *that* or a mother *this*. And he could care less who heard it. He resembled a darker version of Mr. B, with the same green eyes, and he could really draw the women. But whereas Billy always showed respect, or at least more or less knew where to draw the line, with Wynonie, forget it.

Once while touring with the Clovers and the Buddy Johnson Orchestra he picked up the wife of a well-known entertainer in Tennessee. Obviously, nobody had warned her about Wynonie. After going out for a bite to eat after the show, the rest of us arrived back at our hotel to find him dangling out his window, half-naked—the bottom half—and yelling about what a goddamn waste of time the woman had been. He then proceeded to throw her undergarments out the window one by one.

He took to carrying a tape recorder wherever he went, and if he made a conquest he'd hide it under the bed, record the whole business and play it back on the bus next morning. On another tour we did together he struck again, gleefully spying on Dusty ("Open the Door, Richard") Fletcher and gospel singer Clara Ward as they got it together in their hotel room, then detailing their every move, with lip-smacking relish, to anyone who cared to listen.

He really was the limit, and even Ella Johnson, Buddy's singing sister and a real home girl, fell victim to Wynonie's taunting. Ella was never seen without a black slip under whatever outfit she was wearing. Wynonie's judgment as the tour moved along? "That bitch don't have but one slip and she don't ever wash that slip. It was black the day we started this goddamn tour and it'll be a damn sight blacker by the time we're through!" Anyone else but Ella, some folks might have listened to that nonsense, but that girl had been raised right, I swear. She was completely non-showbiz; her brother was the Svengali, and without him she'd never have gone within a mile of a stage. She was a nice girl, a real plain Jane who sang her songs, even her biggest hit, "Since I Fell for You," rolling her goo-goo eyes and looking to her brother for approval, without ever displaying one single ounce of charisma. That she should be the butt of Wynonie's twisted sense of humor was just too much.

There's two kinds of artists on tour, and Wynonie was strictly the other kind. His ego was a match in every way for his libido. I saw him enter a restaurant once and fill a jukebox up with coins so nobody could hear any records but his. He had a neon sign on his lawn at home in St. Albans proclaiming, "This is where the greatest blues singer in the world lives." Until the authorities forced him to pull it down, that is. He *was* a darned good singer, but on the road he was also the all-time pits.

On the road with Thelma Manley, my brother Bennie, me, Harold Lucas of the Clovers and Vernon Vass (a Virginia boy— Mr. B's valet on my recommendation).
(COURTESY OF B.J. JONES)

* * *

CHUCK JACKSON HAD BEEN a member of the Del-Vikings, but when I got to know him he was staying close under Jackie Wilson, who was his mentor and for whom he had enormous respect. Chuck had one heckuva voice for such a skinny guy, deep and powerful and resonant. (He became known as "the Peacock" first for his fussy struttin' around, also as "Thimble-ass." That last was coined by Yvonne Fair, for no matter how neat his suits were tailored, he always seemed to end up with several yards of fabric flappin' round his rear end.) I had just met Jackie when he was with Billy Ward and the Dominoes as Clyde McPhatter's replacement. He darned near got himself fired that night after offering me a drink at the bar. Miss Rose Marks, manager of the group at the time, bawled him out in front of everyone, and that was the beginning of the end as far as Jackie was concerned.

After our first show together at the Apollo, Jackie, Chuck and I were getting ready to travel to the Howard in Washington. It seemed that both those heroes were short of the train fare. I had a good guess where their money had gone, for the backstage crew at the Apollo gambled nonstop between shows and performers often lost their money before they even saw it. Naturally I found room in

At the 845 Club, Brooklyn—Thelma and me, Virginia's double threat!
(COURTESY OF RUTH BROWN)

my Caddy for both guys. Jackie and I became the closest of friends, and I can see him now, paradin' his stuff and drivin' the ladies hysterical in those skin-tight mohair and silk suits he favored. "Mr. Excitement, Mr. Delightment" was no exagerration.

While Jackie lay in a coma after his stroke in the mid-seventies, I used to call and ask about him all the time. I also made several trips to New Jersey to be close to him, but I could never enter the room he was in. I could not face seeing what had been such a fine, vital man in such a hopeless condition. There had been so much in the tabloids of him laying there, muscles wasted and slowly fading away, and it hurt me so bad. When they went through the farce of fundraising to place a headstone on his grave, I had to speak out in disgust. A *headstone?* How much did that cost? Why couldn't his record company, who'd no doubt made millions off him, pay for it?

Another wonderful artist who died before his time was Roy Hamilton. My first sight of him was quite something. At the last minute I had rushed back from California to open at the Apollo, entering the theater through the back door on 126th Street. Tarzan of the Apes could have been on the bill with me for all I knew, and as I left my dressing room ready to take the stage I heard the audience screaming and whistling. Curious, I decided to take a peek from the catwalk, and there was this tall, *outstandingly* handsome image in a blue tuxedo singing "You'll Never Walk Alone" in a voice to die for. The audience was going crazy, refusing to let him go, yet this was the act I was supposed to follow! I thought, "Oh boy, here we go again."

I did follow him that one time, but I made darn sure there was a comic between us for the second show. I went to Roy's dressing room to explain my action, and told him, "The day will come when you'll understand." Years later he was playing in New York at Basin Street and they had Juliette Greco on stage immediately before him singing the blues in French. The audience was cheering fit to raise the roof, and when I saw him afterwards he just looked at me, burst out laughing and said, "You know what I'm going to say!" I had the distinct impression *la belle* Juliette would be followed by a comic at the next show.

It was ironic that Roy fell ill soon after telling me he intended to give up the business and concentrate on singing spirituals. By the time I reached his bedside he was on a life-support machine, suffering from malignant hypertension, high blood pressure and pneumonia. Chickie and I spent a whole day and night there with his family and showbiz friends like Brook Benton and his wife Mary, Godfrey Cambridge, Ruby Dee, Sidney Poitier and his wife Juanita, and Ossie Davis. They said Roy was unable to recognize anyone, but I took a crucifix and placed it in his hands and he was able to hold it.

Ray Charles shares the same gospel roots as Roy. When my little troup arrived in Austin, Texas, for a gig Dave Crew sidled up as I prepared for rehearsals, smiling that smile of his that indicated he knew something I did not. It seemed that promoter Billy Shaw had put together a new band for us. "I've got a surprise for you," Dave informed me. "The band's here, all right. But the keyboard player is blind!"

"*What?*" I yelled. "Dave, is this your idea of a joke? How's he goin' to read my music if he can't see? What *is* that?"

Ray and I laugh about that introduction every time we meet. He wasn't doing his jazz and blues stuff back then—this was '52, and he was sounding just like Nat "King" Cole—but that was about to change once he signed with Atlantic and found his true metier.

Ray and Al Hibbler, another blind singer, were appearing with me in New Jersey a few years later. When Ray's set was over he parked himself behind the wheel of my car, waiting for the two of us to finish up and join him. I got into the back seat, ready to relax and talk for a while before we took off for our hotel, while Al got into the passenger seat beside Ray. "Okay, Ruth," said Ray, "we're goin' on a sightseein' trip!" So saying, he took off, cool as coffee— two blind guys in front, one driving, me in the back—and drove fifty terrifying yards down the track while I sat there screaming and Hibbler laughed his socks off. They were a real pair of jiveass jokers. Every time they met me it would be, "Girl, you sure lookin' good! Pretty as ever! And I just *love* that dress you're wearin'!"

At Chicago's Regal, Ray got into an argument with Dave. He wanted the dressing room with all the mirrors, leaving me with a mirrorless closet. I couldn't make head nor tail nor sense of that one, but I guess genius neither requires nor offers explanations. I let him have his way. Not the next time, though.

Ray may not be able to see, but he sure can sense, smell—and run. As soon as the rest of the band left us behind in my suite at the Stardust in New Orleans, he upped and chased me round and round the room, yelling, "You can't get away! I kin smell you!" When the band reappeared I asked Ray, "What would you have done if you'd caught me?"

"Ain't no tellin'," he replied, shakin' that nappy head of his from side to side.

When a tour I was on visited the Paradise Theater in Detroit, the same venue all the big gospel shows played, it became the custom for the Reverend C. L. Franklin to invite my gang to his house for dinner. The two of us became steady friends, or to put it another way, he had a thing for me for quite a while. And if you're busy picturing a conventional preacher man in a starched white collar, forget it. This man's cloth was silk, and I mean made to measure. He sported a "konk", and was tall, fine-looking and very, very suave.

His teenage daughter Aretha, all shy, gawky and hesitant, emerged from her room one night and was coaxed into sitting at the piano, where she played and sang for us. Her father turned to me when she was through: "Well, what do you think, Ruth?" I was simply stunned. "If I had to follow her," I replied, "I'd break both her legs, young as she is!" I didn't know it at the time, but she'd already cut a couple of gospel numbers for Leonard Chess before Columbia signed her, long before her amazing run on Atlantic.

Mahalia Jackson and I got to know each other at a religious fair, and when we met again it was at a benefit held in Carnegie Hall in the early fifties to raise money for the Southern Christian Leadership fund. You name them, they all turned out: Frank Sinatra, Sammy Davis, Jr., Peter Lawford, Joey Bishop, Tony Bennett, Harry Belafonte, Sidney Poitier. I was invited to be part of that, together with Nipsey Russell and the Sy Oliver Band. After my song Mahalia and I got to talking backstage. "I'd love to meet Dr. King," I told her.

"Why, sure you can," she replied. Just then he walked up the hallway. "Martin," she said as he approached, "I'd like for you to meet Ruth Brown. She's—"

He put his hand out to shake mine and looked straight at me. "I *know* Ruth Brown," he declared. "I *know* who she is, and I'd really like to thank her for being here tonight." Before he walked on he had one more thing to tell me. "You've got a great voice," he said, "but you should give more back to the Lord."

I did not know whether to feel complimented or humbled, and I was too busy being overwhelmed to care. I swear that when he put his hand in mine, it was like I had touched the hand of God.

BEFORE RONNIE WAS CONCEIVED Clyde McPhatter and I had worked in the studio just once together. He was one of the unbilled Drifters on my version of "Old Man River." Clyde was shy and sweet, and despite his high, girlish voice and mannerisms there was an innate manliness about him that I found tremendously appealing. We became close friends, strictly platonic, and I was astonished when he volunteered to stand in as Ronnie's father. Fond as I was of him, and acutely aware of the gravity of my situation—it was unthinkable in those days for someone in the public eye to have a child and no husband—I thanked him from the bottom of my heart, but turned down his suggestion.

By the time we recorded "Love Has Joined Us Together" and "I Gotta Have You," six months after my split with Willis in '55, things had progressed to the stage where Clyde and I both knew something had to give. It was there in the way we greeted each other whenever we met, in the way we hugged when a session had gone well, in the way I teased him about those little "stingy brim" hats he used to wear, in the reluctant, lingering way we began to say good-bye.

Pfc. Clyde Lensey McPhatter had been drafted in '54 and was halfway through his stint for Uncle Sam in Buffalo, New York, when the dam keeping us in check burst. Atlantic was aware of his decision to leave the Drifters and pursue a solo career on his return, and realized that his duet with me was part of the process. When it began to gain airplay I suggested to Tommy "Dr. Jive" Smalls that he try to get Clyde and me down to New York to promote the disc. He did, and of all people Willis "Gator" Jackson turned up playing sax behind us.

Rather than risk being seen in the city, Clyde asked me to join him in Buffalo and spend the weekend in a friend's house he'd borrowed. We both knew exactly what we were doing, we had no illusions we were embarking on anything but a "tingum," but unlike so many of those short-lived affairs, this was premeditated and born out of deep affection for each other. And if anticipation was sweet, consummation proved even sweeter. When we got ready for bed that first night I watched as he took off his battle dress, slipped off his tie and began to unbutton his shirt. As I caught sight of his chocolate chest under the khaki, he looked up and smiled his dazzling smile. "Ever unwrapped a soldier boy before?" he asked, beckoning me over.

"Can't say that I have," I lied. This was no time to be thinking of Walter Laboeuf!

Next day he took me shopping and bought me a friendship ring. "You're my lady now," he teased, "my secret lady love." We dined and danced at the Moonglow Club until the early hours, made love all night once more, then prepared to say our farewells. Our "tingum" defied convention, lasting several more weeks, and while it did we were both going around like kids with this big secret. Then it was over, and we moved on. The friendship and regard never ended, though. It continued until the day the world lost Clyde.

Like everyone else I had heard rumors of his bisexuality, and I believe towards the end he was ashamed and terrified of the outside world having his gay tendencies confirmed. He began drinking to drown the guilt and shame he felt, sinking his career into the doldrums. I wish I could say that the last time we appeared together, at

The only time Clyde and I were billed together on a record. (COURTESY OF RUTH BROWN)

the Apollo in '68, was a happy occasion. It wasn't, for two reasons. Also on that show were the Five Keys, the Ruben Phillips Orchestra, George Smith and Vivien Reed. There was another act scheduled to open with us, Frankie Lymon, and when he failed to turn up Mr. Schiffman sent a couple of stagehands round to get him. That's when they found poor little Frankie in his granny's coldwater flat in Harlem, dead from a heroin overdose.

Clyde arrived at the theater the worse for wear and continued drinking until the minute before he took the stage. His act dragged on and on, his announcements becoming more and more slurred and maudlin. Every time Ruben cut the orchestra he just launched into another number. Finally, Mr. Schiffman begged me to get him off. I did, by strolling on and asking him if he'd like to sing "our" song, "Love Has Joined Us Together," as a final encore. First he flung his arms round me. "This gal, this Ruth Brown," he announced, "she always been my special friend. Don't nobody but she and I know what there is between us." He turned to me, swaying ever so slightly: "Ain't that right?" I laughed it off like a trouper. "Hey, maybe one day you'll tell *me*, Clyde," I jived him.

After his death at thirty-nine years of age I spent some time talking with his pianist, Cliff Smalls. We discussed the anguish Clyde had felt on returning from his less-than-triumphant British tour at the end of the sixties, the shame he experienced after being arrested for "loitering with intent," even though the charges had been subsequently dropped. He cut an album with his original producer at Mercury, Clyde Otis. "Welcome Back" might have revived his career, but it got overlooked when Decca released it in '71. A year later, shattered that his request to rejoin Atlantic had been turned down, and separated from his second wife, Lena, he literally drank himself to death. His unique voice was hushed forever.

"I always knew Clyde loved you," was one of the last things Cliff told me that day. That meant so much to me.

11

MAMA, HE TREATS YOUR DAUGHTER MEAN

MY RELATIONSHIP with Earl Swanson was romantic, dramatic and, as it turned out, extremely foolish. He was another tenor sax player, and a good one when he wanted to be. When we got to talking on a tour I was on with the Griffin Brothers Orchestra, he said that he had spotted me that time in Houston when Little Richard and our all-star choir had filled the night with glory. Before joining the Griffins he was a member of Richard's band, the Upsetters—they both hailed from Macon, Georgia—and he didn't seem too upset when I said, truthfully, that I hadn't noticed him at the time.

He came over as charming, complimentary and very presentable, and all I can say is that I needed someone to fill the void Willis had left. On the surface they were dissimilar. Unlike Willis, Earl was no fashion plate. He was always neat, but without that flair Willis had for putting good clothes together and making an ensemble. I passed a lot of what I learned from Willis on to Earl, without ever volunteering where it had come from, of course, but Earl had a different style, mixing Jackie Wilson silk-and-mohair suits willy-nilly with Clyde's stingy-brims.

Although I was attracted to him, a prime consideration in my decision to accept his proposal of marriage was Ronnie's not having a father around. Second, way below that, I didn't want to be by

136

myself and have the world look at me that way. We were married in Baltimore between the matinee and early evening shows at the Royal Theater, with the exotic dancers on our bill, the Spence Twins, standing witness for me. The reason I had to ask them? Dave Crew and Lee Anderson point-blank refused. "He's *nuthin',*" Dave told me. "Why are you doin' this? You don't need this guy." Trouble is, I did. And they were all right, I was all wrong. Earl, I quickly discovered, didn't even get along with his sister Claudia, the vocalist with the band, nor, it seemed, with his brother Rudolph. Talk about rushing in! Although it was Earl that young Ronnie walked to on his first birthday in January '56, ours was a doomed relationship. He became domineering and pushy, and it was soon clear that he did not see Ruth Brown, the woman, all he saw was Ruth Brown, the star. Our marriage had not one of the necessary ingredients.

There was something seriously wrong with Earl, something eating him up inside, and I should have realized that from the beginning. Eventually I got the whole thing from his sister, and Earl himself confirmed it one night in his cups. It was a tragic story, and my heart reached out to him when I heard it. It went all the way back to his childhood, when he was separated from a family unable to support all three of its kids. It was three-year-old Earl his parents chose to be brought up by his granny. He kept a terrible rage bottled up inside at this injustice, a rage primed to explode whenever a new frustration arrived. And drink popped that cork every time. "He could have kept me! Why did Daddy send *me* away?" he'd repeat over and over, smashing his fist against whatever object was handy. His story drew me to him for a while. It wouldn't have if I had known that the handy object would soon be me.

The two of us visited my mama whenever we passed through Virginia, and this return to near his roots aggravated Earl's need to assert himself, even though I had officially made him my manager, as something other than "Ruth Brown's husband." "Where's the money?" he would demand of promoters. I knew it was necessary to play rough with some of these characters, but he picked on the wrong ones, he picked the good guys. If a reporter wanted to do a story on me after a show, he'd be the one to decide whether or not we had the time. Often he would turn to me in front of them and say, "I'm tired. Let's get outta here." And he would simply explode

With piano man Lee Anderson in 1954. (Courtesy of Ruth Brown)

if anyone called him "Mr. Brown": "The name's *Swanson*, not god-damn *Brown!*"

I knew Earl was sampling cocaine, which I am sure did nothing to help his increasingly violent mood swings, and smoking pot had the same effect on him as drinking, unleashing the demons inside. He became so mean, with all the resentment he felt toward his privileged brother and sister vented on me in torrents of verbal abuse, that it got so friends of mine refused to come round if they knew he'd be there.

Matters came to a head in Richmond when he physically attacked me in our hotel room, beating me to my knees after a bout of heavy drinking and drug-taking. I called my brothers, and they drove eighty miles to hand Earl their ultimatum face to face: *"Never* as long as you live do you lift your hands to her again." To reinforce the message they brought along a notorious cousin of ours, Booty Green, a guy who was into every kind of racket in Portsmouth—running numbers, making corn liquor, pimping, you name it, every vice imaginable. If anything had happened to Earl it would have been jes' another killing as far as Booty was concerned.

For a while Earl was contrite, not to say downright scared. I was relieved, and considerably impressed, when he announced that he wasn't going on the road with me again, that he intended to stay home and take care of "our" son. Fine, I thought. I left my white Cadillac with him when Dave and the gang arrived to pick me up. Back in Richmond, I got a call from a woman who ran a hotel in Norfolk. "If I wasn't your friend I wouldn't be tellin' you this," was her line, "but your husband's just checked in here with another woman."

Without even stopping to think I drove straight back there, arriving to find my Caddy parked outside the hotel. Earl almost fell over backwards with surprise when he opened his door, but recovered mighty quick. "What the *hell* are you doin' here?" he yelled, jumping right on me, fists flying. To add insult to injury, I even knew the woman he was with.

When he turned up at my brother's doorstep next day I was still hopping mad and kicked him out. After he left with his suitcase and saxophone, the picture of dejection, heading in the direction of the bus station, I had a swift change of heart, accompanied by a crying fit. "Will I go fetch him?" Benny asked. "Would you do that?" I answered tearfully. (You can imagine the three-act play Chickie made of all this when it was relayed to him!) I know it was pathetic, but hope surely does spring eternal, and I refused to give up that easy.

Thelma got in the middle of one of Earl's beatings, and it was spectacular. He had me backed up against the window on the fifteenth floor of a hotel in San Francisco, his hands tight around my throat. When Thelma entered the room and saw what was going on, she tugged at his arm and said, "Earl, please don't kill Ruth." Although she had spoken quietly, Earl's eyes almost popped out of his skull at her interruption. He let go his grip on me, spun around and slapped Thelma across her head with the back of his hand. Thelma took him by surprise when she bopped him back, then turned and walked out. When he chased after her and tried to grab her from behind, she picked up a chair. "Do it! Just do it!" she dared him. Wisely, he backed off. I believe some of that spitfire mentality was beginning to rub off on my girl!

As I sank lower and lower under the weight of Earl's abuse, the question on everyone's mind became, "Why doesn't she fight back? What's happened to the original spitfire?" The answer lay in Earl's softening-up process, the verbalistics that assured me I was a falling star, that he was the one who made our shows work. He plastered either "Earl Swanson Presents" or "The Earl Swanson Band, featuring Ruth Brown" on our billings, always with his name first and in larger print. If I appeared too breezy or defiant before going on he would punch me in the stomach, then as the tears started, at the humiliation as much as the pain, and my mascara began to run, he'd say, "Holy Jesus, look at you! What an almighty mess! And you call yourself a star?" Other times it was black eyes, which I covered with shades by day, with makeup by night. Long sleeves may have covered the worst of the bruises, but not the hurt that went deeper and tore up my self-esteem.

A separation was inevitable, but I was pregnant again by that time. And it was a difficult, heavy and painful pregnancy. With the increase in weight my legs started acting up, all of which combined to make the physical abuse that never stopped even more difficult to take. I went home to have my baby, hoping he would be born in the peace of Mama's house. It turned out he was reluctant to come into this world by himself—in my condition, I couldn't exactly blame him—and I had to be taken by ferry to the maternity hospital in Norfolk, where he was delivered by cesarian section. Young Earl was a blue baby and had to undergo a complete blood exchange.

By the time I resumed touring, five weeks after Earl Jr. was born, I had become a very small person in my own eyes. The abuse continued, and I began to take a drink before going on stage for the first time in my life. Thelma knew about it. She had to, for she was the one I got to run out and fetch the bottles of Seagram's Golden Gin. Although there certainly is no salvation in the bottle, it did get me through that terrible spell, for it's hard to go on stage and act happy and carefree when you've just been cussed out, knocked down and you've just got up off your knees.

As a woman I was ashamed that I had become so obsessed and weak that I would allow a man to treat me that way. I had seen the outer edges of it with my dad, and had always sworn it would never happen to me. By that time, I guess, I was trying to protect my professional name, but the truth had a habit of sneaking out in performance.

On stage and pregnant with Earl.
(COURTESY OF RUTH BROWN)

I never had drunk before and I did not handle it well. The warm-up swinger was no problem, the trouble started with the ballad. With my confidence leaking all over the place, there was one song I was really scared to sing, believer in lyrics that I am. It was "He's Funny That Way." Every time I went ahead and did it anyway I waited, after the line, "I'm not much to look at, nothing to see," for someone out there to come right back at me: "You said a mouthful, bitch! You sure ain't!"

I weaned myself off that drink behind the curtain soon after Earl and I separated. Lawdy, I could pick a good song, but I sure couldn't pick a man worth a damn. After the divorce I tried to make sure that his son was no stranger to him, arranging regular meetings wherever possible. It still took until Earl Jr. was eight years old before he got together with his father properly, spending the summer with him at his new home in the Bronx. A surprise for me was just how paternal Earl was, and how well the two of them hit it off. You never can tell.

THERE WERE BLACK DEEJAYS APLENTY by 1953, especially in the New York area, each of them approachable to some degree or other.

Jack Walker of WOU was known simply as "the Pear-shaped One," Hal Jackson of WMCA was an ex-auto salesman from Washington, Bill Cook of Newark's WAAT was an ex-dance promoter who discovered Roy Hamilton. Guys like them were all-powerful, their names often a marquee-draw bigger than the artists they featured.

The problem for black artists was that these people preached to the converted, since the white audience had its own programs that stuck rigidly to artists such as Perry Como, Guy Mitchell, Teresa Brewer, Al Martino, Don Cornell and Eddie Fisher, most if not all allied with the powerful "majors" of the record business, Columbia, Decca, Capitol and RCA. There was no such thing as the white equivalent of a black-artist "indie" like Atlantic, and simply no way for Atlantic to break into these white playlists. Or was there?

What helped black music on its way to asserting an identity well beyond the "race records" tag, and achieving that vital breakthrough, was WLAC's *Randy's Record Shop Show,* hosted by deejay Gene Noble. Randy was a white aficionado of our music, and since his show could be picked up all the way from California to Virginia, it really began to turn things round for R and B. The message that spread through the network of white radio stations was that our music was here to stay. Randy set the fuse, but the detonator for the explosion of black music was Alan "Moondog" Freed, a deejay I met a couple of times at Cleveland's WJW.

Freed was smart enough to realize that kids could care less what color your face was as long as the music hit the spot. Soon he was promoted to the big time, New York's WINS, and before long every city had its own white deejay savvy enough to follow. Freed's live shows, mixing black and white chart acts regardless, swept all before them as R and B became rock 'n' roll.

The unfortunate side effect of Freed's live "Supershows" was to turn performing into a rat race. You no longer did an act, it was, "Here's seventeen people, each singing one song." On one of Alan's extravaganzas I sang "Lucky Lips" seven times in one day. And *nothing* else! It was a fiasco, a rock 'n' roll circus, but it was a huge business. There was little of the camaraderie we were used to, for we'd meet each other running. I'd bump into the Platters and

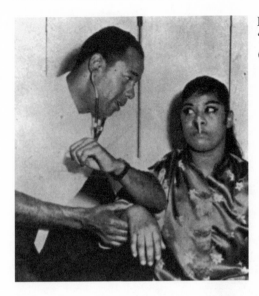

Deejay Jocko Henderson
"taking my temperature."
(COURTESY OF RUTH BROWN)

they'd barely get to the chorus of "Only You" before they were off
and it would be Buddy Knox going on about his "Party Doll," then
the Chiffons, the Turbans, the Crows, even Pat Boone with them
white bucks on his feet, running in late from school.

In no time others were copying Freed's formula, and I followed
that date with "The Fantabulous Rock 'n' Roll Show of '57" for
Shaw Artists, hustling 'round thirty-four dates in thirty-four cities
with the Coasters, the Drifters, Bo Diddley, the Schoolboys and
Smiley Lewis. We did blockbuster business, with one Texas show
alone attracting twelve thousand fans. I was still a hot item, so much
so that I was asked to do several television commercials, pretty un-
heard of for a black lady at the time unless you happened to be
Lena Horne. I made five black-and-white kinescopes in a single day,
all meant to look as if they'd been filmed on separate occasions, the
game given away by the same faces in the frenziedly applauding
audience. Paul Williams backed me, with that reprobate Jimmy
Brown added to his line-up for the occasion. The emcee was Willie
Bryant, who deejayed from the window of the Baby Grand as the
self-styled "Mayor of Harlem." I was featured in a color featurette
for Studio Films, Rock and Roll Revue. I was the Lucky Strike girl for
a while, and when I did my jingle, "Light up a Lucky! It's light-up
time!" the band behind me was again led by Paul Williams and

Giving it my best shot on Alan
Freed's rock and roll show at
the Paramount in 1956.
(COURTESY OF RUTH BROWN)

included a young unknown named James Brown. I was also, so help
me, the poster girl for Jax Beer.

Doing so many "Supershows" had a bad effect on my throat, and
it was Billy Eckstine who referred me to his specialist, the head
surgeon at the Harlem Eye, Nose and Throat Hospital. I ended up
having a tonsillectomy under a local anesthetic and worried that the
Ruth Brown sound would change as a result. It did, deepening it a
fraction to a Marian Anderson contralto, but not so's anybody noticed.

IN ALL THE YEARS I was with Atlantic I made just one album from
scratch, all the rest having been assembled from singles, and I really
had to fuss and fight to get *Late Date with Ruth Brown* off the
ground. It was my vehicle to take me back to the ballads and standards I loved, and I was lucky enough to be assigned Bobby Darin's
arranger, Richard Wess, to do the charts. I had little Earl with me in

Band leader Paul "Hucklebuck" Williams on sax, Riff Ruffin on guitar and me in an early dress design by sister Delia. (COURTESY OF RUTH BROWN)

the studio during the sessions, and Sid Bernstein came along to do some PR for us. He held my baby during one number and was wet on for his pains. Years later, when Sid was responsible for bringing the Beatles to America, I chided him that he was the guy who put all us black acts out of work. "Serves you right for what your kid did to me," he replied, chuckling.

Signing a white artist like Bobby Darin was a departure for Atlantic. He joined what was a strong roster, including myself, LaVern, Clyde, Big Joe Turner, Ray Charles, the Drifters and the Clovers. Herb's return from his army stint in Germany in '55 with a pregnant girlfriend had caused a lot of strain, not least on his marriage to Miriam. To avoid conflict with Jerry Wexler, who occupied the desk beside Ahmet previously reserved for him, Herb was given a separate office, separate artists, even a separate label, Atco. One of the artists placed under his wing was ex-Brill Building songwriter Bobby. Herb had so little enthusiasm for Bobby he wanted to drop him after several records did a nosedive. Ahmet remained convinced he had a winner and proved it spectacularly, much to Herb's mortification, personally producing Bobby's first in a long line of smash hits, "Splish Splash." With his other endeavors at Atco heading no place, this proved too much for Herb, and when he asked to be bought out it solved everyone's problems, on a personal and business level.

One of the first "45s."
(COURTESY OF HOWELL BEGLE)

Of all the artists on the label I was the one who missed Herb most when he bowed out. He was a soft guy, quite a contrast to hard-as-nails Miriam, and some people considered him eccentric, but he was always good to me. Although we got on well enough, I never reached the same level of rapport with Jerry. At the same time Ahmet was becoming a little remote.

Bobby, meanwhile, became a good friend. I often came across him in the studio, trying out little things on the piano. "I hear you're a songwriter," I jived him one day. "Why don't you write me a song?" He did, and the record was produced by two other ex-Brillers, Jerry Leiber and Mike Stoller. "This Little Girl's Gone Rockin'" not only made the R-and-B chart, but crossed over to Billboard's Hot Hundred and became a hit.

It was Bobby who first tipped me off that all was not as it should be with regard to the royalty situation at Atlantic. Following a surreptitious dig through their accounts file before taking off for Capitol, he took me to one side. "I've been shortchanged, Ruth," he told me, "and while I was in there I had a look at your stuff. All I can tell you is that if I were you, I'd push a little harder." I didn't know whether to laugh or cry. All I'd ever had over the years were advances to keep me going, combined with either blank stares or cries of, "Hey, don't push it. Taking our expenses into account, you're in the red."

12

"MRS. SHOWBIZ"

ALTHOUGH CHART HITS kept coming towards the end of the fifties, they became less frequent and smaller potatoes. "Why Me?" made some noise in '58, with "Don't Deceive Me" proving the last of the line in '59. Regardless of this, I never thought my relationship with Atlantic would change that much, for I hadn't stopped to realize how big they had become. When you're part of the foundation stone I guess you don't keep looking up to see how tall your building is. The changes were brought home to me one day when I called Ahmet's secretary Noreen, who had been around when I first arrived, to make an appointment. All of a sudden I had to speak to *her* secretary to get to Noreen, let alone her boss. It became demeaning, the lengths I had to go to, for the child did not seem to know Ruth Brown from the wallpaper.

Through Ray Charles, who'd switched from Atlantic to ABC-Paramount, I heard that the label was extremely interested in the possibility of signing me to a contract. I had to at least check it out, but detected a distinct chill in the air when I finally met with the ABC execs. "Never mind from whom," they told me, "but we've just heard from a *very reliable* source that you've recently re-signed with Atlantic. We shouldn't even be having this conversation."

"My contract's got only a few months to go," I protested.

"Not what we heard," they insisted. "We took enough flak on the last go-round with Ray. Thank you for dropping by, Miss Brown."

Matters came to a head at Atlantic only weeks later when I went to see Ahmet in the company's shiny new offices at Columbus Circle and was kept waiting in an outer office for four hours. Miriam—now Mrs. Freddie Bienstock, but just as much the embodiment of "Tokyo Rose," her old office nickname, as ever—passed by me several times, bustling between offices. On the first occasion I got a nod, after that no further acknowledgment. It was as if all those years of socializing and working together counted for nothing. I went through anger, and way beyond, reaching well past disgust by the end of that wait.

It certainly gave me ample opportunity to review where I stood with the company. Through successive contracts my advance for each side had been raised from $69 to $350. In '54 I was presented with my first gold record by Ahmet and Herb. I swear I held that disc for all of five minutes and never saw it again! A year later, on stage at the Apollo, Ahmet and Herb presented me with a plaque to commemorate sales of five million records. That I kept. During the fifties I had a total of thirteen Top Ten R-and-B hits, including five number ones. Three of those, "5–10–15 Hours (Of Your Love)," "Mama, He Treats Your Daughter Mean" and "Lucky Lips" were certified by Atlantic to Billboard as million-sellers. When I joined the company in '48 they were ranked twenty-fifth in the R-and-B field; by '51, and from then on, Atlantic was the undisputed number-one label. Through all this I had to ask, like I was begging for a handout, for every advance on royalties beyond the flat contract sum. And indeed, that was the purpose of my current meeting with Ahmet. I got some money that day, but I knew it was over, that I was through at Atlantic. Who had scared ABC-Paramount off? After losing Ray Charles, I was convinced Ahmet was determined not to lose out again.

I met Brook Benton that afternoon in Beefsteak Charlie's, a bar between Broadway and Eighth Avenue where musicians and actors congregated. Its walls were lined with sheet music and if you waited long enough you met everyone who happened to be in town, Dizzy sitting at the bar, Mr. B at a table, LaVern table-hoppin' with her husband, Slappy White. It was *the* meeting place, with every mother's child, you can believe it, dressed to the nines. Shooting the bull was the name of the game, for in those days we had no PR teams, we did it ourselves. One of the standard excuses for having

been out of the limelight was, "Oh, didn't you know? I've been to
Europe!"

Brook was sitting there sippin' with Clyde Otis, a big, huggy bear
of a man who was Mercury's A and R man (an industry first for a
black guy) as well as his songwriting partner. I was set to tour with
Brook's show on a bill with the James Moody Band and the Shirelles, and we soon got to talking about how things were at Atlantic.
When I indicated they were none too good, Brook said, "Why don't
I take you over to see my manager? Maybe he can work out a deal
for you at Mercury." But first we had a date across town with a
remarkable lady.

Florence Greenberg was busy mothering everyone in sight when
Brook and I arrived at Scepter Records' humble office to discuss
our tour with her Shirelles. In her blue knitted suit with a double
rope of pearls, Florence looked like Barbara Cook crossed with
Molly Goldberg, a real four-star ash-blonde Jewish mama, just about
the unlikeliest head of a record company I ever did see. She treated
Shirley Alston and her group as her kids, and they were indeed a
nice bunch of girls. Shirley was a doll, neat and sweet, whose onstage presence and that killer heartbreak voice could twist you into
knots, then after the show she'd revert to being the quiet, conservative girl we all adored.

Florence was not only their mother at Scepter, but their tax
consultant, team captain, tailor and dietician, masterminding and
supervising everything Shirley and the girls did, every little move
they made on stage, every tiny inflection in their records. Since
Brook was topping our bill—rightly so, for he was ruling the chart
roost with three Mercury discs in the Top Forty—he was in no
mood to go along with everything Flo laid down, for they ranged
from travel arrangements for her "kids" to "suitable" accomoda-
tion, out-of-pocket expenses, even a chaperone (no prizes for guessing who landed that post!). Between me and Brook and Florence,
we worked things out.

She was a real piece of work, this housewife from New Jersey, who
went on to build a sizable empire almost entirely based on black
artists, with Dionne Warwick, Tommy Hunt, Maxine Daniels and
Chuck Jackson among those waiting in the wings for the "Greenberg treatment." If only she had managed to keep clear of sharks,

admittedly close to an impossibility in the record business in those days, Scepter might still be with us today.

Brook was as good as his word, for through him I was introduced to Shelby Singleton, who produced my two records for Mercury's parent label Philips, *Along Comes Ruth* and *Gospel Time. Along Comes Ruth* is one of my all-time favorites. I did Clyde's "Treasure of Love," LaVern's "Jim Dandy," Bobby "Blue" Bland's "Cry, Cry, Cry," as well as other hits of the period like "Sea of Love" and "Shake a Hand," together with a couple of numbers Brook wrote. We had a good time cutting that album, and it shows. After almost twelve years at Atlantic it still felt strange at first even to contemplate my name under a different logo, but everything must change, I guess, and you either change too or fall by the wayside. And I wasn't ready to do that just yet.

WHILE ON TOUR in the late fifties and early sixties, my sons had been living with Mama in Portsmouth. They adored her and called her "Mrs. Santa Claus." We got together at every available opportunity, but I was in for a shock one day when I checked in after a lengthy spell on the road. After hugging me for a minute Earl broke free, crying, "I want my mama!" and ran to his granny. I was hurt, and it really made me pause and think. If I wasn't careful, I was going to miss a lot of my kids growing up. I had never planned to be Mrs. Showbiz who just dropped by occasionally, but it seemed that was exactly what I had become. Mama understood, though she was far from ecstatic about their moving to New York with me.

We were all together in an apartment in Lenox Terrace that spring of '62, Ronnie, Earl, me, and a trumpet player named Danny Moore, with whom I had been keeping company on and off, mostly on, for close on four years. Danny was such a pretty young thing, he had women falling all over him, and despite Chickie's "Oh, Miss Brown, there you go again, pickin' a chicken!" it was fine as wine and twice as mellow while it lasted. Danny's life was his music— Ruth Brown, too, while we lasted—and unlike Willis, he could care less if his jacket was made of cotton or cashmere, or if it came from Saks or the Salvation Army. One day, though, I just looked at that overgrown kid and realized he was just as much a baby as my sons.

Earl Jr. and Ronnie, Colonnade Amusement Center, 125th Street, NYC—between shows at the Apollo.
(COURTESY OF RUTH BROWN)

That single thought did it. Being a mama to your own is one thing, but the heck with extending it to bedmates, no matter how spectacular.

In late '62 I developed a lump on my breast. It was found to be benign, thank the Lord, and there was no need for a mastectomy, but after its removal the treatment I received caused my hair to recede and thin out. I had always worn it straight back, with a pony tail and spit curls, a style that did nothing to hide what was happening. In desperation I took to attaching little hairpieces. The whole process was devastating to me. I'd cry myself to sleep at night, then wake up in the morning scared to look at the pillow and the fresh crop of loose hair that surely lay there. Full of self-pity—"What have I done to deserve this?"—and seeking a ton of sympathy, I phoned Mama. She said, "God gave you your *life*, Ruth. Do what other folks do, buy yourself a wig." I did, and soon it became positively fashionable to wear one.

I had to keep working through all this to keep the money rolling

in, and I began to see how sounds and styles were changing, how far
we had come from the rough-hewn country blues of the thirties and
forties, through R and B and rock 'n' roll, to reach the urban
sophistication of the Motown sound. Was there still a place for Ruth
Brown?

RUDY GUMBS WAS A FAN of mine who never missed a performance if I
was within traveling distance of his home in Huntington, Long Island. It was through him that I met my third husband. Bill Blunt
was a friend of Rudy's I had seen in Rudy's company many times.
He was quite a gentleman, and he and I had an old-fashioned,
romantic courtship through letters and phone calls, with flowers
and candy arriving regularly, together with invitations to shows.
Mama was on a visit one night when Bill arrived at my apartment.
After coffee and talking for a bit, he turned to Mama and out of the
blue asked, "Mrs. Weston, why don't you tell Ruth to marry me?"
When I burst out laughing at this, he said to Mama, "She doesn't
think I'm serious." Shaking her head and smiling, Mama replied,
"Well, I don't think you're serious either!"

"Oh, but I am," he assured her. "I've loved Ruth for the longest
time. Look, I don't have a lot to offer, but I hold down a steady,
secure job, and I'd really try to make a good home for her and her
boys."

That was when my ears pricked up. A good home for me and *my
boys*? I'm sure Bill didn't realize it at the time, but he had just
pressed the button. Of course I was looking for a man, I'd never
stopped seeking a permanent attachment, no matter how many
blind alleys and dead-end streets I'd run up, down and sideways in
the process. Now, however, I mainly wanted a daddy and role model
for my boys. "Let me think about it," I suggested.

He called me up the following week. "Come on," he said, "let
me show you what Huntington is like." I have to tell you I was very
impressed. It was beautiful—lots of green grass, pretty houses,
friendly shopping areas, a well-tended high school. Still I had to up
the ante: I told Bill I wanted some Chinese food, and he even found
that for me. Up to that point we had never talked about how he
earned his living, and he chose that occasion to drop his bomb-

Town Hill Club, Brooklyn—
mid-fifties.
(COURTESY OF RUTH BROWN)

shell: "By the way, I'm a police officer." Seeing the look of blank amazement on my face, he plowed on: "Yep, been on the force twenty-three years. Just outside here, on the corner of York and Maine, is where I started off as a raw motorcycle cop."

After recovering from the shock I realized I had the explanation for his appearing to know everyone in town, for all morning it had been, "Hi, Bill, how ya doin'?" from what seemed like the entire population. I began to think, "Hey, this is not too bad."

I undertook a series of gigs singing at Playboy Clubs in the months leading up to our marriage in '63. Although the money was steady they were not the greatest engagements, for I got no billing. The comedians were the stars, and I got to meet many great funnymen in Flip Wilson, George Carlin, George Kirby, David Brenner, Alan Drake, and, long before the *Karate Kid* movies, Pat Morita. Otherwise I sang the same five or six songs every night, and that was it. Nevertheless, Hugh Hefner was appreciative enough to offer me and Bill a two-week, all-expenses-paid honeymoon in the Bahamas. Bill and I were married in a pretty little church in St. Albans, and after returning from our idyllic trip to the islands we moved into a beautiful house at 2 Plum Tree Lane. The boys were happy in a room of their own, and they liked and respected Bill. I'll never forget the first time they saw him decked out in his uniform, tall, broad-shouldered and handsome, like a black Gary Cooper hot from the set of *Beau Geste*. They gawped at him in awe and cried, "Mo-o-o-m!" Bill was deeply into all kinds of sports and the kids loved that.

There was just one flaw in the equation, and it emerged after a few months. Bill wanted me to turn my back on show business and settle down forever in suburban anonymity. If only I had been able to deal with that, to shut out the dreams I still had, it would have been ideal.

Alas, I simply couldn't.

13

"NURSE BLUNT"

THE CONTRADICTION BILL AND I WERE LIVING involved his being proud of having a celebrity on his arm, in his kitchen and in his bed, while denying me the freedom to explore new possibilities in my career. One of the few times I was called upon to sing during our marriage was at a function Bill's police association, the Guardians, held every year. They spent a fortune bringing in the likes of Count Basie or Duke Ellington to the local Colony Inn for the event, but got the singer—me—for free.

It was strange to work with the Duke under these circumstances, since he had been in at the start of my career odyssey, and just as strange to meet Bill and the members of his band after our adventures on the road together. As this suburban housewife introduced her husband, one of the shining lights on the force, I am sure they thought, "Hey, which Ruth Brown is *this?*"

Getting a taste of the spotlight again was like teasing an alcoholic. No way was one glass ever going to satisfy. I began accepting the occasional gig at a club in town called the Scampi House. They expected me to work for next to nothing, and I did it, hating the fact that I was being exploited but unable to turn them down. They paid fifty dollars a night and drained my professional blood, refusing to contribute a penny to promotion, expecting me to do all of that myself. Then they began booking other artists, using my name —"Ruth Brown presents . . ."—without paying a penny. Unsatisfactory as it was, these were my last remaining links to show business.

Being handed a credit card and running wild with the darn thing did nothing to help. It was the first piece of plastic I'd ever had and I went a little crazy. "Get whatever you need for yourself and the boys," Bill said, and a few thousand dollars later he realized what a mistake he had made. I never stopped to count, and ignored the fact that no matter how high he had climbed—he was the highest-ranking black officer in the history of Suffolk County—he was still on a relatively modest salary. I simply had no concept of being careful after a decade of spending big money as I earned it. My philosophy, okay, my *excuse*, had been that tomorrow would take care of itself. On this particular tomorrow I was faced with a stunned husband disbelievingly plowing through a mountain of receipts.

There were other developments that made me uncomfortable. One was a series of phone calls from ex-girlfriends of Bill's that made it clear how unwelcome I was in some quarters of the community. Bill had been no monk before our marriage and had been regarded as one of the most desirable catches around, so these calls were both persistent and vicious. Then there was the twice-weekly dinners I was expected to host for Bill's friends and colleagues, most of whom were fellow pillars of the establishment. When they started in discussing the rearrangement of school classes to accommodate their professorial duties, or duty rosters that might better serve the needs of the community, I began to drift towards the kitchen, where I'd just sit with the kids. Much as I wanted to, I felt I had nothing to contribute.

Slowly our marriage began to deteriorate. Bill was eight years older than I and a fine man, not in any way an unkind man, a man who got the boys into the Boy Scouts and taught them everything they knew about sports, and not just baseball and football, but track and skiing. To this day they have an abiding respect for him, and so do I. Torn as I was, though, I had to try and get back the career that had slipped away. I believe there's a price for everything in this life, and it's a question of facing that fact and deciding if you're prepared to pay it.

When we eventually separated in '66 I moved with the boys to a house in Deerpark, just five miles away, renting with an option to buy. I was reluctant to leave the area and have Ron and Earl change schools, where they were doing so well, and abandon the curriculum with which they were familiar. And all their friends were there. Meantime I had to support all three of us, for I had no claim on Bill.

After their schooling in Portsmouth, being the only two black kids out of several hundred pupils in Deerpark's junior high came as a considerable shock. Their prowess at sports quickly overcame any initial awkwardness and it was a while before racism reared its ugly head. It came from the most unexpected quarter. A good friend of Ronnie's in fifth grade was a boy named Chip O'Connor. One day when Ronnie was passing by Chip's house, Chip's six-year-old brother came out, stood on the porch and pointed, chanting, "Nigger, nigger, you're a *nigger*. You're black and a nigger, nigger, *nigger* . . ."

Eventually his mother burst through the door, looked at Ronnie standing there frozen to the spot, grabbed her son and pulled him inside. Ronnie ran home to me, baffled, and asked what on earth was going on. Where had that little boy got his hatred? I had no answer for him, except that ignorance was bred in the most unlikely places, and when Ronnie put the same question to Chip, the reply was that sometimes his parents came out with stuff like that. Although Chip apologized, Ronnie never felt the same towards him. And after that, he told me, no matter how nice anyone was to him at school, he'd wonder what they were *really* thinking. It was his first taste.

The incident left me more protective of my kids than ever, maybe overprotective. I most certainly was that when I went along to watch Ronnie playing football on the high school team. Watching him earlier in the pee-wee league had been fine, but now we were into serious business! When I saw him tackled and buried under a mountain of heavyweights I rushed on to the field yelling, "What are you doin' to my baby?" Ronnie was mortified, but his teammates made a cute joke out of it, leaving a spare helmet perched on the end of the bench in the locker room thereafter. "That's your mom's spot," they informed my son.

Kids, of course, can sock it right back to you as well. Little Earl did that to me when he was just ten years old. In my heyday with Willis I had smoked Dunhill's brand of colored cigarette, yellow to match a yellow dress, all that nonsense, and when that died down I took up Kools mentholated, the favorite choice of singers. I had given up soon after breaking up with Bill, then came across a discarded pack of Kools one day that must have been lying around for months. When I lit up the smoke was not only stale, but went straight down the wrong pipe, and I immediately began spluttering and choking. That was Earl's cue to enter the room. Snatching the pack from my lap, he flung it across the room. "I thought you loved me!" he hollered.

I truly didn't understand at first what he was talking about. "I do!" I protested. "You know I do!"

"How could you do that?" Earl continued in a tone that just pierced my heart. "You'll die! I don't understand how you can say you love me and smoke. What would I do if anything happened to you? How can you say you love me and do this?" He had caught me totally off-guard, and for a moment all I could do was sit there like an idiot. Then I gathered him to me, we cried and cried together. And I never, ever smoked again.

In our new, independent family existence it did not take long before debts of all kinds had piled up, and it soon got to the point where I was seriously wondering if I could ever cope. Even with engagements that did come my way there was often next to nothing left after I had paid the band and settled traveling expenses. From time to time my mama and brothers and sisters got together and put five or ten dollars each in an envelope for me. Sometimes it was more, for I was far from shy in asking, if the need was dire enough. I knew I had earned more in a decade than most of them might see in a lifetime, but I had to deal with the present, after all.

Many times I was unable to meet the rent, but I always had a plan somewhere, some brilliant idea to cover it and get through. The boys knew they were living through rough times, and there were days when they had to count their lunch-money pennies, or go collect a can of kerosene to heat the house. When the lights were turned off that first winter because I was unable to pay the electricity bill, I found a metal tray, sat about forty Pepsi-Cola bottles on it and stuffed tallow candles in every one. That gave us light, together with a certain amount of heat. Come spring the boys simply sat outside on the porch as the evenings grew long and studied out there until the light failed.

I got involved with the church all over again, joining the nearby Pentecostal and traveling to neighboring houses of worship. I did everything for them, hurling myself right back into it, cooking, cleaning, decorating, just trying desperately to be part of something. I was made to confess all my sins at the altar for having been out in the showbiz world, and it was, "Wash your face, take all these rings off," that whole scenario. They prevailed upon me to sing a couple of times at funerals, proceeds to go to the church, and that led them to ask that I become part of their regular funeral package, bookable in advance. I drew the line at that. I wanted to belong simply as a member; they wanted Ruth Brown, the star.

One man I had been fortunate to meet during the marriage was a friend of Bill's, Bob Washington, head of the Community Action Center in Wyandanche. When I bumped into him at the grocery store one day we got to talking, the conversation progressing from, "I can't believe what happened to you and Bill, I thought you guys were together forever," to a discussion on how I was making ends meet. "Not very well," I summed up.

I leveled with Bob, for he was someone I instinctively felt I could trust. While trying to re-establish myself in show business I needed a steady paycheck that would at least take care of essentials like the rent and food. Qualifications other than my voice? I could cook, I was a good listener, I was a person who loved children. "Let me think about that," Bob said when I was through, "I'll keep in touch."

Two days later he called me up. "You might not want to consider this," he began, "but there may be a vacancy for a teacher's aide in our Head Start program for young kids four and up. No, you don't need any education certificates, you assist teachers, look after the kids in the playground, oversee their play periods, help out generally. The biggest challenge you'll have to deal with is someone recognizing you."

I got started a few days later and began performing all the most menial tasks. I accompanied the youngest kids to the bathroom, set up their lunch trays in the kitchen, that sort of thing. Slowly but surely I started to get to know each child individually, and they in turn began to realize that "Miss Blunt" would always take the time to listen to their problems. A school bus picked up all the kids and delivered them in the morning, and when I heard that job was open I took it on as well, early start and all. I loved the work, in fact I didn't regard it as work at all. I still needed the occasional gig to enable us to survive financially, and they were few and far between.

Things got so bad that I sat down one night and wrote a ten-page letter to Ahmet. I'd heard that he had sold Atlantic to Warner/ Seven Arts, but that he was still around running the company. I marked it Private and Confidential and phoned Noreen, told her it was on its way and asked her to get it to her boss personally. I hesitated to write what I did, for I laid myself naked. It was a declaration of desperation, pleading, begging for help. I still insisted I was not asking for anything I was not entitled to, but I was in a bad way, I needed money to pay my grocery, fuel and rent bills, I was having a real hard time, I'd even pay it back if I had to. Ahmet responded by sending me a check for $1,000.

Six months down the line at school a teacher was being transferred and I was asked if I'd like to replace her, take over the class and leave the driving to someone else. I stressed my complete lack of academic qualifications but was told that the dedication and love of the job I had demonstrated were considered enough. Well, I turned that schoolroom into a miniature storybook, a fairy-tale dream. I painted all the kids' desks and chairs a rainbow of pastel colors, and ran up matching curtains for the windows. With all their names stenciled on their lockers, Miss Blunt's room became the favorite by far in that school. I helped the children make cut-out faces from whatever material I could lay my hands on, be it pumpkin shells or old cereal boxes, and I took them on field trips.

I was more than capable of writing an extremely chatty, informative and interesting report on these activities, but not, alas, in the style required by the school administration. As a result I found myself back on Head Start detail by day and on the bus doing my rounds. At nights I took to sneaking out to Sonny's, a local nightspot, to sing for a few dollars.

* * *

GRATEFUL AS I HAD BEEN for Ahmet's $1,000, I was convinced I was entitled to more than crumbs from the rich man's label. It was another chance encounter, this time at a supermarket checkout in Wyandanche, that began my twenty-odd-year battle with Atlantic, their new owners Kinney, and eventually the mighty Time-Warner. There was a lady in the checkout aisle alongside me who looked familiar. Sure enough, it was a face from my childhood, Ensley Stevenson, daughter of Ethlyn, a good friend of my mother's; the two had met all the time on the street corner with their baby carriages. *"Girl,"* she said, "it can't be *you!"*

We stood outside the market telling our stories for so long that the frozen goods began to melt. I told her that my latest marriage had failed, but omitted a lot more, like how close we were to being flung out for non-payment of rent and other such niceties. Ensley was married to a man named Alfonso Sands, the principal of Wyandanche High School, and Ensley was teaching there. I knew instantly I had found a friend.

I still did not want Ensley to see me destitute, but she managed to con my address out of me and said she would drop by. She did that the very next day, leaving me with no alternative but to come clean with the whole truth about my circumstances. I admitted that my career had gone to pieces, that I was having a real struggle to make ends meet. I stressed that I had not given up, that I was still out there kickin', but it was a question of how much longer I could keep a roof over our heads.

The first thing Ensley insisted upon was giving me the use of her second car, a station wagon. I had been using public transportation since leaving Bill, and her offer was a tremendous boon, for my legs had never stopped giving me trouble. Her next question: What on earth had happened to the fortune I must have made off record sales? She listened in amazement as I explained where I stood with Atlantic, a has-been charity case, due precisely nothing, according to them. Ensley immediately suggested I get a legal mind on the case.

Within a week I was reeling off everything I considered relevant to a lawyer she knew in Babylon. The first thing he laid on the line was that I had, after all, signed a contract. Why had I accepted the conditions if I didn't like them? I told him that part of the answer was an unwillingness to let folks higher up get even a hint of that last school report card, admitting the limit of my education. So many of the black groups and singers who catapulted to fame in the fifties, I explained, came out of the backwoods and were delighted to sign any piece of paper that was shoved in front of them. It was a case of, "Wow, we're getting records released, if they hit, we're made! Let's go!" The lawyer agreed to write Atlantic and request a complete accounting. That was one contract condition certainly unfulfilled since the fifties.

We waited and waited after that first official letter went out, and after four months the reply came back from our lawyer. To put it mildly, it was not encouraging.

"Ruth Brown," it ran, "is in debt to Atlantic Records, and for a very considerable sum. We strongly advise against any further correspondence as there is always the possibility Atlantic may pursue her for this debt. We enclose our bill, payment of which is due forthwith."

Looking back now, I can see this as a kind of beginning, although it could also have been the end. As for the threat that Atlantic might come after me for the money they said I owed, hah! If they could extract it from my hide, they were welcome.

Together with Ensley and Alfonso I worked my way over the years through six more lawyers. I never once considered giving up, because I was convinced that right was on my side. Sure, I'd had handouts instead of royalties throughout the fifties, but I simply could not conceive that these relatively modest sums, even with production costs added in, could cancel out royalties from millions of records sold. And those records were continuing to sell, as any visit to a record store could bear witness. Any further personal appeals to Ahmet were now out of the question, of course, for our legal correspondence had long since burned that bridge. Trouble was, each and every new legal brain we hired came back with the same answer, expertly stonewalled by the powers at Atlantic. And always, *always* there was the constant threat from them: Leave off, get lost, *drop it,* or we'll sue for recovery of the money you owe.

It was Alfonso who suggested forming Miss Rhythm, Inc. From

this angle we dispensed with lawyers. We had little choice; I was crippled by debt. Alfonso took over the correspondence himself, utilizing the one weapon Atlantic had provided us over the years, the contradictory sums they quoted. They did not amount to all that much, but we seized on every *i* they had failed to dot and every *t* they had failed to cross in an attempt to keep the dialogue alive. We never stopped, right through the seventies, but I don't believe for one minute, despite the sincere efforts of all concerned, that we even caused one tiny ripple of concern at the Kinney Corporation's head office, where, as new owners of Warner/Seven Arts, all matters Atlantic were now referred.

THE SALARY I GOT from Head Start, tiny as it was, served one advantage: it enabled me to apply for government assistance to get my kids through school. Then there were food stamps and rent aid to dependent mothers. Later I got a state loan, allowing me to attend beauty-school classes. It was a case of anything and everything just to keep hanging in.

Salvation also arrived in the form of an organization called the International Art of Jazz, IAJ, run by Miss Ann Sneed with a supplement from the National Endowment for the Arts. They organized workshops in schools, sometimes two or three a week, covering every level from kindergarten to college, the idea being to give pupils a taste of that good music, a word on its origins, and a run-down of the dynamics involved. A typical presentation would be at an eight A.M. high school assembly, starting with a talk on harmony, rhythm and melody, accompanied by samples from top musicians like Clark Terry and Thad Jones. Ann gave everyone a chance to participate. We covered the state of New York from Long Island up to Rochester and Syracuse, and the IAJ became my survival kit, enabling me to keep my sanity and self-respect. And it introduced the kids to the music, continuing that vital thread in our culture.

When the school term ended I signed up with a local agency that allocated one's services wherever they were required, for babysitting, housecleaning, bathing the sick and elderly, helping take care of the retarded and disabled, whatever. After an initial interview you didn't have to visit them any more, they just called up and told you where to report that day. When it was confirmed you had carried out the work satisfactorily, the check was in the mail. No muss, no fuss, and your dignity was left intact. Except I kept my latest breadwinning position from my sons in case they would be upset. That was my intention, but you know what they say about the best-laid schemes of mice, men and mamas.

Since the job was steady, varied and going well, I decided to stay into the new school term instead of returning to the crèche. I waited until the kids caught the school bus before donning the little white uniform the agency supplied, jumping into my car and taking off. Ronnie missed the bus one morning, doubled back to beg a lift and caught me just as I was leaving. "Mom, where you goin'?" he asked. "Out," I replied, trying to look unconcerned. "No," he persisted, "I mean where you goin' in that *white uniform?*"

I took a deep breath. "I'm a nurse. I mean, I'm going to beauty school," I lied, badly as usual. I had been thinking about training as a beautician, and I later did, but for the moment most of my work was as a domestic. It was what Mama had done, me too as a girl for that matter, and I was in no way ashamed of it, just concerned with my sons' feelings. I need not have worried, for when we talked it over that night I discovered what I should have realized all along. They were behind me in whatever I did. And oh, how they crumpled up with laughter at the very thought of "Nurse Blunt."

When business was slack I took whatever else I could get, and one proved a real low point. The owner of the candy store and newspaper stand made a great show that he had no idea who I was, and got a mean, perverse kick out of employing me. I served behind his counter and enjoyed it well enough—at least I was meeting people —until one day some friends of his dropped by. Grabbing a broom, he pushed it towards me and said, "Here, go sweep the sidewalk." Usually one of his sons performed this task, and I certainly hadn't been hired for that, so I protested. "Look," he said, "I don't give a good goddamn if you *are* Ruth Brown. When I say sweep, you'll *sweep!* Take this broom!"

I stood my ground, looked him up and down, and replied, "No, *you* take this broom. And you know what? If you got the time I'll tell you what you can *do* with this broom." No need to tell I was out of there and unemployed one hot minute later. There's an amusing coda to this tale: close on fifteen years later, when I was starring on Broadway in *Black and Blue,* this candyman called me on the backstage phone and requested three complimentary tickets to the show. On the basis that he had known me back then! I do not believe I am a vindictive woman, and I am certain no court in the land would blame me for telling this character the show was sold out as far ahead as anyone could see.

DURING WHAT I CALL my "wilderness years" I made several albums. After my two-record deal at Mercury was up, a mercurial little guy named Bob Shad signed me up for an album he called *Ruth Brown '65.* I was impressed with the trouble he took and the instrumentation he used, with a fine arranger and conductor, Peter Matz, and names in there like Clark Terry, Urbie Green, Roland Hanna and Hank Jones. There were two Nellie Lutcher tunes, "Hurry on Down" and "He's a Real Gone Guy," and a slow, dreamy version of the old Shirley Temple classic, "On the Good Ship Lollipop."

During the IAJ gigs bass player Ben Tucker and I got to talking one day. He was working with Peggy Lee at the time and asked, "Girl, who you recording for now?" When I told him I was between contracts he mentioned that he and Grady Tate were partners in a small record label, Skye, with Norman Schwartz and Gary McFarlane. From that came *Black is Brown and Brown is Beautiful,* less elaborate than Bob Shad's production but containing some good stuff. One number was Paul McCartney's "Yesterday," for which I copped a Grammy nomination for Best Rhythm and Blues Performance in '69. That caused a ripple for a hot second or two.

Producer Sonny Lester lived nearby in Half Hollow Hills. I had worked in his house as a domestic through the agency, but luckily he had never recognized me. When we met afresh at an IAJ festival, it led to *Fine Brown Frame* with the great Thad Jones/Mel Lewis Orchestra. Boy, did this one swing, although a couple of my favorite ballads, "Be Anything (But Be Mine)" and "Black Coffee," also benefited from those marvelous brassy sounds.

My luck ran out with the fourth album. A guy named Jerry Williams, a.k.a. Swamp Dogg, introduced himself one day. He said I had attended high school in Portsmouth with his mama, that he had worked at Atlantic, and that he would like to produce me. His set-up was impressive. He had a beautiful house in Long Island, with limos and town cars always at the door, and he mentioned a wealthy backer putting up the bulk of the money for his "Ruth Brown project."

I was not about to ask to see his line of credit at the bank, eager instead just to grab at whatever straw came along to keep my career alive. The album, with every track written by Jerry, was recorded with only basic rhythm tracks in Muscle Shoals, Alabama. The intention, he assured me, was to sweeten it later when his backer coughed up more loot.

A few weeks after returning from Muscle Shoals, Jerry phoned me to say that Mr. Money had backed out. Since the tapes he had were unreleasable in their present state, he told me he had no alternative but to abandon the project. Oh, and a check for $600 for my services was in the mail. I was disappointed but philosophical. He had tried his best, after all.

As soon as that check arrived I rushed across the street to Wheatley Heights, a garage run by a real friendly bunch of guys I'd gotten to know. Owner Joe Caldwell cashed it for me, allowing me to pay off my longest-standing debts. A few days later he called me. The check had bounced. I suggested he re-deposit it, that it must be a mistake. It bounced again.

Frantic, I tried calling Jerry. A machine took every message, but no reply came. I contacted my brother Leonard and asked him to accompany me to his house in Hempstead. I had often visited when the album was in the planning stages, and I had played with Jerry's children in their front room and broken bread in their kitchen. This time was different. When he saw the two of us on his doorstep Jerry went crazy. He screamed at us like a wild man, threatened to set his German shepherds loose and to shoot us if we as much as set foot in his house. Then he slammed and bolted the door in our faces, leaving us standing there, shaking and powerless, completely taken aback at the savagery of his reception.

I had been through a lot, but in many ways this was the worst of all. I had to make amends to Joe at the garage, paying him off slowly, and I was mortified to have been humiliated like that in front of Leonard. A year or so later someone called to say the album, *Brown Sugar,* was in the stores, and exactly as laid down at Muscle Shoals, no strings added, nothing. Having discovered that Jerry Williams had moved from Long Island, I spoke to his stepfather when I visited Virginia soon afterwards, and asked if he knew his whereabouts. To quote him directly: "Don't ask me."

With no phone of my own, Joe and his station attendants, Mike and Louie, continued to take my messages and run across the street whenever someone called. "Wheatley Heights" is how they answered, and I guess everyone assumed it was some kind of security apartment. Perception is everything, especially in showbiz!

14

REDD FOXX TO THE RESCUE

IN THE MID-SEVENTIES I applied for a government loan to get Ronnie through a semester at Howard University, in Washington, D.C. He gained a full engineering and partial football scholarship, then made their team and took himself through from that point. Earl had always had a hankering to go to university in California, and on his own he successfully applied at UCLA. I refused to let him go. "If anything should happen to you," I tried to explain, "I couldn't afford to fly down." Earl listened to me, bless him. He had ambitions to be a newscaster and I obtained a grant to get him instead into the New York Institute of Technology in Hempstead, a well respected school. With Ronnie doing well at Howard and self-supporting, and Earl settled on the Hofstra campus, I felt I could relax just a bit for the first time since my break-up with Bill. My first priority, my boys, had been taken care of; they were getting the chance I had turned my back on. I harbored no regrets for myself, but they would never be denied the benefit of a sound education.

The old house I rented still seemed awfully empty without them, and when a neighbor offered me a ride to the closing day of the Westbury Music Fair I gladly accepted. It was a chance to say hello to Billy Eckstine and Redd Foxx for the first time in a very long time. And, if I had only known it, to have my life turned upside-

168

down yet again. I dressed in my smartest outfit for the occasion, a two-piece black pants suit with matching bandolero hat and pretty yellow blouse, and I did my makeup professionally, something I had not bothered with for ages. The fact is, I was nervous about meeting these people and figuring a way to get round their inevitable questioning. Redd had reached the top of the tree with *Sanford and Son* on TV and Mr. B was still riding high, whereas the only success I could talk about was getting both my boys into college from a poverty-stricken home base. Then again, that was no small thing.

I talked to Billy first, and he was charming as ever, then I asked the security guard if I could speak to Mr. Foxx. He walked down the hall, knocked on his door and hollered, "Lady here says she knows you, Redd. Name of Ruth Brown." I heard the reply loud and clear through the door: "What you say? *Ruth Brown?*" Redd stepped into the hall wearing just a pair of white boxer shorts covered with great big red hearts, and walked towards me in his bare feet. "You come here!" he told me, hugging and squeezing me to him. "What you mean standin' out there in that hall? You ought t'be ashamed of yourself! Where the hell you been, anyway?"

When we sat down I explained that my marriage had long since broken up. "Uh-oh," he said, "here we go again." I said no, it had not been like that this time, no re-run either of Jimmy Brown, Willis or Earl, simply that I was not and never could be a typical suburban housewife. "You're lookin' great," he told me, then leaned forward. "Listen, Ruth, I'd like you to come to California and work with me there. There's all kinds of things you could be doin'." When I tried to explain that I had no money to travel, and even if I had I couldn't leave anyway, that my kids were both at college nearby, he waved both objections away. "Ruth, everything's gonna be on me. I'll send you your ticket, and if there's any emergency and you gotta get back here, that's my treat too."

"Redd, I couldn't—"

"Don't tell me that! It's the least I can do. Have you forgotten I owe you?"

"What you talkin' about?"

"Oh, you overlookin' that little incident in San Francisco 'bout twenty-five years ago? Let me refresh that memory of yours. There was this comedian really struggling, down on his luck, name of Mr.

Redd Foxx. He been locked out of his hotel! Then he saw that an old acquaintance of his, a real cute young singer he first met at Newport News, was headlinin' at the Fillmore East. Name of Miss Ruth Brown, I believe. So he finds out she's at the Robert Lee Hotel, walks his ass over there, comes right out and asks for a hand-out. She is kindness itself and, as luck would have it, has been paid in cash for her performance. Pointing to a dresser with a towel sat on top, she explains that underneath that towel is the night's tak-ings, that I should help myself and take whatever I need. When I look, there must be close on three thousand dollars sat there. I remove exactly four hundred and fifty, enough to fly me back east and make a fresh start with a career that's headed no place. Ain't nobody ever done nothin' like that for me before or since. Does that jog your memory, Miss Brown?''

It did, but it was something I had not thought of for a quarter of a century. "Look, stay for the party at my hotel after the show," he suggested, "and we'll talk some more." Sitting through Redd's per-formance I found myself sliding further and further down in my seat, for anyone expecting to see him come on like *Sanford* must have had a terrible shock. Lord knows he had always been blue on stage, now he was way beyond that. When a bunch of nuns got up and started leaving, he yelled at them "Yeah, get the hell out, you're all half-dead anyway. Bunch of motherf————' bitches!''

Back at his place I gave him the phone number of Wheatley Heights, all the while protesting that I would have to think about his offer, as well as talking it over with my sons. Back home I could hardly contain my excitement, although part of me was already playing Redd's offer down. He had been carried away talking about old times, he would forget the whole deal once he was back in Los Angeles, who was I kidding anyway? I made up my mind to table the whole thing until it was confirmed; only then would I seek my sons' advice. I should have known better than to doubt Redd for one second.

Three days later my buddy Mike ran across from the garage, eyes popping out his head like a kid: "Ruth, I swear I ain't kiddin'. Redd Foxx is on the phone for you! *Redd Foxx!*"

Sure enough, it was the man, calling from NBC in between tap-ing segments of his show. "Ruth, I don't want no bullshit," he began, "I want your butt on the first plane to California. Don't ask no questions, come down here for two weeks an' give it a shake. You don't have to bring no clothes, no money, nothin', the ticket an' five hundred dollars will be with you any minute now. Gotta run, Ruth, call as soon as you know your flight an' I'll have you picked up at the airport."

First I called Ronnie. His response was immediate: "Go, Mama." Earl followed suit: "Why are you even asking? You should have been on the plane two hours ago!" But what about the house, I asked. "What house?" he replied. "Just *go!*" That telephone summons from Redd began a five-year stint on the West Coast.

THE CHAUFFEUR who picked me up at the airport was Junior, Redd's right-hand man. Off we swept in his Mercedes, straight to Redd's palatial home on Mulholland Drive atop the Hollywood Hills. As soon as we pulled up Redd walked out, hugged me and said, 'Welcome to Hollywood.' Inside were Clifton Davis, Della Reese, Sarah Vaughan, his regular gang of poker players, who all greeted me in turn.

Redd had booked me into a suite at the Bel Air Hotel and my mouth fell open when I saw it. I arrived carrying the cheapest suitcase I'll bet they'd ever seen, and the first thing I made sure of was I didn't have to pay no bill. Next morning I was driven out to NBC's Burbank Studios, the first movie lot I'd ever seen. There was a parking space with Redd's name on it, and I bumped into Ed Mc-Mahon and *Chico and the Man*'s Freddie Prinze before clearing reception. Redd arranged for me to share a scene in *Sanford* that very first day with the *Beverly Hillbillies* star Nancy Kulp. I stayed a month in the luxury of the Bel Air before settling into a small apartment down on Wilshire, fitting it out with furniture from a thrift shop.

As soon as Earl heard I was settling in for the duration he was on the phone. A college friend of his had transferred to the University of New Mexico in Albuquerque and had invited him down for a look-see. I agreed to the visit, although I could see what was coming a mile off. On his return he told me he had fallen in love with the place, and when I followed up with an inspection trip of my own, I came away mightily impressed. I had stopped him from going to

UCLA on the basis that it was too far from home. Now that he would be close enough to visit on weekends, how could I refuse? I involved Bob Washington, my Head Start benefactor, to help with the application paperwork. With the necessary testimonials obtained from our local minister, Earl was enrolled at Albuquerque for the 1976–77 semester.

Redd became executive producer on a show about Martin Luther King called *Selma,* and got me cast as Mahalia Jackson. The play ran for four weeks in a theater on Vine Street, off Hollywood Boulevard. Apart from that and walk-ons in *Sanford and Son,* I was left to my own devices and started to look around for work on my own. I had no band, but there were plenty of clubs with their own musicians, and I began picking up the occasional gig. The only thing that bothered me was Redd's excluding me from attending his live shows. Not only that, he offered no explanation.

Out of the blue, just as things were really slowing down, came a lifeline from Europe. It was from Jonas Beerholm and Slim Notini, a couple of rhythm and blues freaks from Sweden, partners in a reissue label, Route 66. They had put out unauthorized compilations of old recordings by various artists, myself and Charles Brown included, and wanted us over there to tour and boost sales. Although it seemed they had not bothered to license the material, they intended to follow up with royalty checks to all concerned based on sales (I know what you're thinking, but they did).

So began my first trek to Europe, together with Charles, whom I contacted on their behalf, and Floyd Dixon. Jonas and Slim put us up at their home in Stockholm, and on the road we were accompanied by a raw but extremely energetic band of young American musicians. Although the partners' prime purpose started off boosting sales of our old material, we all recorded live sets in Sweden, mine emerging as *Takin' Care of Business.* Jonas and Slim's sales technique at the open-air gigs we did was to arrive on their bikes, laden down with albums, and peddle them to the assembled multitude. The trip was great fun, and a refreshing change from the pro hustling that goes on in the States.

Once I was back in Los Angeles, Earl came out to join me during his summer break from college and we both took day jobs as shipping clerks to keep some money rolling in. By the time Redd an-

My baby brother Alvin, the
sweetest kid you could know, and
his musical hero Quincy Jones.
(COURTESY OF ALVIN WESTON)

With "Q" during the European
Jazz Festival Hour.
(COURTESY OF ALVIN WESTON)

nounced his intention to do his act in Las Vegas for a season I had
taken on the cleaning and cooking in his house. In return he paid
me a small retainer, gave me the use of a car when I needed it and
was otherwise good to me. Okay, I was not doing exactly what I'd
expected, but I had been worse off. Much worse.

Billy Eckstine arrived one night to see Redd and found me in the
kitchen with my apron on. "What *in hell* are you doin' in here
working?" he asked, totally stunned.

"I'm just trying to give something back to Redd for all the things
he's done for me," I replied.

Billy flashed that devastating smile of his. "Okay," he said, "since
you're here anyway, peel me a grape, Beulah." I burst out laughing.

"Eckstine," I said, "you got five seconds to vacate this here
kitchen unless you want your ass served up on a bed o' grits!"

It was Billy who explained why Redd refused to have me sing at
his live shows. "Don't take this badly, Ruth," he began, "but the

simple truth is you don't look the way Redd thinks a chick singer should. He's got this thing about ladies bein' petite. He feels that the glamor vultures in spots like Vegas won't buy anything else.''

I was left in charge of the house when Redd took off, the Cinderella who had not been invited to the ball. A few weeks later Herb Jeffries, the one-time Ellington singer and ex-Bronze Buckaroo from the all-black westerns in the thirties, dropped by the shipping department where Earl and I worked. He was a friend of our boss, Gino, and asked to put a call through to Las Vegas. I overheard enough to gather Herb was begging off a singing engagement. A jazz club was short one singer? I waded straight in. "Let me go in your place," I badgered him.

"You're R and B, they want jazz," he told me.

"I can sing anything," I replied. "Look, Herb, I don't care about the money, get me that job."

He did, and he got a plane ticket to get me there as well. It turned out that the Tender Trap wasn't on the Strip, but over on Flamingo Road, and it was the only jazz club in the city. I also found out that I had to do what they called "ups," meaning that every hour I was required to sing for forty minutes, then take twenty off. For six hours on the trot! I was shocked, but that was the deal. It led to a booking at the Gilded Cage at Circus Circus. The place really was a circus, with acrobats, clowns and all; when the circus acts were off, the music was on. What gave me tremendous satisfaction was our position on the Strip, slap across from the Thunderbird, where Redd's show was still running. With my name on a marquee just a stone's throw from his, there was no way he could miss it. So only Les Petites could make it to Vegas, huh? And check out the irony to end all ironies: the vocalist the Thunderbird had chosen to share Redd's bill was none other than the far-from-svelte Della Reese!

Soon the word was out, the phone lines buzzing with callers saying, "Hey, is that the Ruth Brown who did "Mama, He Treats Your Daughter Mean" and all those others back in the fifties?" Strolling outside a day later, I saw that the management had taken down the sign reading "Ruth Brown and All-Star Show." It now read, "Yes, This Is the REAL Ruth Brown!" That night it was impossible to even get near the Gilded Cage for black folks from across the tracks lining up six-deep.

With Sidney
Poitier at Rod
Steiger's home,
post-"In the
Heat of the
Night."
(COURTESY OF
RUTH BROWN)

During our run I read in the trades that auditions for an all-black
staging of *Guys and Dolls* were being held in Los Angeles. With our
act held over at the Gilded Cage I had to fly back specially to attend
them. It was worth it, for I was cast as General Cartwright, head of
the Salvation Army. We ran on and on at the Cage, they had never
seen anything like it, and when *Guys and Dolls* began its run at the
Aladdin I had two shows running at the same time. After the curtain went down at the Aladdin, everyone trooped over to pack Circus Circus. With this double success, and *Guys and Dolls* getting set
for an extended run, I decided to drop my anchor in Vegas for a
while and move into an apartment.

Soon after *Guys and Dolls* closed a friend told me that auditions
were being held for a new production at Meadowbrook Playhouse.
It seemed like a good idea to go along, until I discovered the name
of the play: *Livin' Fat.* You can believe I saw red immediately. "So
they're lookin' for fat people!" I raged. It turned out to be about
finance, not weight gain, and I cooled down. I read for the role of
the grandmother of the house, someone with a great love of rhythm
and blues. Typecasting if I ever heard it! I landed the role.

The young black girl who wrote the play was Judy Ann Mason,
and it had won her a Norman Lear award. The man himself showed

up in Vegas to see the production, along with *Roots* author Alex Haley. They came backstage after the curtain. "You know," said Norman, "I've got a project you might like to consider." Well, I had had enough build-ups leading to let-downs to last a lifetime. Tell it to the marines, I thought. *Wrong again*—proving yet another of my mama's sayings: "Whatever you do, Ruth, never get cynical. That's destructive. Always think the best of people until they give you good reason to think otherwise."

A couple of days later someone from his Tandem Productions called to say Norman wanted me in Los Angeles for camera tests and readings. How could I refuse one of the most successful television producers of all time, a man who had made millions correctly guaging public taste? Here we go again, I thought, New York to L.A., L.A. to Europe and back, L.A. to Vegas, now back to L.A. Heigh-ho, heigh-ho, it's off to work we go! It was a fond farewell to Circus Circus, that Gilded Cage of theirs, the Aladdin, the Meadowbrook Playhouse and my tiny apartment. The anchor was lifted once more and before I knew what was happening a Tandem limo was sweeping me from LAX to the studio.

I read for a part in *Hello, Larry* alongside McLean Stevenson, the *M*A*S*H* veteran. I landed the role and the work was fun at first, with Norman the perfect gentleman, kind and encouraging at all times. It was Stevenson who turned out not to be the easiest person in the world to work with. One of the gossip columnists came out with a story that he was prejudiced against blacks in general, and unhappy in particular with the black woman who'd joined his show. Nobody asked me about this, but if they had I could not have denied the distinct chill I felt whenever he was around. The straw that broke his back was Norman's bringing in ex-Harlem Globetrotter Meadowlark Lemon to join our happy band. This was just too much. Stevenson refused even to pose for a group publicity photo, although he did it indirectly. He made an excuse that he had to visit his dentist that day, but those gossip hounds checked that one out and alleged it was untrue. Whatever, he was the star and it got to the point after a few months where my lines got fewer and fewer. Then the show was canceled.

It was the beginning of the end of television for me during this go-round. There was one more show, *Checking In,* a spin-off of *The*

Jeffersons, but that came along in the middle of a writers' strike and we were only able to film five shows before the scripts ran out.

I had enjoyed a fair run during my years in California and Nevada, dry spells and all, but now I saw the writing on the wall. L.A. and Vegas had been interesting side excursions, a whirlwind of highs and lows. My plan for a return to the East Coast did not include burying myself once more in the sticks. New York City was still where the music played, and it was time to get back to my old day job, to re-establish my singing career. I had one more engagement to fulfill before leaving for the Big Apple. It proved a lulu, with skeletons tumbling from that cupboard I had never dreamed would see the light of day again.

15

BUNDINI RETURNS; SWANSON TOO

BY THE TIME I opened at the Parisien I had both Ronnie and Earl with me in Los Angeles, and they planned to stay to pursue their own careers after I departed for New York. Ronnie's ambitions were on the musical side and he began opening my shows, initially unannounced, singing a trio of songs before I introduced him as "my new find. My son, Ronnie Jackson." Earl had joined a law firm but was hampered by psoriasis, the skin complaint that had dogged him for years. It had started as just a little lump on his head way back in Deerpark, and he kept it to himself until he got to Albuquerque, where it became really serious. Cortisone shots helped initially, then it came back twice as bad, spreading all over his face, neck, chest and body. When it flared up and was at its worst my son was overwhelmed in an agony of itching, flaking and coping with blood-stained clothing and sheets. Although there had been praise from no less a talent than Richard Burton during a visit to Burton's niece and nephew, a talent for acting in college had lain undeveloped in Earl in the crisis of confidence that followed.

As Ronnie was halfway through his set that first night at the Parisien, a name from the past re-entered my life. It was none other than "the Great Bundini," Drew Brown, long since transformed into the world-famous trainer-jester at the court of Muhammad Ali. He came and stood about twenty feet from Ronnie, who recognized

With Thelma and
Ronnie.
(COURTESY OF RUTH BROWN)

him as a famous personality, apparently transfixed by his performance. Drew's manager appeared backstage as soon as my son hit
his dressing room: "Mr. Brown would like to talk to you. Would you
care to join him at his table?" Ronnie's reaction was, "Wow!
Bundini must really have liked my singing!" Drew didn't say too
much to him that night, merely asking how his career was going,
and what kind of things did he enjoy doing in his spare time, what
sports did he follow. All of that seemed innocent enough, if a little
puzzling to my son. Drew made no attempt to speak to me, and
although I was dying to hear what they were discussing I was not
about to crash the party.

Next night Drew was back with several friends. Again he sent for
Ronnie, and this time Ronnie was invited to spend a series of weekends with him, golfing and fishing. "You'll have to forgive him,"
one friend told Ronnie, "this is a very emotional thing for Bundini."

This was too much for my boy. "Would someone please explain
this to me?" he asked, getting up and pushing his chair aside. Receiving no reply, just a series of anguished stares, he left them sitting there and made for my dressing room. I was adjusting my
makeup, and as I looked at him in the mirror and saw him glaring,
my heart sank. "He's back again," said Ronnie, "and this time he's
talking get-to-know-each-other weekends."

Ridiculous and inadequate though it may have been, all I could
think of to say at that moment was, "Do you want to?"

"Maybe I do," Ronnie replied, and although he sounded be-
mused I could sense a dawning light. "But *why?*"

He could tell that I was getting more and more upset, and as I broke down and began crying I looked at him in the mirror and saw in his face that he was on the verge of discovering the secret I had harbored for over a quarter of a century. I was still too choked to speak, and after a minute Ronnie turned his back on me without a word, walked through the door and slammed it shut.

Next morning was like walking on eggs, with Ronnie and me studiously avoiding each other. I knew I had to say something, but how do you explain to your son that the man he always thought was his father is nothing of the kind, that he's been living a lie all his life? All day I steeled myself for the ordeal I knew had to come. When Earl came home early from work that particularly hot and humid afternoon—he'd been forced to excuse himself, he was in such torment—he said something like, "Mom, this thing's really getting me down. It's driving me crazy. We've got to talk about contacting another specialist," I wasn't even looking at him, I was too steeped in my own misery, and I snapped, "You think *you've* got problems? Look at me. I've got to tell Ronnie that Willis isn't his dad!"

For the first and only time in my life Earl broke down and cried in front of me. "How can you *be* so insensitive?" he asked, between racking sobs. "I know it'll be tough for Ronnie, but this is my *day-to-day* existence. I'm a monster, *a side-show, a freak.*"

As I drew him to me and tried to comfort him I realized the inexcusability of what I had said. My attitude had been, "Earl can handle his stuff." He was strong, I knew that. But how strong can anyone be, suffering as he was?

Ronnie kept well away before the show on that third night and Drew was back again, this time with Muhammad Ali himself. Ronnie was again summoned, and as he approached their table Ali got to his feet, gave him an enormous bear-hug, then kissed him on the cheek. "David, David, David," he began—Ronnie's middle name—"it's so great to see you. Listen, kid, you musn't be mad at your dad 'cause, you know, things happen, and I know he's been planning to contact you for the longest time. Just don't be mad, 'cause things like that have happened to me too."

Ronnie decided to play dumb. "My dad?" he asked, staring straight at Ali. "Who's *my dad?*"

Ali turned to Drew, an expression of disbelief on his face. "He doesn't know? You haven't talked to him yet?" Drew shook his head: "You never gave me a chance."

"I never gave you a chance?" Ali echoed. "What have you been tellin' the boy the last two nights?"

"You came out with it so fast," Drew complained.

"You told me it was all sorted out," Ali said.

Ronnie gave both of them a look, then silently turned and marched once more into my dressing room. He had no need to say anything, and I was suddenly calm. "Ronnie," I said, "if it had been up to me you'd never have known."

"It's true, then?"

"Yes, it's true."

My son told me later he felt as if someone had kicked him in the stomach. He had gone through a lifetime of folks saying, "Oh, you're Willis's boy, all right!" Now it all came back to sting him like a swarm of bees. As the news sank in, of course, there were compensations. Like being acknowledged the son of a celebrity, a hero of the sporting world, a larger-than-life force whose progress, erratic though it had been, had been minutely chronicled over the years. Ronnie's acceptance, when it came, was no starry-eyed adoration. On the contrary, he had a knock-down, drag-out fight with Drew before the air was cleared. Where had he been, he wanted to know, when his mother had been scrubbing floors and close to destitute? Flying off to Monaco or Zaire with no expense spared? Had he never once thought to send a check, even anonymously, to help out? And why *now*? Drew had no answer, except that advancing years, twinges of regret, and Lord knows what else had finally dictated his action, ham-fisted though it had been.

There was another major surprise in store when Drew's other son, Drew Brown, Jr., began calling Ronnie. "I always knew you were my brother," he informed Ronnie, "but I wasn't allowed to get in touch." Then there was the revelation they were born on the same day, only hours apart. Ultimately the friendship and respect between Ronnie and his true father that endured until Drew's death was a wonderful conclusion to the whole tortured saga.

Before leaving for New York I sought an equally happy end to Earl's problem. UCLA, we both had been led to believe, would provide the answer. A team of no less than eight specialists examined him. Their pronouncement? That he should go home and soak in a tar bath, something our own doctor had recommended years earlier. Of course it soothed, but it was far from the miracle cure we expected from UCLA's cutting-edge research.

His life became unbearable, for psoriasis was entrenched all over his body. He was rejected in public; all he wanted to do was hide himself away. He'd wake each morning with the sheets covered in blood and scales. He was talking openly about suicide, how he could not go on, and I was scared. As soon as I arrived in New York I sought advice on the best place for treatment of his complaint. Then I sent for him.

It was during hospitalization in New York's Columbia-Presbyterian that hope began to emerge. I know that Earl credits them with saving his life. He shared a wing with other dermatological patients there, and the first thing he was taught was how to deal with his affliction emotionally. He saw how others suffered and discovered he was far from alone, that others were far worse off than him. One poor girl had a truly terrible condition, atopic dermatitis, in which the skin turns like leather. It is not only extremely painful, it prohibits movement. He was made to understand that there was no "miracle cure," and he absorbed the technical feedback on his condition. He learned something else too: compassion for others, never to pass judgment on surface appearances. When he was discharged his condition had eased, but just as important, he was in a far better emotional state. A couple of years later he was admitted to Rockefeller Center for further observation, and that was another step forward.

By the time I arrived back in New York mama had left Portsmouth and moved to Long Island to be near Delia and Leonard in Hempstead. With Benny and Leonard running a barber's shop back home, young Alvin involved in photography, and Goldie the head of her own large family, our family was divided equally between New York State and Virginia.

You know the story where the husband phones the wife to tell her their cat has fallen off the roof and been killed? She protests that he should never have broken such dreadful news so badly—he should have made several calls, beginning with the news that the cat was *on* the roof, then it was *refusing* to come down, then it was *slipping,* and

My son Earl, Jr. (COURTESY OF RUTH BROWN)

so on. That's how this here idiot broke the news to my family that I was back with Earl Swanson. I met him soon after returning to the city while looking for a permanent apartment I could afford. With next to no money, that was not the easiest quest. He suggested that I move in with him on Riverside Drive, that we give it one more try, we'd both been young, headstrong and foolish, he'd changed, all that stuff. On the phone with Mama, Delia, or Ronnie or Earl, I adopted the cat story approach. First it was, "You'll never guess who's standing beside me!" then it was, "Would you like to speak to Earl?" They soon saw through that nonsense, and realized all too well what I'd done. So did I before I was a whole lot older.

Nor did my son let me off for any altruistic motives. "Don't say you're doing it for me," he warned. "I've lived without a father for years and I don't need one now. If you're doing this you're doing it for yourself."

I had enjoyed a lucky streak professionally soon after returning from Los Angeles. Thad Jones and Mel Lewis, with whom I'd recorded *Fine Brown Frame* at the end of the sixties, invited me along on a tour of Japan. It was brief but fun, and incredible to be so far away and have our music appreciated so much. A trip to Tokyo's electrical goods district and the record stores there showed Ruth Brown alive and well and living in Japan, at least in record terms,

with several Atlantic compilations, as well as *Late Date*, widely available.

On my return to New York there was more good news. A club in
Greenwich Village, the Cookery, run by the same Barney Josephsen
of the famous Cafe Society years earlier, had Helen Humes booked.
When she fell ill, Barney heard I was in town and hired me to cover
her spot until she recovered. The eighteen-week run there gave me
a hold on the Big Apple again and led to a whole spate of bookings.

Years earlier, way back in the sixties, I had introduced a ridicu-
lously multi-talented youngster named Little Stevie Wonder at the
Apollo. When I was handed a note at Greenstreet's, a Chelsea club,
to say that Stevie was up there on the balcony, I cut the band to
announce his presence. "Ladies and gentlemen," I began, "it's my
privilege and pleasure to acknowledge the presence of a true superstar in our midst tonight. I haven't seen him in many, many years,
and I'm so honored to think that he came here this evening to see
me."

Stevie stood up as the audience applauded, then yelled, "I've
been listenin' to you, Ruth, and you're soundin' real good. Hell,
somebody get me down there to that stage!" There was an uproar
as he grabbed the microphone. "I didn't come down here to sing,"
he said straight out. "I want to tell you something. I did not come
here because I had nothin' else to do. I came here because they
told me Ruth Brown was singing here tonight, and this is the lady,
take my word for it, who started it all. Wasn't for Ruth there
wouldn't be no Aretha, wouldn't be *nobody!* I'm here to tell you this
lady is a true legend."

Complimented as I was, I have to correct Stevie. There are certain people, and Aretha's one of them and Stevie's another, who
are more, much more, than singers. They're nothing less than flat-
out forces of nature, and as such ain't nothing could *ever* have
stopped them.

MY FIRST, EXTREMELY BRIEF TASTE of Broadway came after a successful
audition for a role in an all-black musical, *Blues in the Night*, in
which I was reunited with *Guys and Dolls* star Leslie Uggams. I was
cast as an earthy blues singer à la Bessie Smith, ending her wasted

life with nothing to show for it but scrapbooks and a bunch of broken jewelry, sitting on a bed in a flophouse of a hotel. I had a wonderful song to sing, "Wasted Life Blues," that was just my cup of tea, full of poignant lines like, "Lord, I wonder what my end will be." I looked *terrible*—the desired effect, I hasten to add—dressed in a flannel nightgown and a pair of ancient carpet slippers, my hair disheveled, but my number was so strong I felt I had a really good chance of making an impact. "Are you gonna sing it that way *every* night?" Chapman Roberts, the musical director, asked me after one stunned reaction from the rest of the cast—eerie silence at first, then whistles, applause and cries of, "There won't be a dry eye in the house!"

Then things began to go downhill, with the choreographer insisting that in the middle of this extremely moving song I climb on the bed, teeter there for a moment, then jump off. I protested that this was totally inappropriate, but he had to have his artistic way, and I darn near crippled myself doing what I was told.

During preview performances I got a call at home to say I was "a risk" and I shouldn't come in, and in any case I didn't have the stage presence required, I couldn't project, I couldn't sing harmony. Although these were among the excuses, I sensed that Leslie's husband and manager was behind the whole thing. Leslie was a sweet girl, but she was the star and maybe he was trying to prevent her being overwhelmed. Whatever it was, the producer, writer and director of the show, Sheldon Epps, went along with the decision. It was a real slap in the face for me. To let everyone know that my being dropped had nothing to do with physical fitness, I turned up on opening night and marched right down that center aisle before taking my seat. Judging by the amount of press attention that resulted, the gesture did not go unnoticed.

With Earl I soon discovered that he hadn't changed at all, except in one respect. After a brief harmonious spell the violence was now on a much more serious scale. He was working with bandleader Sy Oliver at the Rainbow Room, and after my run at the Cookery and brush with Broadway I picked up little gigs here and there, enabling me to share the utility bills. Despite this he did everything to let me know it was his apartment we were living in. I had to switch off every light, he told me not to go near the phone, even to touch his car was taboo. The apartment was pretty isolated and soon he was back screaming and yelling at me. Then the systematic beatings began all over again. It was brutality, brutality, brutality. Neighbors opened their doors, listened or took a peek, then closed them again. It was trouble between a man and his woman, and the unwritten code was to let them work it out.

After one incident that began with backhand slaps and quickly escalated to savage punching, I was hurt bad, desperate, and at the end of my tether. I survived it somehow and managed to sneak a call next day to young Earl, back in California after his hospitalization at Columbia-Presbyterian. He called his father and told him, "I heard you hit my mother." Earl snapped back, "Don't you dare talk to me like that!" My son told me later what he'd laid down: "If I fly to New York it'll be for one reason and one reason only, and that'll be to kick your ass. For every scar you lay on her I swear I'll break a bone in your body. I will care less that you're my father, all I'll know is that you've hurt my mother, the one person in this world who's tried to do everything for me. *I'll take you out!*" He added that he'd call back, and if the violence was over, it would be a dead issue. "Be the man you taught me to be during that summer we spent together," Earl suggested, *"and don't hit her no more!"*

One night Mama called out of the blue to say she'd had a bad dream, that I should get out of that apartment immediately. "I dreamed you died in there," she told me. "Please, Ruth, get out while you still can." Next on the line was Earl's sister, Claudia, who'd just heard that I'd moved back in with her brother. "Get out, Ruth," she warned me. "He damn near killed that second wife of his. He's dangerous, girl, like a mad dog."

When Earl arrived back from the club early next morning he took one look at me and seemed to sense what had been said, that he had been discussed with others. I got the worst whippin' ever, a knockdown, drag-out beating so bad I did think I was going to die. He ripped off every stitch of clothing I had on, beat me to the ground with his fists, then began kicking. I was in agony with my legs anyway, and I just lay there, praying for it to stop. It did for a moment, but only so he could haul me out the door and into the hallway, where he pressed his foot hard down on my neck and twisted one arm behind my back as I lay there whimpering. Then he began to

With Earl Swanson, 1980—
The calm before the storm.
(COURTESY OF RUTH BROWN)

lay me out verbally: "You're the ugliest, sorriest excuse for a woman I've ever seen. And you're fat, black, wrinkled and ugly." Reaching down, he snatched the wig off my head. "And you're damn near bald, and I don't want no woman that looks like you." My face was being pressed into the carpet grit as he cursed away.

Earl broke my spirit that night. He left me with nothing. The great Ruth Brown, rhythm and blues legend turned song stylist, television and stage performer, lying naked on her belly, eating dirt, swallowing every taunt and insult life had to offer, aching with pain from the bruises that covered her body, from the blows that had blackened her eyes, split her lip, loosened her teeth, but that had strangely, mercifully, numbed her legs.

I KNEW I had to get out there if it killed me, for if I didn't Earl would do it first. I began moving my stuff out slowly so he wouldn't notice, calling Paul Williams, who lived five blocks away, to come over in his car each night and take a little away at a time in the trunk. Earl left for work at 6:00 each night and returned the following morning at 1:15, so everything had to be moved during these hours. Lord, I was never so scared.

Earl got into a habit of phoning between shows to make sure I was there and question me about the electricity I was using. It was another fault if he found the number engaged, and there would be all hell let loose when he got home, since I'd been using the phone without his authority. Paul phoned one night to say he'd just heard what had happened to Earl's last wife, that he'd beaten her unconscious and she'd had to flee their house with her two children. "I know," I told him. "His sister told me." Paul couldn't believe his ears. He'd known it was bad, but he'd never imagined how bad. "And you're still there, girl?" he asked me incredulously. "Okay, enough of gradually moving out. Get out now, this minute, before he kills you. I'm coming over."

The words were no sooner out of his mouth than the door opened and Earl, home early, caught me on the phone. He didn't know who I was talking to, he didn't even care who'd made the call, it was enough that I was defying him by using the phone. His face contorted with rage, he strode over and yanked the receiver away with one hand, the other readying a backhand slap. I dodged it, screamed, ran to the bathroom and locked the door behind me.

Paul heard my scream over the phone, gathered what had happened, and it took him only a few minutes to arrive outside our building. I heard the buzzer sound in our apartment over the noise of Earl trying to batter the door down. Paul told me later that he'd pressed all the buttons and some other party had let him in. He ran up the stairs, found our front door open and confronted Earl. "Get away from that door, you stone-crazy bastard," I heard Paul yell. That was my cue. I opened the bathroom door and ran past Earl, then Paul and I took off. Scared as I was, my first question as we sat together in his car was, "What'll I do about the rest of my stuff?"

"Write it off," came the reply, without a moment's hesitation, "just like you should write that crazy sonofabitch out of your life!" I gave him no argument.

Paul took me to his place and I called a girlfriend of mine, Birdie Green, a singer who lived on Central Park West. She offered me a couch in her apartment to sleep on, and I stayed with her a month. Mighty grateful as I was for the shelter, it was a low point for me. Earl had sapped the last ounce of my self-esteem and confidence. All the lipstick, powder and paint in the world could never turn this "fat, ugly bitch" into something anyone in their right mind would want to look at. I was wrecked, down, dumped, finished, *forget it!*

The trough lasted until I was able to rent a tiny room of my own from one of my girlfriends. Unfortunately it had no door, it was just a room adjoining hers, and I never got a moment's privacy. All I heard was, "Guess who's stayin' with me! Ruth Brown!" It took me back to what I've always said, "Lord, just give me somethin', even if it's no bigger than a phone booth, just to get my dignity back." If only I'd remembered to specify a door. Paying the rent, and making a world of difference, was two nights' steady work a week at the Baby Grand.

One day I was out buying groceries when a lady approached me. "You're Ruth Brown, aren't you?" she asked. "I sure am," I replied, "but please don't hold that against me." She turned out to be a friend of the singer Valerie Carr, a buddy of mine from the fifties who'd enjoyed a big record, and a good one too, with "After Midnight (When the Girls Talk About the Boys)." What was I doing these days, she wanted to know. "To be truthful," I replied, "not a whole lot. Things aren't too good right now." I explained my situation and told her I was searching for an apartment of my own. "I don't care if it's just one room," I added, "just as long as I can get a bed in there and lock the door behind me."

She fell silent for a moment. "I got a friend in Atlantic City, and she has a one-room apartment up on 165th Street," she explained. "I keep the keys while she's away and she hasn't stayed there for almost a year. You could ask her if she's prepared to sublet. Let me give you her number."

I called her as soon as I got to a phone and when she came over with the keys to show me the place I hardly even looked at it before saying, "I'll take it!" And I have that apartment to this day, my little bolt-hole in New York City. I got my strength back there; that single room was my sanctuary, my bedroom, my living room, my prayer room, my everything. There was no kitchen, but I fixed that up as well, together with a corner where I could worship and give thanks to the Lord for what he'd found for me. And always, always there was an open Bible at the door. When anyone visited, my family included, and asked how on earth I could live in such a place, I'd reply, "I'm fine here, thank you, and if you don't understand that, don't ask." I had my own tiny corner of the planet, and with Mama nearby and calling every day, it was more than enough.

16

A BRAND-NEW BITCH

NORMAN SCHWARTZ, the man behind my *Black Is Brown and Brown Is Beautiful* album in the sixties, cut *The Soul Survives* with me in 1982 before I was cast in *Amen Corner,* a musical version of James Baldwin's play. Earl Swanson backed me on Norman's session, recorded live at Washington's Blues Alley, for the first and most definitely the last time. Goodbye to all that!

Norman and I were together in a deli on Fifty-seventh Street when he spotted a friend of his, a tall, elegant brunette named Kathy Hammer. What struck me immediately about Kathy was an unmistakable, indefinable air of "born to rule," but in the nicest way imaginable. As soon as he introduced us she looked at me as if she had just discovered the lost chord. "Oh my goodness," she declared, "my fiancé's birthday is coming up and you've simply no idea how much he *loves* Ruth Brown. Could you possibly put a little group together and sing at Arthur's party?" She then proceeded to name an unbelievable fee she'd be prepared to pay. I naturally agreed and when we talked again a few days later she dropped the bombshell that oh, by the way, the birthday party was being held in Columbus, Ohio. 'Don't worry,' she hastily added, 'we'll fly you all there.' She did, and it was a truly wonderful occasion. We were put up overnight in her fiancé's beautiful home and treated royally.

When *Amen Corner* hit Washington soon afterwards something extraordinary happened. It did not seem that way at the time, only later would I realize its significance. A young man named Howell

Begle presented himself backstage one night, a pile of Ruth Brown albums tucked under his arm. He was short, slightly built, with sandy-colored hair and the bluest eyes this side of Paul Newman. He explained he'd been a rhythm-and-blues nut since his school-days, ever since dragging his mother along to one of Alan Freed's rock 'n' roll Shows. That was where he caught my act, brief though it was, and he'd remained a fan ever since. He was friends with Kathy Hammer, and I soon gathered she had filled him in on how we'd met, our appearance at her party, all of that. I hadn't seen some of the albums he wanted me to sign for years. "Where on earth did you get them all?" I asked him.

"All over," he told me, "and I paid dearly for them."

"Really? That's interesting," I said, " 'cause I'm not getting a penny."

"Kathy told me as much," he replied, "and I find that quite unbelievable."

"I wish I was," I said. "Oh, friends of mine have tried to help, but between us we've got exactly nowhere. I haven't had a royalty state-ment in over twenty-five years. And there's a whole bunch of other artists in the same boat."

Howell said he'd like to call me next time he was in New York, that he'd be talking to Kathy and would be in touch. We left it at that. Soon after his visit Atlantic would be the last thing on my mind.

I AUDITIONED for the role in *Amen Corner* soon after moving into the tiny apartment that became my haven. I had no big part, but it was visibility, and I needed that badly. And I got to sing a number called "There's a Man Sleeping Close Somewhere," sitting at a table, wearing a simple housedress and apron. The song was about the man my sister, the show's star, was in love with, and it was a stone knockout. I gave it everything I've got, and apparently it showed. When director Philip Rose was interviewed during our run in Wash-ington and asked why Ruth Brown was unbilled, the question threw him at first. "She's not a trained actress," his reply began, then he added, "but I've never worked with one before who has the timing and knack that she has." When I read that my heart leapt. Let me tell you, these little things you hold on to!

They chopped the show up, adding and subtracting as we went along, and it was destined not to last. When it hit New York just before Thanksgiving, Clive Barnes of the *Post* listed its shortcomings like everyone else. They had tried to make a musical out of something purely dramatic, and he reported that it simply did not work. But he added something else: "If you want to take my word for something, pay for a ticket and go just to hear Ruth Brown. I don't know what the director was thinking about to make her just sit there at a table and sing only one song, but that alone is worth the price of admission." When I finally got to meet Barnes you can bet I gave him a big hug for that.

Mama and Leonard came to see the show at the Nederlander and climbed three flights of stairs to reach my dressing room afterwards. When I scolded her for making that climb, she quickly hushed me up. "Long as I've waited to see you on Broadway, I wouldn't have missed this for *nuthin'!*" Suddenly she caught sight of our male star, Roger Robinson, whom she recognized as the black detective from *Kojak*. Nudging me furiously, she said, "Ruth, have you any idea who this *is?*" She was so excited.

When she was admitted to hospital in Mineola with heart problems a few days later, Mama asked my family not to let me know, convinced I'd walk away from the show as soon as I heard the news. She was in intensive care for several days, and by the time she came out of there the show had closed, during the first week of December. Only after that did they decide it was safe to tell me, and I was frantic as I rushed to see her, as well as in considerable pain from my legs. The journey up and down subway steps was a nightmare. When visiting time was over I watched as she lay there on her plumped-up pillows. There was talk of having a pacemaker fitted, and I was just so relieved to see her responding favorably to all she'd been through. "You're looking good, Mama." I told her. "I'll be back tomorrow and bring you a nice new nightgown and bathrobe, and some bedroom slippers."

As I left and said goodbye at the door, she waved me out with that wonderful smile of hers. Downstairs in the lobby I found the gift shop about to close, and the girl counting her cash-register receipts. Something told me to go in anyway. "Could I pay you to see that my mother gets one rose on her breakfast tray tomorrow and one on her lunch tray?" I asked her. She said that she would and I paid for the two roses. Then I spotted a little basket of flowers and asked how much that was. "Oh, I'm just closing up," she said, "you're welcome to take them."

I made my way back to Mama's room with them, slipped inside and placed them in a bowl at her bedside. "This will take care of you until I get back tomorrow," I said. "They're beautiful, Ruth," she replied, "but do one thing for me. Sit them by the window so the sun will hit them in the morning." I did that, and we waved again at each other as I left. "I'll see you tomorrow, Mama," I promised. "I'll be with you by suppertime."

It stormed the next day like I don't know what. To get to the subway I had to walk three blocks from 165th to 168th Street, negotiate a series of steep stairs and walk through a tunnel there to catch the train to Penn Station that connected to the Long Island Railroad. I couldn't walk that fast in the driving rain, and I missed the connection. Rather than wait an hour for the next train I hiked all the way back to my apartment and called Mama to tell her I'd be over the following day instead. Someone in her room picked up the phone, held it for a minute without saying anything, then laid it back down, leaving it off the hook. As I sat in my apartment, still dripping wet, I was scarcely able to believe what I was hearing. They were trying everything to revive Mama. "Come on, Martha, breathe, *breathe*," someone said, while I screamed for someone to talk to me. Instead, I heard the click of the receiver being replaced.

I immediately called Delia in Hempstead and told her what I'd just heard. "No, no, that can't be right," she told me, "Leonard and I just left her an hour or so back and she was fine."

"I don't care," I screamed, "something's happened. You have to go back there right away." I'll never know how I passed the next hour and a half in my apartment before my sister called back. It was the longest ninety minutes of my life, and I summoned every prayer and exhortation I could think of. When the phone did ring I leapt at it like a wild thing. "Ruth, Leonard and I are coming over," was all Delia said.

"For what?"

"We're both coming over."

"For what? Why tonight?"

Delia fell silent, and it was a silence I had to break even if it meant spelling out the unthinkable. "Is Mama dead?" I whispered.

"We'll be over soon, Ruth," was all my sister replied.

I knew. Putting my hat and coat back on, I walked out into the rain. Delia and Leonard found me wandering sixteen blocks away, at three A.M., soaked to the skin and out of my mind. That was the only time in my life that I cursed God and show business both. I had not been able to pay for a car or to call on a friend to take me over to see Mama, and there was a terrible anger mixed in with the overwhelming grief I felt.

For the next few days I just went off into a different place emotionally. I was never going to sing again, I was never going to make it back. I even took to wearing my mother's clothes. I was on the verge of a nervous breakdown.

Her body had to be flown to Virginia for burial and I did not even have the money for a plane ticket. A neighbor looked at the coat I was proposing to wear and told me flat-out that it was not good enough for a funeral. "Okay," I said, "lend me one." She did, and I wore that borrowed coat to Mama's funeral, and flew to Virginia on borrowed money.

On the journey I said very little to anyone and just listened when we got to Portsmouth as all my brothers and sisters made polite conversation. I was unable to contribute, for I was simply unwilling to deal with the situation, to come to terms with the fact of my mother's death and burial. Delia was the authoritative one, deciding who the funeral director was going to be and organizing Goldie and me to select a coffin at the parlor. I found it difficult to believe I was in a funeral home, for it was more like a furniture showroom, they had coffins of all different colors and materials, with dainty matching outfits to match, complete with all-inclusive price tags. I took a seat and watched as Delia and Goldie moved from one to another, then I heard one of them murmur, "This is a nice color . . ."

That was it for me. I just went *off*.

"This is *not* a supermarket!" I exploded. "I could care less if the dress don't match the coffin, understand? What's Mama taking with her? Have you both forgotten what she always taught us about material things?"

I knew I took them aback and upset them, and I knew they were only doing what they felt right and proper, but it cut right across what Mama had always preached: "You can't take nothin' with you, and when you get ready to go you're not even given a say on what they put on your behind." Or: "The first time you attend a funeral and see a Brinks van drawin' up, then you'll know that material stuff matters."

The morning of the funeral we all gathered at Benny's house, and as I looked out the window I saw the hearse coming to a halt outside. There was a light rain falling and as I lowered the blind I said, "Blessed is the corpse that it rains on," another expression of Mama's. As we moved outside, a watery sun peeped out from behind the clouds. I'd never consciously beheld a rainbow since my childhood, and the one that came out seemed to stretch from one side of the house to the other. Being the eldest I was in the first car and I watched as two bluebirds fluttered on either side of the hearse all the way to the church.

The congregation waiting for us was a revelation. After being away so long I'd forgotten the many organizations Mama had been involved with, like the Deacon board, all of whose members were there, heads bowed, resplendent in their uniforms and regalia. The first thing the minister came out with had me crumbling. "We're going to open the door to Heaven today," he declared, " 'cause that's where our dear sister Martha is heading." Someone behind me mistakenly tried to hush me up: "Don't cry, don't cry." I turned around, tears rolling down my cheeks. "I beg your pardon," I said. "This is my mother and I'll cry if I want to."

As we went through the whole graveside thing time just seemed to stop. That night we re-assembled at Benny's house, ostensibly to talk about all our memories of Mama, as well as how we planned to stay together as a family. After a while a hush fell on our little assembly, and I sensed Benny picking up some kind of unspoken cue. "You know, Ruth," he said, "we have to get together to fulfill Mama's wish."

"What wish was that?" I asked.

"Well, we weren't going to tell you so soon after the funeral, but I don't see any point in delayin'. Mama was very concerned about you being alone and havin' a bad time. And she asked us to see that nothin' happened to you, that you were taken care of.''

Borrowed cash or no, borrowed coat or no, I turned on my brother, at the same time including the rest of my family in one all-encompassing glare. ''Really? Well, thank you very much,'' I replied, ''but let me tell you something. From here on in, there'll be no need to worry about me. You guys may not be able to understand this, for I've always been easy-goin', but hey, you're about to see a brand-new bitch out here, especially where my music is concerned. I made it in the first place with that gift that was given to me, and I'll make it again, 'cause it's still there. Now I'm goin' back to get what belongs to me, but before I do, listen to me and listen good. You will *never* have to get together and pay for me no more!''

It was like I was emerging from shock. The truth is I had forgotten that my mother could die, just blanked the thought out. Now that I had finally bought it, now that I had been forced to face the truth, it was suddenly crystal-clear that there was only one way the void could even be partly filled. I could see the startled expression on the faces of Benny, Leonard, Leroy, Goldie, Delia, even young Alvin as I spelled out the last of my pronouncement: ''Whether you're aware of it or not, I have just become the African-American Rose Kennedy, the head of the clan. From this day forward you will look to me, and where I am you will gather. *Understand?*''

SOON AFTER I GOT BACK from mama's funeral, Kathy Hammer called to say that Howell Begle was due in town. She invited me to lunch before we both went to meet him, then asked, ''Did you know, by the way, that he's an attorney?'' I replied that he hadn't told me, that it had never come up in our conversation. ''Let me tell you,'' said Kathy, ''they don't call him 'Beagle' for nothing. When he puts his nose down and starts looking for something, he'll find it. He told me he really likes you, Ruth, and he'd like to help in any way he can.''

We met Howell in a Madison Avenue boardroom he was visiting, sat ourselves around a borrowed table, and began talking about record royalties, Atlantic's in particular. I detailed the endless correspondence Ensley, Alfonse and our appointed lawyers had entered into over the years, and showed him how our latest sad-sack attempt had ended. Someone named Lewinter at Atlantic had forwarded my correspondence to the company's attorneys. Their letter, dated May 1983, ran:

> We have carefully reviewed your letter, and find that it principally addresses events which transpired as long ago as twenty-eight years . . . Furthermore, most of the issues which you raise relate to very vague and highly speculative matters. It is unlikely that further investigation would result in any monies becoming payable.
>
> As both a legal principle and a purely practical matter, it is not feasible for a business concern to be indefinitely subjected to inquiries and complaints regarding the performance of its contractual commitments. For this reason, the state legislature has enacted a statute of limitations which precludes such inquiries and complaints.
>
> While it appears that our client has made every attempt to accommodate you, and to provide you information which you desire, the statute of limitations protects companies such as our client from having to bear the extremely costly and genuinely impractical burden of answering for every accounting and payment over long periods of time. Accordingly, please be advised that our client declines to take any further action with regard to your requests. We hope you can appreciate our client's position.

That end-of-the-road correspondence summarized how fruitless the whole exercise had been, I told Howell. Maybe even worse than fruitless, for according to a royalty statement I'd actually managed to squeeze out of the company I was *in debt* to Atlantic.

Why? Well, the original agreement had called for a flat payment up front for every side I recorded, starting at $69. That sum was against royalties, which were calculated at a straight five percent of sales. For me and Bing Crosby both, according to Ahmet. The snag was that those royalties commenced only when Atlantic's production costs were recovered, for I was responsible for both the musi-

cians' fees and arrangements. Whatever Atlantic calculated this figure to be was something that I, like dozens of other artists, was in
no position to dispute. Then there were so many records allocated
for promotion, which always seemed to me an amazingly large
amount, and no royalty was paid on them. On top of that there was
a ten percent allowance for breakages. Understandable in the days
of shellac, it was less easy to comprehend as we moved into vinyl.

What none of us understood was that cutting so many sides, with
fees of an unspecified amount to be paid for before we saw a penny
in royalties outside of peanut advances, did not mean their guaranteed release. If only one side out of every three cut was released,
that one side was loaded with the expenses incurred for *all three*
sessions. If you cut twenty and only ten saw the light of day, you still
got stung for the cost of twenty. The computation of those expenses, of course, was entirely in the hands of those in charge, and
was never spelled out.

Leaving school at fifteen, Lord knows I was no rocket scientist,
but there were people like Big Joe Turner, next door to illiterate,
lining up like lambs to the slaughter. Only corporations had access
to lawyers in those days, I told Howell. And besides, we *trusted* these
contracts and the people who drew them up.

Those old "session costs," according to the royalty report I'd
gotten out of Atlantic, far outweighed what they claimed I'd earned
in over twenty years. Would you believe those earnings amounted to
$785 domestic and foreign combined? Specifically, $354 at home,
$431 abroad. Howell's expression when I reached that point was
priceless.

"I can't believe what I'm hearing," he declared. "They say *you*
owe *them* money? And that the total sales of your stuff both home
and abroad amounts to just *seven hundred bucks over twenty years*?
Look, Ruth, I'll tell you what, I can't make any promises, I don't
want to do that and raise your hopes again after all you've been
through, but I want you to go home and go through everything
you've got. I don't give a good goddamn how old it is. Dig it out,
and if it's got *Atlantic* written on it, send it to me in Washington."

He also asked me to prepare a list of everyone else he needed to
contact, like other record companies I'd been associated with over
the years, so he could inform them that as of now he would be

representing Ruth Brown, that she had a legal adviser protecting her interests. When I pointed out that I didn't have any money to pay him, that I was still settling old lawyers' bills, he smiled. "Forget it," he told me. "I'm doing this for Ruth Brown and the pleasure you've given me for years." Despite his obvious sincerity and determination, I took his advice and tried not to build my hopes up.

I did have some reason for optimism about the future, although you might be forgiven for filing it under Clutching at Straws. Through a friend of mine, the singer Doris Troy, I'd been introduced to an astrologer named Lynn Palmer. She made six very specific predictions about my future, together with a seventh that, while tantalizing, seemed utterly ridiculous to me at the time. Among other things, she claimed that I'd be back at the top of my profession before the eighties were out. Oh, *sure!*

17

BLACK AND BLUE

WHEN YOU TAKE someone's childhood away from them and make them adults prematurely, what's left when they do grow up? In January 1953 an act named Etta James and the Peaches joined a tour Willis and I were on in Dallas, Texas. Etta was barely a teenager at the time, and her mama was along to look after her. Her daughter was no screamer, but I thought she had one of the strongest young voices I'd ever heard. The only thing that disturbed me was Etta being so young and singing all those songs of grownup love. She was far too young to know what she was singing about. At least I hope she was.

The general attitude in those days, to be honest, was not to be overly concerned with such matters. We were there to put on a show, not deliver philosophical theories. And I daresay someone could have taken a look at me and said the same, unaware of the underpinning my mother and father had provided as I grew up. Nowadays, with all the water that's flowed under the bridge, you'd think we'd probe a little deeper into the psychological scarring process. We don't. Instead, we're happy to accept what's on display at face value. And holler blue murder when things don't turn out that way.

THAT FIRST MEETING with Howell apart, I was privileged to meet another wonderful character in Washington, courtesy of *Amen Corner*.

200

None other than the author of the source material, James Baldwin. When we opened in that city, at the historic Ford Theater, where President Lincoln was assassinated, he was already *persona non grata* with the show's production team, having opened up to the press on his dissatisfaction with the distortions he felt had been wrought. I was angry at his treatment by the muckety-mucks in charge, and appeared proudly on his arm at the press party after the show. The show had been financed by Gil Gerard, TV's Buck Rogers, and he and his wife Connie Selleca turned up at the bash, held on Embassy Row, where the guest of honor was President Ford.

James got the visibility he deserved at the party, and we remained friends thereafter. Much as he enjoyed Retta Hughes in her star role of my sister, he maintained that I could have played Sister Margaret. "You can act," he told me. I thanked him, but protested —not too much—that I was not a trained actress. "You would be *real,*" was his response. "It would come across so natural."

We had lunch together several times during those months in Washington, where the cast was based in little self-catering apart-ments in South East overlooking the Potomac. Later, during a meal in New York, he invited me over to visit him at his home in France. I might have taken him up on the offer, except at the time I would have had trouble raising the fare to Paris, Texas. James was a brac-ing companion, very outspoken, always coming out with the unex-pected comment while demonstrating dramatically with his hands. Sometimes he would seem to be hiding his lifestyle, other times it would be damn that, and he would open up and become extremely campy. Give him a glass of wine, especially his favorite, Pouilly Fuisse, and you could stand by for a nonstop stream of prose and poetry, none of it ever written down, all of it just popping into his head. Amazingly, he knew all of Ruth Brown's history, and talked about Blanche, the car crash and my record career.

He was an incredible little guy, and watching and listening to him I had to continually remind myself that this was not your run-of-the-mill individual running off at the mouth, this was *James Baldwin.* One thing he wasn't was a cutie, and he knew it and got there before anyone else did. "God sure don't love ugly!" he told me once. "Yeah," I replied, "but sometimes he ain't too thrilled with beautiful either." There he was again at the opening night on

Broadway. I wish it had run, if only to pay tribute to James's original, but it was a bird with a broken wing. Which reminds me . . .

Just before the show closed I was on stage with Retta singing a duet, she standing dressed in choir robes, I kneeling in prayer. Just as I turned my head at the halfway point of our number, "Love Dies Hard," a bird flew down the auditorium and right across the stage. It was an unmistakable sign someone was about to die. That was Mama, only days after we closed.

FOR A VARIETY OF REASONS my mother and father are not buried together. Back in '53 cemeteries were miles from home. Mama is at rest near the center of town at a place they call the Woman at the Well. It occurred to me every time I go home that I would always find time to visit Mama's grave, yet something always got in the way of getting out to Dad's resting place at Fisher Hill. Now Leonard is the only one of us still reluctant to do that. "Oh no," he'll say, "I don't want to look at no tombstone and see my name there."

Mama's death brought a whole change in me. Although I went to the brink of manic depression, it never got to the stage of contemplating suicide, at least not seriously. For a moment in time I hated the world with a terrible bitterness. I felt that God had turned his back on me, and that's a desperate, lonely, dreadful feeling. Out of it, apart from a faith that is stronger than ever, came an absolute determination to get what was rightfully mine. I have never believed in the politics of envy, but a phrase Howell used kept coming back to me. It was the efforts of the Ruth Browns of the world, he said, that had formed the base of the multi-million-dollar pyramid Atlantic had become. For one time in my life, I was encouraged to take a look at *me*, to know who Ruth Brown really is.

As soon as I arrived back in New York I began calling every agency I knew: "This is Ruth Brown." "What Ruth Brown?" *"That* Ruth Brown!"* I was aggressive, yes, to the point of being greedy. I started looking round me and saw a lot of phony friends, excess baggage, albatrosses, people who patted me on the back for their own gain. Lots of them had mistaken kindness for dumbness. Now it was time to shake off those negative elements that were holding me back. And hey, I had a lawyer ready to fight for me. Well, I was ready too.

I studied the trade papers, checking out every casting call I thought might be remotely suitable. It paid off, for at the Baby Grand one night I got a visit from an agent named Ted Gegis, bearing a treatment for a show called *Black and Blue,* an all-black musical revue of Cotton Club days. It would be opening in Paris, he explained, and I should read it and get myself along to the auditions. My first thought was, "Shucks, this'll be another cattle call. There'll be dozens of hopefuls lining up."

By the time auditions were scheduled I was already down in New Orleans doing *Staggerlee,* a workshop show written by Vernell Bagneris, with music by Allen Toussaint. The storyline was based on the public domain blues, "Stack O' Lee," that Lloyd Price had turned into a smash back in the sixties. Vernell, hot from portraying Jelly Roll Morton in *One Mo' Time,* lured me in over a fish dinner in New York. As with *Amen Corner,* I guess the marquee value of having Ruth Brown featured was behind it, rather than any acting ability they felt I might have. Although Lord knows I was no stellar attraction at the time, my name certainly would not turn people away. Vernell was playing Staggerlee and the music, with tunes like "Ruler of My Heart," was incredible. Way before *Sister Act,* we had a gaggle of nuns, myself included, tearing on to the stage and filling the place with an exultant mixture of gospel and rock.

We were reaching the end of six weeks of rehearsals and the run was about to start when I had to fly to New York to audition for *Black and Blue.* "As soon as they see I'm not size nine, it'll be, 'forget it,' " I grumbled to myself during the journey. The treatment gave no clue as to what they were looking for and I turned up wearing a blood-red pants suit and sporting a long curly wig. I'd been told to have two songs ready, a ballad and a gospel number, and when I walked in there had already been several singers before me, among them Linda Hopkins, Carrie Smith, Joyce Bryant and Sandra Reeves Phillips. They were performers based in New York, and I understood they had been auditioning in California as well.

As I walked on stage I saw two guys sitting in the stalls, taking it all in. I delivered "Yes Sir, That's My Baby" first, then followed up with "You'll Never Walk Alone." When I finished there was an encouraging response. They actually stood up and applauded. I knew they were Argentinian gentlemen and thought this must simply be a custom of their country. Not a bit like New York! There was nothing said, though, beyond the usual "We'll be in touch." I made straight for the airport, not really knowing what to make of it all.

Two days later I got the answer. Claudio Segovia and Hector Orezzoli wanted me for their show, and could I double back to New York? I was semi-installed in New Orleans by this time, even had my mother's cat, Ginger, down there with me, but I asked permission to leave. There was no problem, for I had a good understudy and they appreciated the great opportunity I was being offered.

The next time Claudio and Hector wanted to hear me sing a few different songs. They had Linda Hopkins back as well and asked us to duet on a couple of items. Also in place was the amazing taps wizard Bunny Briggs, and piano man Lloyd Mayors, who had worked with Sammy Davis, Jr. for years and had a real feel for what I did. Next thing I knew the whole thing was wrapped up. "We're leaving for Paris on November fourth," they announced. This was in late September. I had less than two months to get ready. It was way down yonder to New Orleans for a couple of weeks, then back to New York. There the deal was signed, Howell having cast a friendly eye over my contract. On top of our salaries, our board and all expenses were paid and there was a guaranteed run of eight weeks. Off we went, the three female leads—myself, Linda Hopkins and Sandra Reeves Phillips—together with the other singers, dancers and musicians who made up the show.

From the beginning Hector and Claudio were wonderful twin pillars of support. Both were perfectionists in their own way. Hector had the finesse for staging, Claudio's genius lay in costumes. They were "me and my shadow," having been school friends initially, then roommates and friends for life. They had already tasted success with their previous shows, *Flamenco Puro* and *Tango Argentina,* and were set on making it three in a row. Claudio took to watching me from the wings when I was singing "Body and Soul," his favorite, and he would put put his fingers to his lips as I finished, kiss them and mouth, "Diva!" *Very* gratifying! My magnificent beaded costume for that song, incidentally, tipped the scales at thirty pounds and cost $30,000. During rehearsals Claudio played me audio and video tapes of Maria Callas, and urged me to try for her presence and strength. Everything, as far as both of them were concerned, had to be the best it could be, and that feeling was contagious.

Ours was not a show that allowed any individual to be a star, on the surface, that is, because so much of what we did was ensemble stuff. All we could do was give our individual best. Parisians loved *Black and Blue* so much that we ran way over our initial booking of six weeks, staying for an record-breaking eight months. One of the reasons for our success in France was the complete absence of dialog. It was one hundred percent song and dance, and I guess these are international languages anyone can understand. In any case we acted out the songs, and most would have been familiar to any hip international audience in their own language. Claudio's gorgeous costumes set the whole thing off. There were high hats, feathers, sequins, pearls, the works, with forty people on our chorus line and a full stage band. The entire affair was as authentic as anything Paris had seen since the days of Josephine Baker, and maybe it outdid even that. It was so gratifying to discover the great respect and affection the French had for the music, as well as the elements of black culture that were on display.

On a visit to the famous Lido Musique in the Champs-Elysses I was taken aback at the Ruth Brown albums they had in there, European pressings mixed in with Japanese imports. The majority came from Atlantic's foreign licensees, and I listed each of them for Howell's perusal. In many ways it was like a trip back in time, for here too were the Drifters, the Clovers, Joe Turner, Clyde McPhatter, LaVern Baker, a virtual Atlantic reunion. Why, I asked myself, would stores like these be giving such items shelf space unless they were selling healthy numbers?

Sipping a drink in one of the pavement cafes on the Champs-Elysees and watching the world go by, visiting the Tuileries Gardens and the Sacre Coeur, or strolling along the Left Bank and watching the artists at work, were all part of the thrill of living and working in one of the world's most beautiful and exciting cities. We were put up in apartments in the Chatelet district, and from my dressing room I had superb views of Notre Dame to the left and the Bastille to the right.

"Preacher" Robbins, me, Linda Hopkins and Sandra Reeves Phillips,
"Black and Blue." (COURTESY OF RUTH BROWN)

Before we left Paris the demand for an cast album became overwhelming. There was even talk of an imminent Broadway transfer,
which unfortunately turned out to be way premature.

WHILE HOWELL WAS CHIPPING AWAY at Atlantic, and keeping in touch
regularly, I found work back in New York wherever I could. I began
hosting a radio program for National Public Radio, *Harlem Hit
Parade,* and accepted whatever gigs came my way. It was a case of
anything to keep my profile high. Howell and I both knew it was
going to be a long trail a-winding, but all along I was encouraged by
the mixture of diligence, ingenuity and the pure, cool nerve he
displayed.

Ahmet and his partners at Atlantic had collected in excess of $17
million from Warner/Seven Arts in 1967 before realizing that even
at this price they had practically given the company away. "We sold
it for seventeen and a half million when it was worth thirty-five
million," Jerry Wexler has claimed. His reasoning? The year after

the sale, Atlantic enjoyed gross earnings of $45 million, prompting Ahmet's offer to buy his company back for $40 million. "No dice," was the understandable response.

The opportunity for redress came when Steve Ross at Kinney, Warner/Seven Arts' new owner, was faced with the prospect of Ahmet and his crew jumping ship. In no time flat a "sweetener" on the original deal was rushed through. As a jubilant Jerry put it: "We almost sold it a second time!"

How could Howell impress on Warner Communications that ours was a case that wouldn't go away? The problem with straight-ahead suing was that it would tie the affair up in litigation forever and certainly cost more than any imaginable settlement. If, that is, we didn't get slaughtered at the outset, for on the face of it Howell was representing someone of no business significance whatsoever. If he started a dialog with lawyers, their instinctive reaction would be to push him through the usual initiation process: depositions, hearings all over the country spread over years, a minimum outlay of hundreds of thousands of dollars, what Howell referred to as the "wear the bastards down" technique.

Instead his strategy was to begin with low-level information-gathering approaches, then to choose his battles, utilizing his various contacts in the worlds of business, politics and entertainment. Luckily, and to me amazingly, they were worlds that converged with surprising regularity. Necessity was about to prove the mama of invention. If a legalistic approach was out, the concentration had to be on moral policy issues. Warner, in short, had to be persuaded they had a real PR problem on their hands. A headache that wouldn't quit.

My role was to grab as big a share of the limelight as possible. If mine was just the story of a down-and-out oldie who got a bum rap back in the fifties, what was the big deal? My case would be so much more effective if I was someone to reckon with all over again in the eighties. I had a double incentive to get my career re-launched.

Howell had first had to convince his partners at his Washington, D.C., law firm of Verner, Liipfert to cut him enough slack to work my case on the side, balancing out the income he would continue to generate from his "day job" in mergers and acquisitions—general counsel to the Media News Group, which he helped set up, and

"Ruth Brown and Friends"— my all-star line-up: "Tootsie" Bean, Bill Williams, Carlene Ray, their singer! Bobbie Forrester and Charles "C.I." Williams.
(COURTESY OF RUTH BROWN)

representing them in the purchase of several dozen newspapers— for what was essentially a *pro bono,* uncompensated effort requiring considerable advances for travel and other expenses. "Don't begrudge me this," was the message. Fortunately, his partners listened.

One of them was Harry McPherson, a gentleman who had once been Lyndon Johnson's White House Counsel. At the end of the Johnson administration McPherson had been appointed trustee both of the Kennedy Center for the Performing Arts and the American Film Institute. Keenly interested in every aspect of the arts, Howell had worked alongside his partner in helping put together these organizations' television spectaculars, the "Kennedy Center Honors" and AFI's annual "Life Achievement Awards" presentation. By the time I met Howell he'd been the lawyer for dozens of other high-profile television specials, including five annual NBC "Christmas in Washington" specials, and ABC's Fiftieth Presidential Inaugural Gala for Ronald Reagan.

After our meeting in the fall of '83, Howell first got together with Sanford "Bud" Wolff, President of AFTRA (American Federation of Theatrical and Radio Artists). The union also represents recording artists. Atlantic, in common with every other record company, forwards pension contributions to AFTRA in respect of their roster, all of them subject to audit by the organization. Howell's work in the arts had introduced him to Wolff, and it was his help he enlisted in prising details of my contracts out of Atlantic. When these confirmed everything I had told him, Howell made his first direct contact with the company. Before his initial meeting he asked for copies of my royalty statements, together with a full accounting, for all my years on the label. Then we simply stood back and waited until we saw what the company came out with.

There was a token response from Atlantic by the time we next met, in March '84, when Howell indicated that it might be advantageous, working on the theory of strength in numbers, if other artists from the same period with the company were added to his list. For starters I introduced him to Joe Turner and the Clovers, contacting Joe in Los Angeles and Bill Harris of the Clovers on Howell's doorstep in Washington.

Big Joe, the undisputed "Boss of the Blues," was a giant in more than mere physical stature. As a kid after the first World War in his native Kansas City he'd led a blind guitarist through the city, his blues singing leading to introductions to Count Basie and Ben Webster before his legendary teaming with boogie-woogie pianist Pete Johnson produced such classics as "Roll 'em, Pete" and "Cherry Red." After a long spell on Decca Records, Joe was drifting, his career in the doldrums, when Ahmet saw him at the Apollo in '51 and signed him up. Off Joe went again, producing one beauty after another—"Chains of Love"; "Sweet Sixteen"; "Honey, Hush"; "Flip, Flop and Fly"; "Corinne, Corrina"; with Jesse Stone's "Shake, Rattle and Roll" providing the bluprint for Bill Haley's watered-down worldwide smash.

Howell had been six years old in 1950 when Atlantic signed the Clovers, a band fresh from a Washington, D.C., high school. By the time the group had racked up their eighteenth hit nine years later with "Love Potion No. 9" (soon after leaving the label) he was playing guitar in a Detroit high school band and was one of their many fans. My lawyer was a rocker from way back!

Between Joe, the Clovers and myself we had, his research revealed, landed Atlantic thirty-six Top Ten rhythm and blues hits, including eight number ones. In short order Howell entered into a formal attorney/client relationship with them, and arranged for Joe to travel from his home in Los Angeles to Washington to appear with me in concert. The idea behind the showcase, I guess, was to convert any remaining doubters among his colleagues at Verner, Liipfert that we were worth fighting for.

We succeeded in putting that over, and with that behind us we were really off and running.

18

HOWELL IN ACTION

SOME PERFORMERS YOU NEVER FORGET, they're woven into the warp and weft of your mind so tight. One such for me was the irrepressible Sammy Davis, Jr. The first time I met Sammy was at the Oasis, a club I worked in Los Angeles during my first visit to California in the early fifties. He was still with the Will Mastin Trio and had the terrible accident in front of him he overcame so gamely. Sammy, I quickly discovered, was an inveterate flirt. It came as natural as breathing to him and was strictly not to be taken seriously. After making goo-goo eyes at me for half the night, he invited me to dance and began whispering all kinds of vooterooney in my ear. We were snapped together while this was going on, and I was towering over him, my chiffon dress and coat teamed with high-heel shoes with platform soles. "I'm comin' by after your second show and taking you out for the best dinner you've ever had," he informed me.

"I've already eaten," I sassed straight back.

"Supper, then," he insisted, then continued talking all kinds of trash.

During my second engagement in the city, this time at the Shrine, he arrived backstage with the tobacco heiress Doris Duke, who invited all of us over to her place for drinks. Everyone took up the offer except me, because in the audience that night was the famous black Shakespearean actor William Marshall, over whom every black female's insides (and doubtless several of our white cousins' too) had flip-flopped over in the movie *Lydia Bailey,* where he played the Jamaican rebel Toussaint. Pictured standing on the dock in one scene, with his magnificent frame silhouetted against those gathering storm clouds, you can bet that touching the hem of his garment was merely the start of their fantasies. Mine too!

When William strode backstage and invited me for a bite to eat I waved goodbye to Sammy, Doris and the departing multitude. He took me first to a club owned by jazz pianist Dorothy Donegan and her husband, where we relaxed to the music, danced a little, and talked some. He was a dream on wheels, though I have to tell you he came up short in the dinner department; this turned out to be a chicken sandwich. Next evening the male members of my entourage were at a loss to explain my ducking out on them. "You passed up an opportunity to check out Doris Duke's home to have a sandwich with Marshall?" was one bewildered response. I sure did. Who needs fancy food with company like that?

Years later, by which time Sammy and I had been together on numerous occasions, he unfailingly continuing to drop his old jive on me, I decided it was time to lay him out. Taking him to one side, I said, "Hey, what happened? You married another woman! You told me you was goin' to love me forever, never let me go!"

Flashing that mile-wide grin of his, he said, "Ruth, stop *quibblin'!*"

HOWELL FIRST HEARD from an artists' rights representative named Chuck Rubin soon after taking on the Clovers as clients through Bill Harris. Another of the group, it turned out, had already been in touch with Chuck, who had been out in the field trying to raise money for a variety of artists since the seventies. Chuck was coming from a different place than Howell. For a start, there could hardly be a greater contrast between Howell's quietly luxurious Washington base and Chuck's decidedly funky New York premises.

Chuck had grown up with the music as a teenager and become an artists' manager as well as a packager of talent. He had managed Wilbert Harrison for years through his hit-making "Kansas City" and "Let's Work Together" period—the latter becoming the sixties anthem through a version by Canned Heat—and toured all over with him when Creedence Clearwater Revival, great fans of Wilbert's, had insisted he open for them on their world tours. After ten years together Wilbert approached Chuck and requested his help in finding a replacement for his lawyer, who had died while chasing unpaid royalties.

To his surprise Chuck found great difficulty in finding a mainstream attorney prepared to take over. Most regarded the whole thing as a complete waste of their time, not worth the trouble. Either that, or it meant taking on a fight with major companies who put lots of business their way. Why mess up a good thing? Instead, Chuck decided to consult with other artists he knew to compare their royalty levels. The unanimous response: "Royalties? What royalties?"

In ten years with Wilbert, Chuck had assumed he was collecting regular income for his recordings, and if Wilbert's first lawyer had not died on him, and his "problem" had never been aired, Chuck might still be booking acts today. Instead, he took up Wilbert's case, secure in the knowledge that there was plenty of similar business out there.

The next watershed arrived via the enormous success of *American Graffiti*. The oldies soundtrack from that hit movie produced a ton of money for the companies who'd leased their tracks to Universal and MCA, but hardly a cent to the artists who'd laid down the music in the first place. Pursuing their share of the payday got Chuck into the business with a vengeance. He eventually signed up dozens of artists on the basis of the percentage he'd collect from any settlement. No lawyer himself, he was obliged to employ a battery of courtroom attorneys to help him pursue his various claims.

Initially he was unceremoniously shown the door by every record company, and with a mixture of utter disdain, callousness and undisguised glee that spoke volumes for the disrespect in which they held the artists he represented. He had very little leverage in the early days, and many years passed before he was able to chalk up his first victory and collect a single dollar. With a relish in his delivery that would do Walter Matthau proud, the rangy, laid-back Rubin likens the tactic he often takes with companies to Go Fish. Although this is only a humble children's card game, he maintains it teaches a lot about life, depending as it does on the truthfulness of one's partner. Hugging his cards close to his chest, it's possible to imagine him confronting some record company accountant and asking, "Do you have any *fives?*" Before replying, his opponent has to figure out whether or not Chuck already knows the answer.

While conceding that initially a very great deal of "chasing" took place, he is sensitive enough today to resent being described as a chaser, since that implies someone forever behind in the game. "Call me a confronter," he'll suggest. "That's a more accurate description of what I do. I'm more comfortable with that."

To his critics, and there are many who consider his fifty percent fee in perpetuity plus out-of-pocket expenses extortionate, Chuck will first point to the cases where his best efforts achieve nothing but a pile of bills. Then he'll ask, "Isn't fifty percent of *something* better than a hundred percent of *nothing?*"

Despite their differences Howell immediately saw a mutuality of interests, for Chuck had been up against the might of Atlantic on a number of issues. Whenever there had been an excuse, the company held back money that was due.

In the case of Clyde's widow, Lena McPhatter, they refused to part with funds she desperately needed until a bond was posted indemnifying them against potential claims from other quarters. After many years of this delaying tactic Chuck helped raise the money to post the bond.

And they had seized on an internal disagreement between the Coasters. The group had not been paid since 1968, the company retaining $30,000 until every single *i* was dotted and *t* crossed. Chuck was still in the process of trying to extract the money when we met him. He had a copy of the Coasters' contract, which Howell was able to compare with Joe's, the Clovers' and mine. That was useful in itself, and a whole lot more would follow.

HOWELL'S FIRST MEETING at Atlantic's offices, in April 1984, began uneventfully. Apart from anything else, he was immediately aware that a wealth of material was missing, not least any record of sales from my best-selling period, the first half of the fifties. After a couple of hours of shuffling papers, however, the gears suddenly shifted into overdrive. As he later pointed out to me, issues do not come wrapped in pretty paper and neatly labeled.

Instead, it was a relatively innocent-looking handwritten scrawl spread across a copy of the typed royalty statement I'd been sent in 1983 that made him sit up and take notice. The first message read, "We did not go back to pick up royalties earned between 1960 and 1971 on foreign. *We had no way to check*" (the italics are mine).

Atlantic, it seemed, had routinely failed to record my foreign sales throughout the sixties before its accounting systems had been computerized. Despite this, they had furnished the statement showing foreign royalties for the period as $431. It was a figure they must have plucked out of thin air.

The second message was, if anything, even more damning: "We didn't post information to deleted accounts when we were on the manual system."

I can only picture Howell's expression when he read this. This was a crucial discovery, for it proved conclusively not only that there was an inherent flaw in their system, a gaping hole with eleven years' missing data, but that they had been fully aware of it and had sent out intentionally false royalty statements.

If they had skipped foreign royalties for Ruth Brown for eleven years and failed to post other sales information, the same would more than likely apply to all their other acts from the same period. Howell decided to keep this hot item under his hat for the time being, and continue to hold out for the most comprehensive accounts it was possible to extract from Atlantic. Who knew what other smoking guns lay in there?

Over dinner with Howell a few nights after his discovery, I could see he was preoccupied. He picked at his food, took a gulp of wine, followed by more picking. "Something on your mind, Howell?" I had to ask.

"Ruth, I think I've found the big stick to threaten Atlantic with," he told me. "It's called RICO."

"I saw a good movie called *The Brothers Rico* once," I told him. "It was about the Mafia."

"Close, *very* close, but no cigar," Howell replied, smiling. "RICO's full title is the Racketeer Influenced and Corrupt Organizations Act. It's an act that allows individual plaintiffs to sue corporations privately. If you win you get triple damages, together with your attorney's fees—if, that is, you can prove activity of the type organized crime gets involved in . . . larceny, extortion—and mail fraud. It's not necessary to prove mob links, only that crimes frequently *associated* with the mob have been committed."

"I don't see where we come in."

"If we can prove that Atlantic *knowingly* sent out incorrect information through the U.S. mail—and I believe we have that proof in the form of those scribbled messages—we have a clear case of mail fraud. And every time we can get them to send more royalty reports, it's a repeat offense."

No, I did not say, "Go get 'em, boy!" But that's what I felt.

HOWELL'S FIRST ENCOUNTER with a senior Atlantic executive, Mel Lewinter, was hosted by Bud Wolff and took place the following September. Lewinter? The name rang a bell. He was the individual who'd passed on my letter in 1983 to Atlantic's attorneys, resulting in the "Forget it, you got no hope" message that might have spelled the end of the line.

When Howell's request for a full accounting was renewed, Lewinter played hardball yet again and highhandedly insisted on Howell's engagement of a "knowledgable accountant." There was no way, he stressed, that they were prepared to be "subjected to an amateur effort." Howell can play hardball with the best of them, and with Wolff's agreement he engaged, *pro bono*, AFTRA's auditors, who performed the same function for the American Federation of Musicians (AFofM). With their help a highly detailed questionnaire was presented to Atlantic in November.

Who was it observed that the wheels of justice grind exceeding slow? For a long time they seemed to have shuddered to a complete halt. Until June 1985, to be precise, when Howell had a partial reply from Atlantic that raised more questions than it answered. Among the juicier items, they now maintained that my "Lucky Lips," which they'd previously sworn to Billboard and Cashbox on a stack of bibles had sold a million copies, had in fact barely scraped 200,000. And the Clovers had been paid a total of only $2,500 since 1960, an average of $100 a year, $20 per member.

Whatever else, we believed Atlantic was in breach of contract for failing to supply us with quarterly statements. Their answer? Sales of all our recordings for the last twenty-five years had been negligible, yielding royalties of less than $9,000 combined for Joe, the Clovers and myself—a total of $360 per year each. Old "session costs"—my, how those union-scale fees had mounted up—wiped out all but $4,000 of that, entitling Joe to his first Atlantic check in twenty-five years. Joe's new-found surplus included a rock-bottom $500 for Atlantic's licensing of "Corrine, Corrina" for the soundtrack of *The Buddy Holly Story.* This raised another question, for the payment seemed ludicrously low compared to the Sam Cooke estate's $7,000 negotiated by RCA Records for the use of "(What a) Wonderful World" in the Richard Gere remake of *Breathless.*

As for me and the Clovers, it was still a case of "Forget it, you got no hope." We still owed the company money, to the tune of $10,000, $20,000 or $30,000, depending on how you looked at it.

Howell's reaction to all this was one of outrage. When is a million-seller not a million-seller? Answer: when royalty payments are under discussion. And the sums quoted from 1960 onwards represented sales of around 2,000 albums a year for all of us combined. Considering the size of Atlantic's worldwide operation, this was highly unlikely; Warner was simply too powerful a force to be wasting its time on marketing the albums to achieve such paltry results. If sales had really been this low, surely they would have taken the stuff off the market completely?

Atlantic had no way of knowing that two handwritten messages by a clerk in their accounts department had already given the game away. To us these memos were nothing less than manna from heaven.

While we were considering our next move, with RICO very much in the forefront of our minds, I took a call from a young investigative reporter named Martin Burke. He was busy pitching an idea to Andy Lack, head of a brand-new investigative series, *West 57th,* planned as a younger, hipper companion show to CBS's established *60 Minutes.* Martin intended in his segment to focus on record company rip-offs, with particular emphasis on Atlantic's treatment of people like Joe and myself. The news of Howell's investigation was getting around.

It turned out that Howell had successfully represented newscaster Roger Mudd in the past, and since Roger was a old friend of Andy

Lack's, Howell prevailed on him to reinforce Martin's pitch. This clinched the deal, and I spent lengthy sessions with Martin deciding on our best approach before taping my contribution to the show in June. Once again Howell got in touch with Chuck Rubin. Would he like an opportunity to have some of his clients appear on a nationally televised show, and perhaps put in an appearance of his own to advance their case? The answer was yes.

We collectively held our breaths until the airing, scheduled for August, for there was a feeling among us that this could bust the story wide open. I'd never gotten this far before, not remotely, although there was still the matter of those unrecovered "session costs." Oh sure, the idea of money was important, but this had long since gone beyond that. The struggle now was for nothing less than getting my dignity back.

WITH TWO MONTHS STILL TO GO before our story on *West 57th* was due to air, Howell was granted his first meeting with Sheldon Vogel, Atlantic's chief financial officer. Tall, wiry and elegant as he was, there remained a distinct element of the New York streetfighter about Vogel, which the hint of "New Joisey" in his staccato speech did nothing to dispel. His reputation as a toughie who ate nails with his breakfast bagels preceded him, and we were only too aware of his nickname of "the Enforcer" at Warner Communications. Even he had little alternative but to concede that certain financial "irregularities" existed, which was a major step forward in itself. Howell was again advised that the royalty accountings for Joe and the Clovers, already furnished for me back to 1955, were "misplaced," and therefore no longer available. For that matter, strangely enough, so were my royalty records before 1955, my strongest-selling period. They had, it seemed, just disappeared.

It was a frustrating case of one step forward, two back. No, make that one and a half steps forward, for Vogel then pledged to reinstate quarterly statements for all of us. Howell was jubilant. Every single one would be capable of forming the basis of a separate RICO claim, for each time a statement was sent out it constituted a brand-new unlawful act. They'd be digging themselves a deeper hole with each mailing.

*   *   *

West 57th was pure, unadulterated dynamite. "Way back then," the voiceover began, "there were few rules when it came to the music industry. And shrewd record company owners could often do just about anything they wanted. Now the old rock 'n' roll is back, but we found for many of the people who created it, the music ended a long time ago."

There I was, in front of a primetime audience of millions, wandering round Tower Records on Broadway above Columbus Circle, picking up domestically pressed records of mine, as well as a selection of imports from the Japanese Warner-Pioneer affiliate, and explaining that none of them was bringing me a dime. "Ruth last had a statement in 1964," Howell declared on camera, "then never received another until 1983. Yet her records are sold internationally, and sales are supposed to be reported to the performer."

Chuck Rubin, Brook Benton, Bo Diddley and Hank Ballard all told their own tales of woe. "Some people can say I *almost* got robbed," said Brook, who was both ex-Mercury Records and Atlantic. "I can't say that. *I got robbed!*"

Hank Ballard revealed that he'd used the same lawyer as his King label chief, Syd Nathan, when negotiating his deal for million-selling records like "The Twist." Ouch! "We *trusted* these people," was the message Bo put over. Looking just a little uncomfortable in the glare of the spotlight, Chuck summed it up: "They trusted *other* people. And a lot of them were the *wrong* people."

Big Joe Turner, looking terribly ill, came on supporting himself on crutches. "I got no way to keep up with it," he declared as they flashed a still of Ahmet and Joe from the fifties, posing alongside a mountain of Joe's discs.

Again it was Howell's turn: "Joe got his first check about three months ago. And that was for four thousand dollars, representing twenty-five years' worth of royalty payments to him."

The interviewer was incredulous: "The first money he'd received in *twenty-five years?*"

"Yes."

Slow fade to black.

I spoke to Joe after the taping. He was really ailing, unable even to stand for long, and undergoing dialysis treatment. He explained that he still had no option except to keep working. "I'm a sick man, Ruth," he told me, "and all I want to do is rest at home. But I got to keep goin' to keep up with the darn medical bills. Otherwise, all I got is welfare."

I had worked with Joe so many times in his heyday, we had shared laughs together on many bills, shared transport too, for that matter. Once in the fifties I was driving, he was in the front seat, and we were traveling from Omaha, Nebraska, clear through to Denver and had just passed through Medicine Bow. Snow had been falling and as we made it over the brow of a hill we could see the stretches of sheet ice that covered the road in front. There was no way to stop and I could feel Joe tense up before coming out with a heartfelt, "Oooooh, my Looord!"

I knew better than to panic and apply the brakes. Instead I rode those skids the best I could, until I felt it safe, three-quarters of the way down, to begin gently pumping. When we finally came to a halt on the grassy shoulder, Joe clambered out of the car and stood at the side of the road, shaking his right hand up and down like he was trying to dislodge a ferret. "Shhhheeeee*iiiittt!*" he yelled, then launched into the longest stream of pig Latin I ever did hear, something along the lines of "Hecktamoneybillyreddyvooterooney!"

I just collapsed at the wheel with laughter, not a little tinged with relief that we had both emerged unscathed. "Ruth," he said as he got back inside, "you're the *baddest* woman driver I ever see! You can handle that wheel!"

Some of us called Joe after his song, "Roll 'em, Pete," for nobody could roll 'em like Joe. Didn't matter what he sang, his instruction to the band was the same, "Key of C, and let's take it where it wants to go." He had a groove all his own, he was incredible. And he had the darndest way of avoiding the fact that he could neither read nor write all that well. "What time is it?" I heard him asking once. Instead of replying, one of the band held out his wrist. Joe took one look and said, "Well, I'll be *darned* if it ain't!"

Tragically, a few months after *West 57th* was broadcast we lost Joe, dead at seventy-four of kidney failure. We often hear the phrase, "We'll never see his like again." In the case of Big Joe Turner, it's the gospel truth.

During the very month of his death in November 1985, Atlantic issued its monumental fourteen-volume set, *Atlantic Rhythm and Blues 1947–74*. Howell went ballistic when he surveyed our reinstated quarterly statements the following March and discovered that Atlantic had improperly debited both Joe and myself for a portion of the costs incurred in the set's compilation—for "remastering, editing and mixing." Was there no end to the abuse? It seemed not. And in Joe's case it was reaching beyond the grave.

"Neither Ruth Brown nor Joe Turner have participated in any Atlantic recording sessions for more than twenty years," he blasted them, demanding an immediate cancellation of the charges, for which absolutely no authorization existed in our contracts.

I subsequently heard that Ahmet personally went out of his way to get these charges rubbed out, also that he paid for Big Joe's funeral and settled the mortgage on his widow's home. Whether he was stung into this, or whether he'd have done it anyway, only Ahmet knows. What I am certain of is that if Howell had not been on the case we'd never have gotten to know about all that "remastering" nonsense, they would simply have blithely hiked our debit balances up, pushing the possibility of recoupment even farther into the distance.

Officially Atlantic acknowledged yet another "error" in making the charges, and when Howell also complained the company had "erroneously" paid Joe in his lifetime only half the royalty rate he was due on foreign sales, they issued a further check to Joe's widow. The foreign royalty rate "oversight" applied to me and the Clovers as well, but in my case I was still too deep in the red to see any immediate benefit.

APART FROM any sphincter-tightening that may have occurred at Atlantic and Warner after the airing of *West 57th*, it really grabbed the attention of the gentlemen of the press, who began requesting interviews in droves. Neither Howell nor I held back.

"They make a mockery of the fiduciary arrangement," he raged to one reporter. "These people are sixty years old. They haven't got expensive lawyers. They're not equipped like Phil Collins to fight the system. The people at Atlantic say they're nice guys? Fine, but there's something wrong when a singer's been popular for twenty-five years and hasn't seen a penny since 1963.''

The next few meetings with Atlantic brought fresh revelations. Sheldon Vogel admitted that the company had for a substantial period of time discontinued tracking sales of my records on the basis that my account would be constantly in the red after "session costs" were deducted. For that matter, Atlantic now claimed that by the time all of their R-and-B acts had left the company in the mid-sixties, virtually each and every one had owed money for unrecovered costs. After a while, therefore, they had simply stopped bothering to keep these accounts up to date, in essence writing everyone off the books because, as with me, they saw no chance of recoupment.

They admitted to having stopped bothering to send the quarterly statements contractually required between 1969 and 1983, claiming it was "an administrative burden to post royalties and send out statements on closed accounts." Ruth Brown—who, together with Joe and the Clovers, had helped build the company—was now reduced to "an administrative burden."

Vogel went into specifics in my case. Although by their calculations Atlantic had paid me a total of less than $30,000 for the six-year period between 1955 to 1961, that was nearly $20,000 more than I'd been entitled to, after deducting recording session expenses of $32,000 and an additional $7,000 in commission payments to Blanche. What I *should* have gotten, according to his analysis, was $11,000, or less than two thousand dollars a year.

Howell countered that it was ridiculous to focus on those session costs. More to the point, how come one of their most successful recording artists had left the label owing all that money after being handed just five thousand dollars a year?

He compared Atlantic's claim that my royalties had totalled under $50,000 over that period with their boast to Billboard that I'd enjoyed three million-selling singles. A five percent royalty on just one of them, "Lucky Lips," would have yielded $40,000 on its own. As for the 200,000 copies they now said were sold, Howell had his answer for that, and he made it in starkly bold print: "They were either lying to the trades and public back then or they are lying to the artist now."

Challenged with this kind of irrefutable logic, Atlantic chose the line of least liability. They had, they now maintained, originally "misrepresented" sales to Billboard.

Quite a confession after thirty years.

19

ON CAPITOL HILL

NOT HAVING SEEN Brook Benton for several years, I was shocked by his appearance on *West 57th*. He was skin and bones, and although he came over strongly enough I sensed the changes he must have gone through from the man I had toured with, the wonderful artist at the top of his game. I was aware of the bitterness that now existed between him and his old songwriting partner and recording mananger, Clyde Otis, to whom he sold—some would say gave away —his publishing copyrights in exchange for $50,000.

Clyde, a decent guy as well as a shrewd businessman, had the wherewithal to bide his time until the catalog struck gold, and as it turned out he did not have long to wait. Within a couple of years "A Rockin' Good Way," originally a duet by Brook and Dinah Washington, was remade by Shakin' Stevens and Bonnie Tyler and became a smash all over again throughout Europe. It was too late to do Brook any good, although I know his widow could have used the windfall.

Brook was good people, and it's a terrible shame that he ended up yet another who died far too soon. I remember him being so deeply affected by Roy Hamilton's death that they had to put him in a separate room and give him something for his nerves, for he literally came apart. The cost of Roy's life support had been enormous and Brook said to me, "I've got to continue to make money, 'cause that's what it's all about. If it ever got to the stage where that became a problem, I honestly don't know what I'd do." I didn't work with him much when he did get on his emotional slide, but I'd heard that his whole attitude changed. He didn't turn up for work, began to drink heavily and take drugs and just refused to listen to anyone. It was sad, very sad.

Howell, meantime, had quietly recruited new support from an artist he had long admired. An introduction to Bonnie Raitt by a mutual friend, a former member of her band, led to initial correspondence filling her in on where we stood. The position was bleak, he emphasized, and he needed pledges of support—moral, not financial—from parties interested in seeing justice done. As the friend had indicated, Bonnie's love for the origins of today's music and acknowledgment of the debt current artists owed its pioneers were deep and genuine. From the beginning of her career she has had a tradition of advocacy on behalf of pioneer musicians like Mississippi Fred McDowell and Roosevelt Sykes, to the practical extent of trying to get songwriting royalties for them. I had seen her on television championing Sippie Wallace. Like most others, I knew something of Bonnie's own troubled history, how she was making her way back from serious drug and alcohol problems, attempting at the same time to rehabilitate her stalled recording career after being dropped by Warner Brothers, her record label.

My first meeting with Bonnie was at Martha's Vineyard, where she was appearing in concert. First off, I was simply blown away by her stage act, by her unique combination of country that was more than a little tinged with blues and R and B. I hate people who simply latch on to the blues and pasteurize it to the extent it becomes elevator music. Instead Bonnie was brilliantly fusing the elements together, in the process creating a brand-new groove positively charged with energy and that unashamedly "bin round the block several times" voice, salty as all get out one minute, piercing your heart the next.

When Howell introduced me backstage, Bonnie welcomed me like someone she had worshipped from afar for years, knocking me back on my heels with her "I'm not worthy!" greeting. I know a phony when I see one, and you better believe it, this was no phony. She was warm, natural, funny and friendly, a real class act. I told her the most famous Raitt in my book up until then had been her father, Broadway's immortal Billy Bigelow from *Carousel* and Doris

Day's leading man on the big screen in *The Pajama Game,* John Raitt. And I had only just discovered that he was her dad!

Howell went on to make two other vitally important contacts. The first, Congressman George "Mickey" Leland, chairman of the Black Caucus, was seated next to him at a Women's Political Campaign Fund dinner he attended in Washington. Red-haired, light-skinned, his tendency to chubbiness more than taken care of by immaculate tailoring, Leland simply oozed charisma. That he hailed from the wrong side of the tracks in Houston, Texas, made his ascent to the giddy Washington heights all the more admirable. His reputation as a gregarious, outspoken, some would say downright brash operator preceded him, but Howell knew he was a man who got results. He was also renowned for the quality of the staff he kept around him, from civil rights activist Patrice Johnson, his chief of staff, to Billy Taylor and Larry Irving, who went on to join the Clinton administration.

Howell was also aware that Leland exercised considerable pull within the record industry, not least since one of his committees had been given the responsibility of deciding the U.S. response to the Japanese threat to flood the market with DAT tape recorders. Since this would enable CD-quality copies to be churned out at will, it was seen by the record industry lobby as nothing less than the end of civilized life as we know it on planet earth. It was a potential revenue drain of billions, something to be blocked at any cost.

When Howell casually mentioned his involvement in the struggle with Atlantic, Leland really sat up and took notice. It turned out he was a diehard music fan, particularly our brand. When he revealed that none other than the Reverend Jesse Jackson was readying an assault of his own on Warner's battlements, protesting their almost complete lack of African-Americans in senior positions at the company, as well as their continuing trade with South Africa, it was Howell's turn to listen. "Why don't I introduce you to Jesse?" Leland asked. "Maybe you could get him to add *Ruth Brown* vs. *Atlantic* to his list of concerns." By the time dessert was served, Howell felt he'd gotten an excellent return for the contribution he had made to the Women's Campaign Fund.

The second crucial introduction came courtesy of the Clovers' lead guitarist, Bill Harris. He still resided in Washington and when

Carla Thomas,
me, Howell
Begle and
Bonnie Raitt at
the Handy
Awards in
Memphis, 1990.
(COURTESY OF
RUTH BROWN)

Howell asked one day how he was making ends meet, Bill said he
was running a talent booking agency, as well as giving guitar lessons
on the side. And he had some pretty impressive clients on that
latter list, among them John Conyers, the influential black congressman from Detroit, Michigan. I guess it took Howell all of two
seconds to work that one out, and without delay he sought a meeting with Conyers, accompanied by Bill, his bass-fiddle professor.

He took along another friend to the meeting. The Orlando *Sentinel*'s Annie Groer, a bright, handsome lady, was a highly respected
member of Washington's press corps, with syndicated access to hundreds of newspapers across the country. She was also, incredibly,
another Ruth Brown fanatic. "I grew up with your music, Ruth,"
she told me. "Howell has spoken of the fight you're in with Atlantic
and I want to do all I can to help."

I'd heard that Conyers was considered a complete eccentric by
many lobbyists. On one level he did come across as a dreamer and
an idealist, on another there was the pragmatic side, the street-savvy
politician from Detroit. The combination equalled unpredictability,
but of a highly principled nature, a bit like a fanatically dedicated
Boy Scout. And he was another passionate music buff, with jazz his
particular bag. In that mode he was the author of the legislation
that led to both National Jazz and Dance Weeks being set up.

Howell summarized for Conyers where we'd gotten with Atlantic
and put the case that their reinstated royalty statements were so

incomplete as to suggest either bad faith or reckless disregard for accuracy. After listening intently and studying the data produced, Conyers' ears pricked up when Howell mentioned he was considering action under the RICO act.

He soon discovered why. Purely coincidentally, Conyers was about to chair a series of hearings of the House Judiciary Criminal Justice Subcommittee relating to a proposed amendment to RICO. The hearings were in reaction to concerns expressed by major corporations and the powerful securities industry lobby that corporations were exposed to huge potential lawsuits if RICO was allowed to remain intact. Damages and lawyers' fees apart, RICO had another deadly sting in its tail. A successful civil action could cancel out the normal statute of limitations in any case involving contracts and accounting records more than twenty-five years old. (Like, for example, *Ruth Brown and Co.* vs. *Atlantic!*) The lobby was determined to achieve nothing less than the complete emasculation of the bill, preventing individuals like ourselves from bringing a private action unless it was preceded by a federal prosecution.

If this attempt to curtail RICO succeeded, Howell saw a vital plank of his strategy being hacked away from under him. Consumer groups—and, in principle, Conyers too—were dead set against the proposed change, arguing that it would nullify the whole purpose of RICO. With Howell adding his voice to the chorus, the congressman replied that it might be politic to have Ruth Brown attend the hearings as a witness. It certainly seemed like a wonderful platform to air our case. And bearing in mind that the hearings were open to the press, the publicity they were bound to generate would continue to raise temperatures at Atlantic.

MAYBE I SHOULD have been nervous as I took my seat at the hearings on Capitol Hill in July 1986. I wasn't. I had flown from New York to Washington the day before, and had rested for only an hour or so before spending the rest of the night preparing what I intended to say. I don't mean a speech, for I had no need of that, I just wanted to be sure in my mind that I covered all the issues. I dressed for the occasion in a navy-and-white coat-and-dress ensemble, and although it was a stifling hot day I felt crisp and composed, altogether ready

to give it my best shot. I was seated behind a table with a microphone perched on top, facing the assembly. John Conyers, elegant
and courtly in a beige suit under his robes, was chairing the proceedings. As I rose to speak he interrupted.

"First of all, Miss Brown," he said, "let me welcome you here
today. And let me say that I know exactly who you are. I should, for
I heard you every morning, even in the trenches, back in the fifties.
Your record of "Teardrops from My Eyes" woke me up for years in
the service. Nobody could change the radio station without peril to
his life."

My next fan was altogether unexpected, the controversial right-
wing Senator Jesse Helms from North Carolina. "I know that nobody will expect this," he acknowledged, "but I too know Ruth
Brown. But the record for me was '5–10–15 Hours!' " Seems we
also had a lock on the white Conservative vote. Any port in a storm,
I guess!

Reverend Jesse Jackson was next, and I'd already heard that
Clyde McPhatter was one of his favorite artists. "Let me be allowed
to speak of this lady," he suggested, "whom I first saw perform as a
youth in a place called the Textile Hall. That was in my hometown
of Greenwalk, North Carolina. It may not have been one of her
biggest dates, but boy, she held nothing back." (His wife, he told
me later, hailed from Newport News. So did my Thelma, and when
I repeated her catchphrase, "Good girls come out of Virginia," he
roared with laughter.)

Before I'd even had a chance to open my mouth I knew I had
tremendous support in that assembly. Even so, I could not resist
making a simple point before getting down to it. "Thank you, gentlemen," I said, "but I'd like to have this opportunity to *speak* today
instead of *sing.*" And that's exactly what I did, for forty-five solid,
uninterrupted minutes.

RICO, I declared, was the only affordable way I had to sue Atlantic, to gain justice not only for myself but for the dozens of black
performers who struggled to push what was once called "race music" into mainstream American rhythm and blues, and its descen-
dant, rock 'n' roll. I ticked off a long list of artists, alive and dead,
and stated that Atlantic and other companies too were guilty of
cheating people like Clyde McPhatter, Joe Turner, Frankie Lymon,

Dee Clark, Etta James, LaVern Baker, Brook Benton, Dinah Washington, the Clovers, the Drifters, the Platters, the Five Keys and the Moonglows. I pointed out that many of these artists had given a great deal to their music and gotten very little in return. Now their survivors couldn't afford to take on the might of record corporations. Without RICO, I added, neither could I. A black woman living in a single-room apartment in Harlem versus the corporate might of Warner?

Even today, I told them, Atlantic was selling my records in Europe and around the world and not paying me a dime on the grounds of "unrecovered costs." I'd seen it in Japan and I'd been in Paris in the spring, I explained, and there they were again—Ruth Brown records still selling a quarter of a century after Atlantic and I had parted company, and yielding me not one thin dime. How could it be? Was that justice? Was that *American* justice? Surely we had moved away from plantation days when we took what the boss massa handed out? Or sharecropping with its accompanying debt peonage? I made the point over and over again: *"Leave RICO alone."*

Annie Groer filed a major story on the event for the Orlando *Sentinel* that was picked up by wire services and ran across the country. The headline said it all:

STAR OF THE PAST FIRES A BLAST AT ROCK 'N' ROLL ROYALTY RIP-OFF

Conyers' counsel, Cedric Hendricks, lent his weight to the report: "Ruth told us how she'd been victimized by Atlantic, and shock was expressed at what happened. Mr. Conyers tried to preserve RICO as an effective tool for people like Ruth. One reason we had her as a witness was to get her some exposure in the hopes that other lawyers would come forth and say, 'I can help some of these performers.' The other reason was to try to embarrass Atlantic."

I certainly believe we achieved the latter goal. Maybe we did both.

There were many taken aback at the frankness of my testimony in Washington, seeing the whole episode as nothing less than a blow against corporate America and the capitalist system. I had no such high-minded stuff in mind. I merely wanted what I felt with every fiber of my being was due me and every other similarly disadvantaged artist as well. Apart from anything else, a lot of people were surprised to discover how articulate I was.

Shortly after the Congressional hearings I was invited by John Conyers to take part in a ten-member music-related panel as part of Congressional Black Caucus weekend, as well as performing in the evening on a double bill with Lionel Hampton and his Orchestra. The panel's theme was jazz and its importance to black America, and I seized the opportunity to speak out again on inequities in the treatment of artists by the recording industry, with particular emphasis on Atlantic and "Howell's list." At the same time I remarked on the blurring of categories that had taken place since I'd ruled the rhythm-and-blues roost back in the fifties.

"I'm better known as a rhythm-and-blues rather than a jazz singer," I pointed out, "except I'm no longer sure what the criterion is. If it means having the privilege of working with top jazz artists like Lester Young, Coleman Hawkins, Billy Taylor, Count Basie, Thad Jones, Mel Lewis and Grady Tate, then fine, I'm a jazz singer!"

My old buddy Dizzy Gillespie was sitting alongside me as I spoke, and I turned to him: "Diz, how many times have I performed with you?"

"Lots of times," he replied, " 'cept you didn't bother showin' up on the first occasion." Lord above, will I *ever* live down that missed date at the Apollo?

I had a wonderful time at the function that night, and it didn't hurt our case one little bit that all the top black politicians were there and I got to bend the ear of every single one of them. I talked to Mickey Leland and his wife, to Charles Rangel, James Farmer, Ron Dellums, as well as ex-President Gerald Ford, Maya Angelou, Dorothy Hyatt, Coretta Scott King, and our hostess, Oprah Winfrey. They all told me they loved the music I represented. If I was the ambassador in person, the music we'd made famous was my calling card.

THE THREAT of a class action suit under RICO, its muscle left intact thanks to John Conyers and his committee after those hearings, certainly concentrated Warner's corporate mind. Howell never let up or the assault, claiming that Atlantic had deprived every artist with a number-one hit of at least $100,000 because of faulty book-keeping, improper accounting of session costs, underreporting of domestic sales and underpayment on foreign sales. Another statistic he produced was that an underevaluation of $500 made annually by Atlantic for twenty-five years would amount to $25,000 in today's dollars.

The company's response was to seek refuge behind a smoke-screen of unrecorded acts of generosity back in the fifties. "He's put us in a position of guilty unless proven innocent. How do we prove advances against royalties?" Sheldon Vogel agonized to one reporter. "I can't produce canceled checks from twenty-five years ago. That's what statutes of limitations are for."

I couldn't help thinking that by the same token it was a pity there was no statute of limitations on session costs. Although Vogel was unable to produce canceled checks from twenty-five years ago, he had no such problem detailing those to the last penny.

HOWELL AND I DID NOT HAVE that many opportunities over the years to relax and chat, but I recall one of the times we did, stuck at Washington airport during a snowstorm. We talked generally about the attraction of organized crime to the recording industry. Anyone capable of taking a piece of plastic and cardboard worth twenty-five cents, selling it for many times that at wholesale and avoiding roy-alty payments was on an incredible winner. It was the closest thing to printing money you could get.

There was also the virtual impossibility with multi-national corpo-rations of individuals being able to keep track of sales, cutouts and the dubious practices associated with them to contend with, a hun-dred percent of production costs charged against artists' average ten percent, all hits thrown into the pot with stiffs or unreleased material, together with freebies, bootlegs and returns.

Then there was the opportunity for label heads to put their names on tunes as composers, and assign publishing rights to houses in which they had an interest. We knew that Chuck Rubin had been fighting for years to get Frankie Lymon's widow her share of the royalties Morris Levy had hijacked for himself. Morris didn't know a B from a C-flat, yet his name was on scores of songs as writer or co-writer. In the end Chuck pulled that one off.

I told Howell that Bill Harris of the Clovers had often talked to me about how cheated he had felt at Atlantic, how he was never given credit for all the songs he helped write. "Look, I'm a *musician,*" I recalled him saying. "A musician who studied with Django Reinhardt." Bill, I told Howell, was not alone. I had two songs published by Atlantic's in-house publishing company, Progressive, under my name: "Rain is a Bringdown" and "R. B. Blues." For another, *Standing on the Corner,* I put new lyrics to a traditional blues tune, and when Progressive put that out it was credited to "Brown/Ahbert."

"Ahbert?" Howell asked.

"One of several pennames Ahmet adopted," I replied.

"Why didn't you protest?" he asked.

"I didn't regard it as a big deal at the time. Like many others, I guess, I didn't realize the potential value of these copyrights. I was a singer, not a writer, I was only dabbling. It was a standard blues in the first place, of course. And believe me, it was common practice to concede credit back then if you wanted your song published. Still is today, for that matter. In some circles, ain't nothing changed."

As our flight was being called Howell explained that he had first met Kathy Hammer while she was fundraising for the American Film Institute, and that her fiancé Arthur, an investment banker, had ironically once represented Warner's boss Steve Ross. I couldn't resist asking, adoration of Ruth Brown apart, what Howell was getting out of devoting such an incredible amount of time to what many had written off as a lost cause.

"Okay, Ruth," he said, "I'll tell you. To have gone through law school, worked for a Wall Street firm, to have acquired all these skills, then to be given an opportunity later in life to apply them to something I love is wonderful. Too often in this profession you're not given a chance to be on the right side of the right issue." The bluer-than-blue eyes twinkled. "Besides," he continued, "my kids had no idea what I did as a mere lawyer repping newspaper magnates in multi-million-dollar deals. Ask them now I'm up to my ass in record legends, and you'll find they have a much clearer picture."

20

MOTORMOUTH MEETS JESSE JACKSON

MANY, MANY TIMES over the years I've watched as people have waited outside a theater or club in line, often protecting themselves against the rain with their umbrellas and plastic coats. And I've marveled at their leaving warm, comfortable homes to come and see performers like myself. I've always detested the arrogance of artists whose attitude is, "Here I am, you lucky people!"

Because the truth of the matter is that all of us would look real idiots if there was nobody occupying those seats out front. You mean *nothing* standing there alone, thinking what a real fine thing you are. Take away the band, and nowadays take away the backing group, dancers, strobe lights and amplification, and go ahead, take a shot at it, try to lift just one person's spirit without all that back-up, wardrobe and engineers twiddling a hundred knobs. As I've said many times to an audience, "You look as if you're glad to see me. Believe me, not half as glad as I am to see you!"

BY THE TIME I arrived back from eight months in Paris in 1986, *Staggerlee* had made it to off-Broadway. Vernell Bagneris intended to bow out as the lead and sought my advice on his replacement. I suggested a handsome son of a gun named Adam Wade, whose experience ranged from being Dr. Jonas Salk's assistant to acting as the first black game-show host on *Musical Chairs*. I managed to slip back in as well, and was the only other member of the cast not hailing from New Orleans.

Although I sang a lot of good original stuff in that show, the highlight was a scene in a prayer grove where I performed a great number that had come to mean a lot to me personally, "I'm Lighting a Candle ('Cause I've Got to Get a Handle on a Life I've Taken Too Far)." Each night before I made my entrance toward the sacred grove with its statue of the Virgin Mary, I would nod to Vernell and say, "It's prayer time again, Vern."

On stage one night a casting agent spotted me and mentioned my name to movie director John Waters as a possibility for a role in his new movie. The character, it turned out, was that of a jive-talkin' lady deejay named Motormouth Maybelle, and the movie was *Hairspray*. I had never heard of Waters, let alone his *Pink Flamingos* or *Female Trouble*, but when I mentioned his name to some of the younger members of our cast they got quite excited. "Be careful, though," one of them warned. "His stuff can be outrageous. He'll probably want you to take your clothes off."

"I got no problem with that," I replied. "Just as long as I get to keep my wig on!" It turned out that John had his own ideas about that.

Howell negotiated a short leave of absence from the show so I could do the movie, and a friend drove me through to Allentown, Pennsylvania, for the first day's shooting. I was allocated a trailer and given my wardrobe, then taken over to the makeup tent. The first thing I saw was this head block with a high blonde wig sitting on top. "What in the name of all-get-out is that?" I asked.

"That's what you're wearing in the show," came the reply.

"No, it *ain't!*" I declared. "You can take that away right now. I ain't puttin' no blonde wig on my head, y'understand?"

Back in my trailer I looked out the window and saw two figures walking towards me. One was lanky and wearing a broken-down ole piece of hat, looking for all the world like Howard Hughes restored to life—okay, make that *half*-restored—the other was portly and bald, his clothes fitting where they met and no place else. They were, of course, my director and the star he had created, Divine.

John quickly got down to the business at hand. "Miss B," he said, "I understand you got a problem."

"You're darn right I got a problem," I replied. "I did not come all the way down here to be made a fool of, playing some damn-fool role with that ridiculous wig."

"We would never ask you to do anything that made a fool of you," John calmly replied. "First off, we have too much respect for you, and second we have too much respect for the real-life lady you're portraying."

"The *real-life* lady?" I spluttered. "What is that?"

"Sure, she's no fictional character, she's based on a lady deejay famous on Baltimore radio for years. And the movie's a take-off, a spoof of those crazy times and fashions of the fifties, but an affectionate spoof, as you'll see."

John was so obviously genuine, so sincere, and now that he mentioned it I did recall some outrageous female I'd heard of back then in Baltimore. "I hear what you're saying," I told him, "but I'm still concerned. I guess I've always played characters close to Ruth Brown before, this is just so different. She's a funny lady, all right, but she's not me, she's Motormouth Maybelle. And I honestly don't know how Ruth Brown fans will take it."

It was Divine's turn to enter the discussion. "Miss B," he said, "for every fan you might lose, I promise you'll gain one of mine. I've seen you on stage and I loved you, and I promise you new fans all over the world will do the same when they see you in this movie."

I was persuaded, thank goodness, for I had great fun doing the movie and meeting so many people, from John and Divine themselves to Debbie Harry (I felt even better when I caught sight of *her* wig! Man oh man!) the wonderful, chock-full-o'-life Ricki Lake, Toussaint McCall, who sang the great "Nothing Takes the Place of You," and two extremely talented choreographers, Ed Love and Kiki Shepherd. And it taught me another lesson, the necessity of leaving Ruth Brown to one side in my acting career. The serious side of *Hairspray*, of course—and there was one, despite the frivolity —was the segregation it portrayed. My nose had been well and truly rubbed in that, and it brought back a lot of hurting memories.

What a gal!
Motormouth
Maybelle in
"Hairspray"
(COURTESY OF JOHN
WATERS NEW LINE
PICTURES)

* * *

WHEN SHOOTING ON *Hairspray* moved to Baltimore on the third day, a young member of the crew approached me during a lunch break. And proceeded to knock the feet right from under me. "My wife was hospitalized here a few years back," he explained, "and her roommate was a lady who said she brought you into the business. Name of Blanche Calloway?"

I had run across Blanche's obituary in 1979 and had shed many a tear in the weeks that followed. I just dropped, I could not believe it. "My wife was with her until the day she died," he continued. "No matter how much she suffered she refused to take any medicine. But the one thing she did was to keep on talking about Ruth Brown, how she taught you this, how she taught you that, how she groomed you, how you grew, how proud she was of what you had made of yourself." I tried hard, but try as I might I couldn't stop those tears from streaming once again down my face.

Blanche had taught me so much, from how to make my entrance on stage to achieving eye contact with an audience, with every conceivable stop in between. And unfailingly she told me always to look my best, with shortcuts out of the question. Lord, how I'd tried to keep to her watchword, "More is less." And how, occasionally, I'd fallen from grace! On stage at the Apollo one night I was unaware she was in the audience. For once I'd gone dead against her advice and had all the wrong things on, dressed fit to rival Daddy's Christmas tree. When I caught sight of her sitting there, she flashed me that reproving look so like Mama's. The bandleader, Ruben Phillips, told me later he thought I'd been transformed into a striptease artist when I began to discard a bracelet after singing one line, a ring after another, keeping on until all that crazy stuff was removed. Blanche's contention was that people would be so distracted by all those separate touches they wouldn't focus on your face and the words coming out of your mouth.

She also used to say, "If you gotta follow somebody, do something dynamic, make the audience scream before you even open your mouth." I remembered her words of wisdom on a bill with LaVern, where I was set to follow her. "Uh-oh," I groaned, "they're gonna make this the Battle of the Blues. Can't you just see the reporters waiting to see who's gonna blow who off the stage?" Blanche looked me up and down and said, "Yep, it's time to get you something real special."

Since this was my first concert after giving birth to Ronnie, I had nothing new to wear, just the same old stuff. And Miss Effie Throckbottom, of course, waiting in the wings for the first throwout! Blanche went out and bought a length of gold fabric, which she presented to a dressmaker named Zelda Winn, who'd run up a few items for me in the past. Zelda put together a stunning dress, held up by a single, teasing strap. I sprayed my hair gold to match, leaving a black stripe, while Blanche huddled with the lighting technicians and sorted out the spot placements and cues. "When you hear your name called," she told me, "stay in the wings and begin your opening number from there."

We chose "Lulu's Back in Town," changing the last line of the intro to *"Miss Brown's* back in town."

When the first spot hit that dress the audience whooped and screamed before I even reached the microphone, and from then on I could do nothing wrong. Every time there was a solo from the band I'd spin to the music, causing more uproar. As I came off Blanche hugged me and said, *"That's* what you call show business. When you *show* up, you must take care of *business."*

Sometimes when you lose touch with people, you never *really* lose touch with them, you know what I mean? It was as if Blanche had reached out to me with that message from the past in Baltimore and said, "I'm up here rootin' for you, Ruth. You're doin' good. Hang in there, girl."

John invited me through to *Hairspray's* premiere in Baltimore, and it was done in fine style, with original cars hired for the occasion. Divine's parents traveled from Florida and were overjoyed at the movie and their son's performance in it. At last he had a film they actually approved of! He was a sweet man and died shortly afterwards. John still sends me cards, and I get residuals from that movie every now and then. Altogether, it was a most gratifying experience, and I'm recognized wherever I go by kids of all ages who love the movie and the character of Motormouth. As indeed I do.

IT DID NO HARM to the Atlantic cause when I began to get a whole lot of press attention as *Staggerlee* continued its run in 1987. *Women's Wear Daily* sent along a young man named David Leader to do an interview, and someone gave my number to another reporter, David Hinckley of the New York *Daily News*. When he first called me I mistook him for one of my most persistent bill collectors and told him that Miss Ruth Brown was not at home. Once we got over that little misunderstanding he became a real champion. Stories were all over the place about the ongoing tussle with Atlantic, and they all wanted to know if I was bitter about the way I'd been treated. I said something like, "Well, it would be something if Ahmet showed up at the show."

An actual photo from the "Battle of the Blues," on the same bill as my dear friend Lavern Baker.

(Courtesy of Ruth Brown)

A few weeks later I was sitting in my dressing room after the curtain, makeup half-on, half-off, when the doorman appeared and announced there was a man from a record company to see me. "Who is it?" I called out. "It's me," was the answer. "Who's that? What record company?" I asked. "Ahmet from Atlantic," came the reply.

If I had been half-drowsing, winding down, I was suddenly wide-awake. I opened the door, and there he was. If anything, his goatee beard was even more immaculately trimmed than before, admittedly several shades lighter, and those hooded eyes were still drooping. "I just had to tell you how wonderful you were in the show tonight," he told me. We hugged, and it was kind of a high emotional thing for a moment, being face to face after so long. So much had happened, so much had changed since our last, tense meeting almost three decades earlier. It was more than a little awkward, for neither one of us wanted to say too much about what was going on in the background. Instead, we came on like a couple of old crocks.

I was still having trouble with my legs, I told him, and he said that he had health problems too. If ever I needed a surgeon, he went on, I should look up someone he knew at the New York Hospital. He congratulated me again, said he'd be back, we embraced once more. "I want you to know that I love you, Ruth," he told me, "and everything is going to be all right. I would never do anything to hurt you."

Then he was gone.

I ALWAYS SAY that if there was one person in my family, outside my dad, who should have been a singer, it would have to be my sister Goldie. She was the one back in those days in Portsmouth who had the looks and the voice, combined with a great natural warmth. Unlike me, who barely scraped through school, she was an A-student, a terrific conversationalist, and she excelled in every sport. Somehow, though, when it came time for church, Goldie was always there. I have deep spiritual values my mama implanted, but Goldie has spiritual lines stretching clear to heaven. If you want someone to pray for you, just call Goldie and stand well back. She truly is the spiritual rock in my family of brothers and sisters, a fact I realize more and more as I get older. And she has never deviated from that role. She has the same strength Mama had, handed down from generation to generation. When we made a mistake Mama never said, "I told you so." Instead, she'd look us straight in the eye and simply ask, "Why?" Goldie has that same serenity.

Nevertheless I do cherish a few crazy childhood memories of her that have nothing whatsoever to do with religion. I mean *nuthin'!* The toilet in our house was situated in the yard outside, and there was no running water in there, just a box at the back to catch the waste. Every Wednesday morning a local worthy we called 'the boom-boom man' arrived to empty the contraption out. We'd be playing hopscotch before school or swingin' from our tree, then

one of us would yell, "Look out, the boom-boom man's a-comin',
let's get outta here!" The only exception was when Goldie swallowed a dime and Mama gave her something to cleanse it through.
That Wednesday morning wild horses would have had a powerful
struggle moving Goldie. Her hands determinedly planted on her
hips, "I want my dime back!" she informed the boom-boom bri-
gade.

I was taking a short cut home from school one day when I came
across her rolling on the ground with a girl named Ernestine Washington, who just happened to be about twice her size. Ernestine was
really giving it to Goldie good, and I flew in there immediately, the
Lone Ranger to Tonto's rescue. Between us my sister and I could
have hogtied Ernestine and had her halfway over to the white
slavers in China before anybody even thought to ask. Instead, next
thing I knew Goldie was disappearing in a cloud of dust, leaving
skinny little Ruth to overcome the mighty Ernestine. What I did for
love! Ernestine proceeded to rake my arm with a rusty tin can,
giving me a scar I carry still. When Dad got home that night he
demanded to know what had happened. Then he ordered me to
get dressed, and frogmarched me all the way to the Washington
household. "I hear that your daughter and Ruth had a scrape and
Ernestine cut her with a can," he said to her father. "Now let's see
what she can do without a can." Then he turned to me. "If your
body as much as touches the ground," he warned, "just wait 'til I
get you home!" Lord have mercy!

Whenever things go well for me, Goldie has her explanation at
the ready: "Well, Ruthie, you got smart and took God's direction.
You got in the back seat and let Him drive." *I swear,* I'm *telling* you,
you better *believe* it, Goldie *knows.*

TRUE TO HIS WORD, Mickey Leland arranged for Howell to meet with
Jesse Jackson in New York in November, 1986. The rendezvous was
the UN Plaza Hotel, where Howell was introduced to Reverend
Jackson, who was relaxed in jeans and a T-shirt boldly emblazoned
"Operation PUSH." Before long it transpired that a meeting had
been set up with Steve Ross at Warner the following morning,
which Howell, out of the blue, was informed he'd be attending.

(Steve Ross, the very top of the tree! As an old friend of mine from the Apollo, the great veteran "Moms" Mabley, would have put it, "Now we'se *gittin'* someplace.")

There had been speculation in the press that Jackson harbored his own agenda, that he intended to tick off the Warner brass for attempting to squeeze a friend of his, Dick Griffey, out of the record business. An independent record distributor, Griffey had been an important financial supporter of Jackson's. Warner, so the story ran, had hired Frank Sinatra's heavyweight lawyer, Mickey Rudin, to see Griffey off.

Jackson was surrounded in his room by a host of young staff, all of them anxious to fill their boss in on some aspect or other of the record industry. Howell watched him soak up the research material his people threw at him in the hours that followed, through the supper that was brought in, through the endless phone calls he was obliged to deal with. According to him Jackson was the quickest study he had ever seen.

Next morning, as Howell walked down the hotel steps with Jackson and his delegation—now looking as if they had stepped off the front cover of GQ—he caught a first-hand glimpse of how it feels to be instantly recognizable. "Yo, Jesse! Right on, m'man!" was typical of the salutes as garbage-truck windows were rolled down, taxi drivers waved and passing pedestrians ogled and beamed. Having misread the breakfast invitation, the contingent arrived at Warner a half-hour early, sending the staff that greeted them into a frenzied mixture of fawning admiration and downright panic.

The Operation PUSH (People United to Serve Humanity) party that descended upon Warners consisted of Jackson, the Reverend Tyrone Crider, Kendall Minter, executive director of the Black Entertainment and Sports Lawyers Association, and Howell. Warner chairman Steve Ross was accompanied by his senior vice-president and music label chief Robert Morgado—to whom Ahmet, in common with the heads of Reprise, Elektra and the other record heads reported—and his general counsel Martin Payson. The broad agenda centered on PUSH's concerns with what they termed "racially exclusive, insensitive and economically exploitative policies at Warner.

Jackson confounded the pundits by never once mentioning his

Howell Begle is on the left, Jesse Jackson next to him, in Ray Charles' dressing room after a show. Ray is coming out of the back room after splashing water on his face.
(Courtesy of Ruth Brown)

friend Griffey. Instead, following the breakfast in Warner's boardroom, he launched into a dissertation on the state of the record industry, mainly along the lines of what a sorry-assed, raggedy-tailed, half-masted bunch of people populated it. He berated them for their "farm team" mentality, how they took someone like Anita Baker away from the black artists and repertoire guys as soon as she started selling to whites, moving her over to their white production "experts." This was typical, he maintained, of how the black team that produced her success in the first instance forever remained the underlings.

He expertly wove Warner's trade with South Africa and the company's lack of black boardroom members into his seamless narrative before returning specifically to how artists from the past—no names, no pack drill for the moment—were continually belittled and exploited. At this point he handed the floor to Howell, who'd been listening, open-mouthed in admiration, at the virtuosity of Jackson's presentation.

Howell said his piece, then watched as the back-and-forth between Steve Ross and Jackson began. Brilliant though Jackson had been, Ross was his match. He came over as well briefed, a great listener, an altogether formidable opponent. He was the consummate CEO, bluff yet concerned, conciliatory yet strong, serious yet capable of producing sudden shafts of humor. Howell felt as if he were watching two skilled, robust gladiators performing. As for the rest of the Warner team, Payson came over as smart and watchful, Morgado polished and bright, an impressive corporate executive.

And by any definition Morgado was a political animal, having served as Hugh Carey's chief of staff during Carey's governorship of New York.

When Morgado later gave his account of the meeting in Warner's tower to reporters, he claimed that the royalty question Howell raised "was the first time I'd heard about it to any degree." That surprised me, since I'd assumed these people would be well aware of a matter already thoroughly aired both in the press and on prime-time television. I guess it must be in how you define "to any degree!" The bottom line was Steve Ross's delegating him to look into all matters raised at the meeting. Where, we wondered, had Sheldon Vogel gone? Maybe he was off roughing someone else up, in between spitting out nails or attending to one of his main pursuits, deciding who were this month's lucky recipients of Warner's cut-outs.

No sooner had Morgado began his investigations than Jesse Jackson began upping the ante in his own inimitable way. Accompanied by Howell and a large contingent of PUSH staff, he attended a Black Radio Programming Convention in Houston. Before the event was over he had lined up one hundred fifty radio stations, all of whom signed a solemn pledge not to report airplay on any Warner records until there was a satisfactory outcome to the Operation PUSH talks. Before leaving Houston he put the Reverend Tyrone Crider in charge of maintaining and spreading the boycott. Crider, I heard, did a bang-up job.

Some things in life you have to work and plan for, others fall into your lap. Howell had singlemindedly charted his way through a maze of correspondence with the company, he had seized on RICO and the possibilities it offered, he had refused to take no for an answer. Then there were the couple of windfalls he had picked up and gleefully run with: the serendipitous seating arrangement providing his introduction to Mickey Leland, and through him Jesse Jackson, together with John Conyers' fortuitous choice of a bass-fiddle professor.

We had one more windfall on the way. And boy, was it a peach!

21

HALL OF FAME

As 1963 WAS DRAWING to a close I was busy dressing the enormous Christmas tree my husband Bill had erected in our living room. Suddenly, a news flash on the radio brought terrible news. The undisputed Queen of the Blues, Dinah Washington, was dead at thirty-nine. I wept as the bittersweet memories came flooding back. The first time I'd seen Dinah perform was at the Renaissance Ballroom in Harlem in '48, but it was several years later, while opening at the Apollo, that I actually got to meet her. She was working in Birdland at the time and Willis and I went there one night after our show. The tiny doorman, the one and only "Pee Wee" Marquette, greeted us and showed us through with his usual flourish. "Miss Ruth Brown and Willis 'Gator Tail' Jackson," he announced, just in case anyone had missed our entrance.

All during her performance I waited, hoping for the acknowledgement Dinah might give that I was in the audience. At last she did, declaring, "I hear that 'Mama, He Treats Your Daughter Mean' gal is among us tonight. Come on, Ruth Brown, stand up an' take a bow." When I did there were immediate cries of, "Let her sing, Dinah!"

"Okay, I could use a breather anyway," she agreed. "Come on up, Ruth, an' sing 'Mama, He Treats Your Daughter Mean.'" I decided to do another number first, showing off that I could do standards, I guess, and sang "Skylark" while Dinah retreated to her dressing room through the swing doors at the back of the stage.

246

When I finished the audience went wild and began chanting, " 'Mama! Mama!' " Before I had time to move a muscle Dinah came flying back through those doors. "Hey, I didn't invite you up here to give a whole goddamn show!" she told me. You better believe I got my butt off that stage in a hurry, for nobody, but *nobody*, not even little spitfire Ruth Brown, argued with the Queen.

Later when we went to pay our respects backstage she said, "Well, I will take the time to give you my autograph, Ruth, 'cause the truth of the matter is you can sing. But you ain't s'posed to come on other folk's shows an' take over. 'Specially my shows!"

Willis and I took young Ronnie along to see her backstage at the Apollo soon after this. After Dinah's dresser and friend Larue Manns had opened up for us, I said to my son, "Tell Miss Washington how much you enjoyed her show." Ronnie, that little upsetter, promptly shook a little finger in Dinah's face and said, "Don't you dare sing like my mom!" Well, Dinah let out a roar, rocked back on her feet and hollered, "GIT *that nappy-haired nigger child outta here!*" Then she and Willis began roaring with laughter. When it died down she turned to me, those saucer eyes a-flashin': "Ruth, you *told* him to say that!"

A few years later we met again while Brook Benton and I were playing Chicago's Regal Theater. Dinah was running a club in the city at the time, Robert's Show Lounge, with its own chorus line, including her discovery, Lola Falana, and we received invites to drop in for the late show. Dinah sang, the chorus girls high-kicked, it was wonderful. Then she began introducing the performers from the Regal, including me and Brook.

When she invited him to join her onstage and they launched into one of the duets they'd recently recorded, "Baby, You've Got What It Takes," a problem emerged. Brook, in a mischievous mood, changed the lyrics to, "Baby, you got what it takes, 'cept I wonder why you can't hold a man," all the while looking pointedly at Dinah. She stormed offstage through the rear swing doors she'd modeled on Birdland's, then came steamin' back seconds later, meat cleaver in hand, making straight for Brook. He took one look and flew for his life, right out of that club.

In her dressing room later I found Dinah in tears. It turned out that her latest marriage, to the young Mexican actor Rafael Campos, had turned sour after a matter of weeks. Whether Brook knew this or whether he was making an inspired guess—it was Dinah's sixth trip to the altar—I do not know, but there was no doubt Dinah was hurting. "You know," she said to me, "it's amazing how people think they know you 'cause you walk around with a reputation for bein' mean. But they know nothin'. They don't know what's in my heart and they never will."

She had some champagne brought in and we both got a little high—with me it didn't take much—and when she recovered a bit she said, "Hey, Ruth, you're all right. An' you're *doin'* all right. Like I told you, you can sing."

When all her staff had gone home we found some chairs and sat for a couple of hours outside the club in the cool of the early hours. She was wearing a beautiful pair of shoes and when I remarked on them she said, "You like them? Hey, I've got a hundred pairs. When you come visit me in New York, I'll give you some."

I did drop by her apartment there a few weeks later and watched her play the organ she had installed, accompanying herself on "Cool Kind Papa." Someone arrived with a rackful of fur coats, all supposedly at wholesale prices, and Dinah picked a couple. She was crazy about clothes and had a habit of turning up at the Apollo's early shows to ogle what the so-called competition was wearing. If she didn't like the way someone was dressed she'd yell out, "I don't know *what* that is you got on!"

We got together another time in Detroit when a self-proclaimed mystic named Prophet Jones, modeling himself after Father Divine, was all the rage. He invited several of us to his home, Dinah included, together with Sugar Ray Robinson and the cast of *Porgy and Bess*. We were curious to see how he lived, and maybe even get a demonstration of his powers thrown in, but after we'd been kept waiting for an hour, Dinah hauled herself to her feet. "The Queen don't wait for nobody!" she declared. "Tell the motherf———' Prophet that if he wants to see the Queen he can come where I'm workin'." The headline in the paper next day ran, THE QUEEN WALKS OUT ON THE PROPHET.

Dinah used to tell me she intended to keep right on getting married until she got it right. I was able to understand the seriousness behind the humor of that, for Lord knows I'd been there too.

Unfortunately women have a tendency to underestimate their own worth. They feel incomplete if they lack a strong man beside them, for ain't that "the way it's s'posed t'be?" Otherwise, how can they possibly be a fully feminine, "complete" woman? Sure, that and ten more tons of bull.

Men out there can do what they like, a woman cannot. My dad used to tell me that the guideline by which I should grow as a woman was always to bear in mind that a man can lay in the gutter drunk for a week, then rise up, clean up, put on a fresh suit of clothes and go back to being a gentleman. If a woman did that just once she'd be labeled a tramp for the rest of her life.

I know Dinah's death was accidental, for that lady had too much life in her to ever put an end to it. I believe she got those pills mixed up because she was desperately trying to lose weight with the aid of mercury injections pumped into her by her "weight doctor," one of the few white men she trusted! The first time I saw Dinah she was a size eighteen. She got down to a ridiculous size five with the aid of those shots, but her voice suffered. And that diuretic was brutal. On our way downtown one night from her apartment in Harlem she had to ask her driver to stop at every second corner store to relieve herself. That was how it worked, the water just poured out of her.

The "doctor" might have been a witch doctor for all the good his quack treatment did Dinah, for the weight piled back on as quickly as it came off. And it may well have contributed to her death, although this was never publicized at the time. We know today that mercury builds up in the system and can cause liver failure, so maybe that final deadly cocktail of brandy and diet pills she took was helped on its way by that build-up.

We've all tried to look like the models in the magazines. Dinah had it bad, and I did too for a while. There was a time I was a size ten, but I was never able to lose the weight after my sons were born. I tried all the diets at one time or another, going up and down. Then my voice started going and I figured, hey, am I gonna keep singing or what? After all, every single one of those divas you see around are large ladies, I ain't never seen a skinny one yet. And when I look back, my mother was no skinny-minny later in life, nobody in my family was. I decided to look my best just the way I am.

The world certainly lost a great singer and a totally unique individual when it lost Miss Dinah Washington. Ladies like her had difficulties the world never knew about. Unfortunately it takes the knowledge of pain to convincingly sing about pain. That's why I see such a fine dividing line between a good singer and a fine actress. People forget that on the other side of that voice is—guess what?— a woman with the same feelings as anybody else.

IT WAS HOWELL'S IDEA to take me along to the second annual Rock and Roll Hall of Fame induction ceremony in New York's Waldorf-Astoria in January 1987. I wore a dress run up, as it happens, by Dinah's sister, Ferris Kimbrough. She used a bolt of cheap but cheerful fabric I'd found that had a hint of glitter running through the weave, and even managed to fashion an Indian-style headband from an off-cut.

I had missed the first bash because of *Black and Blue*'s extented run in Paris, and although I was nominated as an inductee for a second time in 1987 I would never have made the entrance on my own for the price of a ticket. (The actual sequence of events: Atlantic indicated I had to pay; Howell sent them a check for both of us; they came to their senses and shamefacedly returned the check.) The price of admission ($350 then, currently $1,500) prevented several others gaining admission. We met Hank ("The Twist"; "Work with Me, Annie") Ballard and his lady standing at the door on the way in, and promised to make room for them at our table if they waited awhile. Even more heartbreaking, we found Joyce McRae standing outside, one of Jackie Wilson's daughters on each arm.

We'd been introduced to Joyce originally by Chuck Rubin as the wife and manager of Sam Moore, one-half of the Sam and Dave team. She was a striking lady, white and Jewish, liable to spin off on tangents at a moment's notice and undoubtedly at her best in the heat of controversy. There were no half measures with Joyce, whose idea of "coaxing" would roughly correspond to anyone else's idea of bludgeoning. This came in useful on several occasions during our fight with Atlantic, for as well as representing the legendary Sam, she became otherwise actively involved, offering advice and encouragement to Howell at many points along the way.

When she'd first met Sam in 1981 he'd been a mainline heroin addict for over a decade. By the time they tied the knot he'd cleaned up his act, and it has remained that way ever since. The gospel according to Joyce: "Behind every great singer lurks a pushy Jewish broad."

In the late sixties she'd been involved with Jackie Wilson and well aware of of the rocky relationship that existed towards the end with his last official wife, Harlene. As head of the Hall of Fame, Ahmet had decreed that Harlene and the son she claimed was Jackie's—a claim disputed in some quarters—be the sole family members allowed to attend his posthumous induction. This was regarded by many as arrogance on the grand scale, flying in the face as it did of a court decision in Georgia that acknowledged the legal status of two daughters by his common-law wife.

"I'm standing out here," Joyce declared, "until someone offers to smuggle these kids in." I took one look at them and my heart melted. One was nine, the other thirteen and a polio victim, and both, I swear to God, were so obviously Jackie's kids no one would have denied them. I looked at Howell, who smiled and nodded as I knew he would, and Joyce handed them over. "Your dad was wonderful," I told them as we made our way into the Waldorf-Astoria, "and a dear, dear friend."

As we were shown to the table we were sharing with Marshall Chess, the surviving member of the Chess family, and Ewart Abner, head of the long-gone and much-mourned Vee-Jay label, Howell grabbed a couple of extra chairs for the girls. I chatted to Abner for a while, for it was the first time our paths had crossed in many years. Ah, those days at the Regal and Tivoli theaters in Chi-town, when he had turned up to see how his artists, my good friends Jerry Butler and the Impressions, were doing on a bill with me . . . !

All went well, right up until a few minutes before Jackie's induction. At that point a couple of six-and-a-half-foot-tall goons appeared. "The kids are gonna have to leave," they announced. "Only Jackie Wilson's wife and son are involved in the presentation."

"Can't you let us stay?" the older girl pleaded. "We just want to watch our father's award ceremony." In turn Howell and I urged Abner, someone who had enjoyed a real rapport with Ahmet back then, to prevail upon his minions. It was no use. Crying, the kids were escorted out. Our empty chairs did not remain empty for long. Hank Ballard and his wife, still outside, saw what was going on and figured maybe there was room for them. They filled the girls' seats.

I was so upset, I had seldom felt so helpless in my life. My blood was already on the boil, and the mass induction on stage soon after Harlene and her son's acceptance of Jackie's honor was all that was required to really set me off. Bruce Springsteen joined Chuck Berry, Bo Diddley, the Drifters, the Coasters, Ben E. King and Speedo of the Cadillacs on stage, with the band led by Paul Schaffer. As Ben began singing "Stand By Me," someone remarked that between them these guys were responsible for the birth of the music we know today as rock 'n' roll. I had only had one glass of champagne, but that did it! I agitatedly turned to look at Howell. "Ruth, what's the matter?" he asked.

"I belong on that stage," I replied. "If these are the contributors, I belong up there with them."

"What are you going to do about it?"

"What am I going to do? Watch me!"

I got up, pushed my chair back, walked to the front of the stage and put my arm out.

"Anybody gonna help me up?" I asked. I have to admit that my black brothers closely resembled a bunch of deer frozen in the headlights of an oncoming truck. It was Bruce who reached out his hand, pulled me on stage, wrapped his arms around me and gave me the warmest hug. I think as far as the organizers were concerned it was another case of that troublesome Ruth Brown again, but at least the audience seemed to appreciate what I was trying to say.

Back at our table after this unexpected diversion, Howell overheard someone at the next table say, 'Isn't it too bad what happened to Gerry? How can it be? Twenty-five years with Atlantic and the guy's out. Just like that!"

I could see his antenna positively spinning out of control. Leaning over behind our two new guests, he whispered excitedly in my ear, "Gerry? Atlantic? Twenty-five years? They've got to be talking about Gerald Bursey, the head of their royalty accounting division!"

We managed to track Bursey down later that same evening. And, praise be, he agreed to cooperate with us.

The very next day Howell got down to business with him. "What sort of things should we be looking for? What questions should we be asking that we haven't gotten around to already?" he asked. Then, notebook in hand, he sat back and listened as Gerry held forth.

Individual items apart, his answer boiled down to one vital point: Atlantic had converted all their old acts to their new computer system, mixing in old and new artists willy-nilly regardless of the enormous differentials in royalty rates. Unlike our old five percent top, current artists' rates, typically twelve to fifteen percent and up, had been negotiated to stand current practices, such as: getting paid only half-rate on foreign earnings; treating ten percent of sales as "free goods"; charging twelve percent for packaging; bearing the costs of "remastering, remixing and editing." Right away, a minimum of twenty-five percent of sales was being discounted, thrown out the window.

How did Atlantic justify lumping their old artists in with this? Oh, it was impossible to keep two systems running side by side, the wisdom ran, so it had to be one way only. The *new* way. The sales of the older stars, their rationale ran, were not significant enough to justify the setting-up of a separate system. So whether by accident or design they had set things up to pay less than what they should. Howell took a deep breath before summing it up this way: "They've been stacking all the charges of a *modern* contract against an *ancient* five percent royalty."

There was another ticking bomb. Gerry confirmed that Atlantic had been automatically charging back as a recording cost the contributions it made to artists' pension funds. That was in flagrant violation of federal law as well as union contracts.

Not only that, but the company had hundreds of artists on their books they had been "unable to track down to pay." What had they done with the surplus dough, amounting to hundreds of thousands of dollars? Why, quietly kept it, despite state laws requiring that lost property and unclaimed monies be handed over to state agencies.

Whether Gerry still had access to Atlantic's computer records from the outside, or whether he simply had an enviable memory, he was unfailingly able to come up with any additional information we needed.

We made a decision. Now was the time to join forces with Chuck Rubin. Many times, even with Joe and the Clovers included in our case, Atlantic was taking shelter behind, "Well, nobody else is complaining." The strength-in-numbers theory needed reinforcing. They had to be made aware that a groundswell was going on.

A previous problem with Howell's and Chuck's working together had been their widely differing financial arrangements with their clients. Howell was uncomfortable with the fifty percent Chuck demanded. The compromise they worked out was simple. Chuck would agree to give Howell one-third of the fifty percent he collected for several of his important clients, including the Coasters and the estate of Clyde McPhatter. And if Howell chose to return the amount to those clients—which he did—that was Howell's business. With Chuck's agreement we added, either in person or through their estates, Brook Benton, Solomon Burke, the Chords, the Coasters, Clyde McPhatter, Sam and Dave, Chuck Willis, Ivory Joe Hunter, Rufus Thomas, Carla Thomas, Eddie Floyd, Chris Kenner, the Mar-Keys, William Bell and Doris Troy. I added Willis "Gator Tail" Jackson to the list. In the case of Sam and Dave, at Joyce McRae's urging, Howell took on Sam Moore, leaving Dave Prater with Chuck.

Howell determined that collectively his newly enlarged artists' roster represented 23 number-one, 90 Top Ten and 87 Top Forty hits on the rhythm-and-blues charts, together with 2 number-one, 24 Top Ten, 45 Top Forty and 130 Top One Hundred hits on Billboard's pop charts. Between us we'd enjoyed more than 400 hits on both charts combined. Howell also dug out a Billboard survey from 1976 ranking all the rhythm-and-blues artists who had hits on their charts between 1950 and 1966. The only female ranked above me was Dinah Washington. I was placed twelfth, followed by Chuck Berry, Jackie Wilson, Little Richard, the Platters, Clyde McPhatter, Etta James and LaVern Baker.

*   *   *

I CONTINUED TAPING the NPR radio programs I had begun in 1985, with a crucial difference. Producer Felix Hernandez had personally hosted the first series of *Harlem Hit Parade*, featuring the great rhythm and blues artists of the forties, fifties and beyond. When I had mentioned to Felix during an interview that I had always wanted to do a radio show, he invited me to take over. I did over a hundred shows for his Ceiba Productions, signing off by reminding everyone that R and B stands for Ruth Brown as well as rhythm and blues.

The broadcasts brought so many old records and artists back to the public's attention. One of the most remarkable was someone otherwise forgotten, a remarkable performer whose stage name was Little Miss Cornshucks. I'd first heard of her back in the early forties at the Big Track Diner, and when I caught up with her a few years later I could see what all the fuss was about. She'd come on stage without shoes—her feet were the tiniest I've ever seen—and wearing not a scrap of makeup. She had a beautiful light baby skin and wore a wide-brimmed straw hat with all the edges frayed and a checked gingham dress with pantaloons and ruffles showing underneath.

Sitting on the edge of the stage, long before Judy Garland did her concerts singing "Over the Rainbow" like that, and clutching a plain straw basket, she'd sing her heart out. And that voice was tremendous, clear as a bell. I loved her version of "So Long," a number I was already familiar with from the Charioteers' record. Before you knew it that basket began filling up with money, poured in by the appreciative audience. Offsetting her childlike appearance, she performed songs such as "(You Came to Me) In the Rain" like an unmistakable adult. That combination of childish innocence and sophistication was irresistible. Her real name was Mildred Cunningham and she came from a group of singing sisters out of Chicago. She was the true forerunner of artists like LaVern Baker, who followed her as "Little Miss Sharecropper."

Many years after watching her perform I was playing in Chicago and including "So Long" in my act. She turned up one night, took umbrage that I was singing "her" number, and grabbed the opportunity to lay me out. In the middle of the song she marched to the edge of the stage, ripped the wig from her head, twirled it on the end of her finger for a moment, then hurled it straight at me. Startled as I was, I kept right on singing. I'd already heard that Little Miss Cornshucks had sadly gone into retirement following a severe nervous breakdown.

Felix decided to follow up our critical and popular success with *BluesStage,* a show devoted to the live music of today, recorded at venues across the country with artists including Albert Collins, Koko Taylor, Little Milton, Buddy Guy and Johnny Winter. I was back as resident soul sister hosting the proceedings, sometimes live at the clubs, more often providing taped bookends. It was and re- mains a great idea, for it provides vital national exposure to the music and the artists involved.

Chuck Jackson and Carla Thomas were featured live and kickin' from the Village Gate, Little Milton did a gasser from the B.K. Lounge in Rochester, Eddie Bo and George Porter of the Meters cooked at Tipitina's in New Orleans. Keeping the music alive, that's what *BluesStage* is all about, and it continues to this day on hundreds of radio stations coast to coast.

While recording one of the shows in Greenwich Village I was brought face to face with a familiar heap of bones from my che- quered past. Yep, Jimmy Earle Brown, the wild child from my equally wild youth!

On a tour back in the late fifties I'd been close to Topeka, Kansas, Jimmy's hometown. I'd never been there before and I took the opportunity to look up Jimmy's father Leonard and his wife Edna. They were real nice folks. His dad raised greyhounds, and had ken- nels built for them in back of the house. They proudly introduced me to their immediate neighbors, then sat me down in their parlor, where we sipped cool, freshly made lemonade. "That James Earle sure was a crazy cuss to let you go," his dad told me, "but you know, Ruthie, that boy never will settle down. He always had wanderin' ways an' I don't see him changing now." His father had said a mouthful.

When Jimmy and I met again he explained that he was with a Latin combo, and was running with a brand-new name to suit. Would you believe Rio Pravo?

"How many times you bin married now, Jimmy?" I asked him.

" 'Bout four, mebbe five," he replied, grinning broadly. "Depends who's countin'."

As Big Joe would have put it, "Ohhhhh, my Looooord!"

22

SKELETONS IN THE CLOSET

REMEMBER GRANNY DELIA? What happened to her at the end of her life has haunted me ever since. While I was attempting model-sub-urban-housewife status with Bill Blunt in the sixties, Granny was working her way through to her own destiny. Out of the blue she astonished everyone by renting out her farm in Macon and pur-chasing land in Princess Anne County in Virginia. Maybe she wanted to be near Mama and Jesse in her declining years, we never knew, but she went on to make a great success of her new enter-prise, specializing in cucumbers for pickling, for which there was a steady and profitable demand.

Granny D's fatal mistake was in signing the property over to Jesse. Her intent was to avoid any problem on her death. Unfortunately, she had not reckoned on his wife's taking a leaf out of Granny Ruth Weston's book. Although Jesse had been a confirmed alcoholic for years, it still came as a terrible shock when his wife Annabelle had him declared insane and confined to Petersburg's mental asylum, the pit of hell in which Big Papa William had long since perished. Granny D had never considered the possibility of Jesse dying before her and the property falling into his wife's hands. Even if she had, I doubt if she or anyone else could have forecast what happened next: an eviction notice was served by Annabelle that kicked

Granny off her own farm! Granny fought the order but she was powerless, bound by the document she herself had drawn up.

Back in Macon, and well into her eighties, she took possession of her old farm. Determined that Annabelle would never get her hands on her North Carolina land, she had it surveyed and willed to Mama. One morning, despite complaining of chest pains, she declared her intention to walk her property and check the survey markers. She never made it back alive. My brothers Benny and Leroy were summoned from Portsmouth when neighbors reported her missing, but even with a squad of state troopers enlisted they failed to find her body after two days of searching. On the third day her new puppy turned up at the farm, whimpering, then led them to the hill she had been crawling up after suffering a massive heart attack. Granny D was lying face down, her hands dug like talons into the red soil she loved so much, so deep they had to be pried out. We were all down there by then and stayed to pay our last respects to a most remarkable lady.

Her entire life had been spent cultivating land, and whenever I think of *The Good Earth,* and the closing scene where Paul Muni looks at the tree his young bride O-lan planted as a seedling and declares, "You are the earth!" I think of Granny D. My brothers and sisters tell me I get a lot of my self-discipline and strength from that flinty, cantankerous, dictatorial, hardbitten upsetter of a lady. What is certain is that we all respected her, for no matter what impression I may have given in telling her story, she asked us to do nothing she could not do, and did do, herself. And despite all her wrong-headed views on degrees of color, all of us are richer in spirit for having known her.

Mama couldn't bear to keep the land on which her mother had died, and so sold most of the fields shortly after Granny D's death, keeping only the house and a few adjacent acres. She rented out what remained for twenty-three dollars a month, until it became so unkempt and overrun she sold the lot, severing our direct links with North Carolina. For all of us it was the end of an era, a final farewell to a time of youth and innocence, another time and another place that can never be recaptured.

Except, of course, in the indelible mental snapshots we will always carry.

*   *   *

THE TEAM AT WARNER flipped when they heard the news that Gerry
Bursey was on our payroll. The RICO threat still hanging over them
was bad enough; now we had a straight line to all their dealings.
Every time Howell went into any meetings with them thereafter and
listed his concerns, chairman Bob Morgado assumed that he knew
everything, even on the rare occasions he didn't, and voluntarily
authorized filling in the missing pieces. They were really running
scared, and for the first time, starting in the spring of 1987, Ahmet
himself began regularly to make an appearance 'round the table,
riding the elevator to Warner's tower from Atlantic's offices fourteen floors below.

I believe one of the things that had grabbed Ahmet's attention
was an article in a small Greek-American publication which began
to circulate in the music trade. It was titled, "Ahmet Ertegun: The
Skeletons in the Closet Sing Rock 'n' Roll." Journalist Claudia
Wright, noting that Atlantic had recorded profits of over $200 mil-
lion in 1985, compared Ahmet's status in his homeland to that of a
Frank Sinatra or Lee Iacocca in Italy, a man whose wealth made
him an exemplar of the American success story, a prominent
spokesman for his community, and a man whom other influential
Americans sought out and liked to call their friend.

He had been been portrayed by the New York *Times* as "well-
educated, owlishly dignified, unfailingly polite', in the Washington
Post as "trim, dapper, debonair," attending with his wife Mica "the
ritziest social events and parties on several continents." According
to Vanity Fair, an invitation to his summer house in Turkey was "the
hottest ticket in town" when the July heat descended in New York.
He was an avid collector of abstract art, lending pieces out for
museum exhibitions, an ex-president of New York's Cosmos football team, chairman of the Rock and Roll Hall of Fame.

He was also, Wright continued, probably the single most impor-
tant political asset Turkey had in the U.S., a leader of the Turkish-
American community, chairman of the board of the American
Turkish Society, and a member (along with David Rockefeller,
Henry Kissinger and John Brademas) of the National Committee
on American Foreign Policy.

She quoted a Washington *Post* article where Ahmet had claimed, "One thing that set Atlantic apart from many of its competitors was its reputation for paying its artists the royalties they deserved. Frankly, it never occurred to me not to pay royalties to artists. We treated them as stars because we were all fans. I think that's what made Atlantic survive where some of the others didn't."

It would thus be more than a small embarrassment to Turkey, Wright maintained, as well as to Turkey's friends in the U.S., if a group of black American singers, fronted by Ruth Brown and Howell Begle, succeeded in their plan to have Congress maintain, even strengthen, the existing anti-racketeering laws to enable them to sue Ahmet and his record company for millions of dollars for fraudulent dealings, including what she described as "grossly understated domestic sales and non-reporting of foreign sales." If the plan succeeded, if the allegations of mail fraud were upheld, we stood to receive every cent of the royalties withheld for over a quarter of a century, plus punitive damages that tripled their value.

She repeated Billboard's assertion that it was artists like Big Joe, the Clovers and myself who had enabled Ahmet to sell the company to Warner/Seven Arts for $17 million in 1967. We were people, she concluded, that Ahmet and his company would prefer to see forgotten.

Not if we could help it.

I HAD BEEN WARNED by many people of the dangers involved in crossing Ahmet, some of which I had been aware of, some I had not. Certainly if anyone wanted a parallel in history of his ability to turn heavy when challenged, they needed to look no further than the fate of my "Lucky Lips" songwriters, Jerry Leiber and Mike Stoller, staff producers at Atlantic for the Drifters, the Coasters and Ben E. King. The crunch for them had followed their insistence on producers' credit *and* a royalty on sales. Ahmet and Jerry Wexler had finally agreed, much against the advice of Miriam Bienstock. Her telling recollection of events? "As a principal of the company I just didn't want to pay it. That's the whole principle of capitalism. You take advantage of people!" Miriam, the ultimate Iron Lady, had said a mouthful.

If Jerry and Mike had been content to leave it at that, all might have been quiet on the Atlantic front. Instead, they pored over subsequent royalty statements in the late fifties and decided they'd been shortchanged. When they insisted on an outside audit, a shortfall of $18,000 was thrown up. A furious Ahmet agreed in the end to pay, but swore he'd never do business with the team again. "That's the end of the relationship," they were told, "and you can forget about the roster of artists." Jerry and Mike swallowed hard. And backed down. The thought of starting over again elsewhere was simply too much to contemplate at the time.

End of the story? Not quite, for they had not reckoned on the continuing wrath of Ahmet. With the Drifters readying themselves for another recording session a month later, the team assumed—reasonably enough, since they'd surrendered to Ahmet's ultimatum—that they'd be back at the controls. Ahmet and Jerry had a different message to convey. They wheeled in Phil Spector instead, the wonder boy Jerry and Mike had been quietly bringing on. After six hit-making years at Atlantic the Leiber-Stoller team departed Atlantic during 1961, amidst bitterness, recrimination and acrimony. The moral of the story was, you don't mess with Ahmet. As Jerry Leiber put it to the authors of the book *Music Man,* "Ahmet took offense at a situation where *we* were wronged. He has always been like that. I think he was offended because *he* was in the wrong, and I think he was embarrassed." Referring to a speech made at the 1987 Hall of Fame dinner, Jerry recalled Ahmet thanking "everybody at Atlantic down to the secretaries, the receptionists and mail clerks, but he never mentioned us."

Jesse Stone was another who discovered the hard way how unmovable Ahmet could be. Writer, arranger, performer and musical director for Atlantic since it was founded in 1947, Jesse had the temerity to ask Ahmet for a percentage of the company seven years later. His claim was not unreasonable, for to many Jesse *was* Atlantic, and with Herb Abramson off to do his stint for Uncle Sam, the timing seemed right. Maybe the idea of a black partner was too far ahead of its time for Ahmet to swallow, but for whatever reason he turned Jesse down flat and embraced Jerry Wexler instead. "Jesse was ripped off," his wife Evelyn told Annie Groer of the Orlando

Sentinel. "They wanted to give him a lifetime job, but he should have been a partner." Jesse gave up and packed his bags, departing in 1954 the company he'd helped to build, a paid employee to the end. Ahmet could have stopped him, but he didn't. Ray Charles moving to ABC-Paramount? That was a different matter entirely, one that Ahmet deeply resented—and one that led, directly or indirectly, to my deal there being stopped before it was even started.

As for Clyde McPhatter, I know he would rather have stayed with Atlantic because he admired Ahmet so much. It was Irving Feld, his manager, who in chasing MGM's loot engineered the initial switch. When Clyde came back from his disastrous trip to England and called Jerry Wexler in 1972, asking to be taken back, the answer from the company was no. The iron door had been slammed shut. Atlantic, it seemed, were neither into "charity cases" nor the business of forgiveness, no matter how unique the voice. Instead of the contract he wanted and the new chance it might have brought for a revived career in the States, Clyde's call resulted in a check for past services rendered. A few months after that he was dead.

"Doc" Pomus talked to the *Music Man* authors as well, describing the profound change he saw in Ahmet after the sale of Atlantic in 1967: "He became very inaccessible, tremendously preoccupied with business." Years later, in the early eighties, Doc ran into a well-oiled Ahmet at a nightclub. Ahmet was all over him, introduced him to his friends, had their photograph taken together. Doc was unimpressed by all the bonhomie and bet a friend that if he phoned Ahmet next day he wouldn't even be put through. He won that bet.

Music writer Dave Marsh told me recently of a conversation he had with Doc Pomus shortly before he passed. "The guys at Atlantic were not like the rest of them," Doc had declared. "They were better."

"Better enough?" asked Dave.

"No," Doc admitted, "but Ahmet was not Morris Levy."

"So did they stick to what the letter of their artists' contracts said?"

"No, they did not."

* * *

Jesse Jackson, never one to flinch from alerting those in office to their responsibilities, had already written to Bud Wolff at AFTRA, urging him to get more involved on behalf of his artists. Howell's new tack to put the fear of death into Atlantic was to request AF-TRA's assistance in examining the company's handling of our federally insured pension contributions. This was a real hot potato, for charging these contributions back to artists was a possible federal offense, thanks to the Taft-Hartley Act. The result was a meeting a few months later between AFTRA pension fund executives and Howell. My man was now accepted as an accredited representative of Operation PUSH. Yo, *brother!*

What followed was a communique from Robert Jaffe, AFTRA's outside counsel, indicating that the union was finally picking up the Taft-Hartley hot potato Howell had handed them on a plate. AF-TRA, Jaffe announced, would investigate potential pension claims against Atlantic on behalf of all their rhythm-and-blues artists. If it were discovered that Atlantic had failed to make adequate pension contributions on their behalf, or had unlawfully charged these artists for their contributions, the union's pension fund trustees would be authorized to institute federal action against Warner Communications. The charge, he warned, could also trigger an unfair labor practices claim. "We hope it is possible to resolve this through discussions," he concluded, adding ominously, "but there are other means of resolution."

Ahmet's emergence at Warner meetings registered a signal that some kind of settlement might be in sight. Howell called me one night to say as much. "Ruth, I think we've gotten to the point where they may be willing to give us something," he began. "If we go on, though, I believe I could take it further . . ."

"Howell, take it further," I said, "take it as far as it'll go. Sure, I could use some money right now, but what the heck, I've been broke so long it don't make no difference."

"Okay, Ruth," he agreed. "There's just one thing you have to do for me, in that case."

"Name it."

"Try to put out a few brushfires that are starting. I've had calls from several artists on our list prepared to settle for anything I can get right now. They're desperate for any cash they can get. Harold Lucas of the Clovers for one—he can't pay the property taxes on the house he's owned for years and he's being threatened with eviction. And there's a half-dozen others. If I were offered thirty-thousand dollars right now by Warner, these people's instinct would be to take it."

I promised to talk to everyone Howell had mentioned, although my heart was sinking. How could I guarantee to these folks in dire need that they wouldn't be forfeiting everything if they followed my advice and hung on? I did it anyway, but not without a lot of soul-searching.

USING THE SAME TRAIN OF THOUGHT behind his recruitment of Bonnie Raitt, Howell turned an introduction to Dan Aykroyd and Judy Jacklin Belushi, John's widow, into another campaign. Their first meeting, in April 1987, courtesy of Sam Moore and Joyce, is an occasion forever etched on Howell's mind. Dan had agreed to help out a friend of his, Isaac Tigrett, who wanted to create a media event to celebrate his Hard Rock Cafe going public. The venue they chose was none other than the venerable New York Stock Exchange; the performers were Dan with Sam Moore and the Blues Brothers Band.

Minutes after the closing bell had sounded "Sam and Dan" were stomping along the stock exchange gallery, a troop of chorus girls high-stepping, kicking and twirling on either side as the duo belted out Barrett Strong's "Money (That's What I Want)" while tossing handfuls of fake greenbacks to the crowd of financial journalists and celebrities on the floor below. I doubt if the hallowed halls had ever witnessed anything like it.

Sam, it quickly emerged, was someone Dan, a rhythm-and-blues freak from way back, cared a lot about. And having made a pile of money from *The Blues Brothers* movie and the accompanying albums —on Atlantic—Howell got the impression that both he and Judy were ready to give something back. Especially if they could have some fun into the bargain. Judy, it turned out, had a house in Martha's Vineyard, where Howell spent much of the summer. He made sure that she and Dan were kept fully apprised of the situation at Atlantic. The role they might play wasn't yet clear. All we knew for sure was that it would do no harm to have a few more powerful friends.

PUBLICIST ALAN EICHLER first came into my life soon after I returned from the West Coast in the early eighties. He made his entrance as a paying customer during my engagement at the Cookery. After the show he told me he was working freelance, looking for performers with a potential for enjoying reactivated careers. Not trading on nostalgia, he stressed, but capable of developing a whole new generation of fans, pliable enough to bloom afresh in the eighties and beyond.

The next I heard he had moved to Los Angeles and was involved with a jazz club, the Vine Street Bar and Grill, as their press agent. He organized a booking for me after *Staggerlee* ended its run. It's important to explain the differences in clubs in that city, as in many others. Vine Street was known as a *white* jazz club, predominantly but not exclusively frequented by whites, whereas the Parisien, where I had been singing when Drew Brown re-entered my life, was the other way round, predominantly but not exclusively frequented by blacks. And symptomatic of the scheme of things, the way they still are, Vine Street was regarded as the "class" joint. Its patrons were about to get their first look at Ruth Brown, complete with piano, bass and drum accompaniment.

The engagement went well and emboldened Alan to talk to another "white" club owner he knew, Bruno Fava of the Hollywood Roosevelt's Cinegrill, situated smack across from the famous Chinese Theater on Hollywood Boulevard. Bruno had managed several other clubs on his way up, and had but one question for Alan: "Who the hell's Ruth Brown?" On Alan's say-so, and playing his own hunch, he gave him the go-ahead to book me in January of '88.

It could be argued that my career as a name artist took off again from that Cinegrill base. Bruno, a shorter version of Luciano Pavarotti, was pleasantly confounded by the crowds that turned up for my opening night, jamming the lobby all the way back to the elevator. Suddenly, any trace of standoffishness in his manner melted. Leonard Feather wrote a wonderful review in the Los Angeles *Times*' Calendar section, and other favorable notices followed, together with requests for TV and press interviews. Alan got Ralph Jungheim along and that led to deal with Fantasy Records, with *Have a Good Time* emerging as my first for the label. Ken Ehrlich, the producer of Showtime's *Coast to Coast,* as well as the annual Grammy ceremony, turned up at the Cinegrill and booked me for a special. Gil Wiest, the owner of Michael's Pub in New York, came to the Cinegrill, looked, listened, had his ear bent by Alan and penciled me in for his place in March.

After Michael's Pub there was no stopping me, with more TV, more interviews, the Showtime special recorded at the Bottom Line in New York with the prolific Otis Blackwell. And, after years of speculation, the possibility of a move to Broadway for *Black and Blue.* Naturally Hector and Claudio wanted me, but the money guys had three younger women in mind for the leads, thinking that would enhance the show's appeal. They changed their minds as the name of Ruth Brown loomed larger due to the nonstop attention I was getting. The only change in the end was Carrie Smith standing in for Sandra Reeves Phillips, who was unavailable.

The release of *Hairspray* kept the momentum going, for although Motormouth Maybelle only had a few scenes, the character really seemed to lodge in people's minds. Howell was delighted with all this, for I introduced the subject of our battle with Atlantic at every opportunity during my interviews. Fighting the might of Warner from the standpoint of a poverty-stricken housewife in Long Island, or of a counted-out black lady hanging on by her fingertips uptown was one thing. From the perspective of a high-profile club performer and movie and Broadway headliner it was quite another.

BEFORE LEAVING for Los Angeles and the Cinegrill, Howell and I had organized a little bash of our own: my sixtieth birthday celebration. The place was the dear old Baby Grand, the last surviving nightclub in Harlem, and there was a dual purpose to the event. Filmmaker George T. Nierenberg had called me earlier with regard to participating in a documentary, *That Rhythm, Those Blues.*

The idea had originated in a call from Ted Fox, author of the definitive book on the Apollo. As part of a series called *The American Experience,* WGBH Public Television had first approached Ted with the idea of a program on the history of the legendary theater. Since he had no knowledge of moviemaking, Ted approached George, who did. After extensive research the project fell apart when the Apollo management decided to create something on their own. The resourceful George promptly decided to use the material he had gathered, widening the focus to cover a history of our music through the eyes of its participants.

When George put his idea to me I did not hesitate. Having already sampled his work on several occasions, I was a fully paid-up fan. I had thoroughly enjoyed *No Maps on My Taps,* his documentary on jazz tap dancing featuring four greats of the art, Howard "Sandman" Sims, Charles "Chuck" Green, Bunny Briggs from *Black and Blue,* and James "Buster" Brown. And I had returned over and over again to marvel at *Say Amen, Somebody,* his widely praised theatrical feature on gospel music.

Initially we met in the neutral territory of a coffee shop, and it was a while before I felt I knew him well enough to ask him over to my walk-up apartment. I was not ashamed of it, it was my sanctuary, but I wanted him to feel comfortable. I need not have worried. And when we met at his place he always insisted on giving me cabfare home, even though he knew darn well I would take the bus and put the extra few dollars aside. Many times, when I did not feel up to it, he would request a meeting, then keep me hanging on the phone for an hour at a time until I ran out of my repertoire of excuses and just gave in. I believe they call it persistence.

For a male counterpart in his film I suggested Charles Brown, pointing out how we had worked together and how much an integral part of the music's story he was. Through highs and lows, good times and bad, in and for the most part out of the limelight, washing dishes between little gigs here and there, Charles had hung in and refused to give up. Like so many of us.

In the weeks before the gig Charles came over to George as wounded, wary and distrustful. He was going through a real downer and George was fearful that he might duck out altogether. Thank goodness he didn't. When the two of them met I could see

Charles's trust in George's integrity grow. It was well placed, for *That Rhythm, Those Blues* did a lot to bring a wonderful artist back from obscurity. George also collared a pair of record producers in Atlantic's Jerry Wexler and Ralph Bass, the man who discovered James Brown for King Records. There were two black deejays as well, Shelly "the Playboy" Steward and the Reverend Al "Diggie Doo" Dixon, and a couple of promoters, one of them J. J. Beamon himself, still looking chipper after all those years.

I had often mentioned Charles to Howell over the years, but the Baby Grand staged his first encounter with the man and his music live, and I could tell he was mightily impressed. It was an emotional evening all round, not only because of my reaching the big six-o, but because the Baby Grand, my savior on so many occasions, named a Ruth Brown Room in my honor. Remember though, folks, we're talking showbiz.

What happened next reminded me of a legend I soaked up as a kid, the tale of the Egyptian muckety-muck whose tomb was found countless centuries after his death, surrounded by nothing but miles of sand as far as the eye could see. The inscription? " 'My name is Ozymandias, King of Kings. / Gaze upon my works, ye Mighty, and despair.' " Ozzy honey, that ain't the way it works, for you or any other mother's child! Just two weeks after my birthday bash, the Baby Grand, and the Ruth Brown Room with it, closed down for good, and was instantly transformed into a laundromat.

23

LOVE OF MY LIFE

BILLIE HOLIDAY GAVE ME one of the great lessons of my professional life. And how! People kept saying back in the early fifties that they saw more than a slight facial resemblance between me and Billie. I loved everything about Lady Day, and took that as a great compliment. While waiting impatiently for Ahmet and Herb to find the all-important follow-up hit to "So Long," I kept right on singing ballads in my act and was thrilled to land a booking at Cafe Society, the club Billie had made her own. And it was on a bill with folk singer Josh White, a close friend of Billie's. Since there was no competitiveness between me and Billie—at least I didn't think so—I hoped she might turn up to see her friend and catch my act.

Sure enough, in she slipped to the club one night, her big boxer dog Mister trotting alongside. The guy who was setting up the microphones, the legendary sound ace Johnny Garry, winked at me as she made her entrance. Well, I panicked at first. Then I got myself together and thought how overwhelmed she'd be if I sang nothing but her numbers as a tribute. Convinced I was doing the right thing, I redid my set, packing in everything I knew of Billie's. Oh, *complete* overkill!

I went from "Gloomy Sunday" to "What a Little Moonlight Can Do" and "Don't Explain," bending over backwards to show Billie how much I revered her, aiming for the exact inflections she was famous for, bending and caressing each note as she did. All through this performance I could see her table at the side of the stage where she sat, legs crossed, smoking, drinking, every inch the sophisticated lady portrayed so well in Billy Strayhorn's "Lush Life." Dressed in blue-gray chiffon, with that gardenia placed just so, she looked stunning.

As I took my bows at the end of the set she abruptly stood up, noisily pushed her table away and strode off. I was devastated. "Why'd she do that?" was the burning question on my mind. I told myself it was because she thought I was no good. The curse of Lucky Millinder! Once again I saw my career skidding to a halt before it had even got started. My life had ended, all in a split second. The great lady had seen and heard me, and she had hated it. The applause from the audience was meaningless.

As I stumbled off stage, tears blinding me, I almost tripped over Billie, who was sitting behind the curtain with Josh. "Excuse me," I said, and made to pass.

"Just a minute," she replied, fixing me with a cool—no, make that a *real* cool—stare. "Right now I know you're hurt—"

"No, I'm not," I lamely protested.

"Yes, you are," she insisted. How right she was! "Let me tell you something," she continued, "and I want you to remember this. Although you may not understand it now, every time you open your mouth and do what you just did out there, they're gonna call *my* name, not *yours*. And that's better for me, but not for you, honey. Don't get me wrong. I appreciate your likin' me so much you want to be like me. But *you* can't be me, 'cause *I'm* me, there's only one Billie Holiday. You can take my stuff and give it your own interpretation, and on a good day you might come up with somethin', 'cause you got a voice. But don't try to be someone you're not. Be yourself."

I was so mortified, brought face to face with my own stupidity. My intention to pay an artist I idolized a sincere compliment had been genuine. But I saw what she was saying, and it was a lesson I never forgot.

I saw Billie just once more after that, when she was reaching the end of her performing days. It was in a place called Pep's Showbar in Philly, a third-string joint with a bandstand above the bar. She'd lost her permit to work clubs in New York, and this was the best she could get. Just around the corner was the Showboat, the top jazz room in the city, and I found it hard to swallow that Billie was so far down she'd been forced to settle for Pep's instead. I'd appeared there in the past, and it was fine for me as a struggling act. Not for a legend like Billie.

I went backstage to see her afterwards, sat there in her cramped dressing room, looking utterly drained. Although she hardly looked up when she spoke—her attention seemed concentrated for the most part at a fixed point on the grubby floor—she was friendly enough. "Ruth, it's good to see you," she said. "Did you notice I didn't sing so loud tonight? I really made those suckers listen!" She laughed wryly. "Honey, you ready for some more advice? You should be, you did wonders with the last dose I dished out. Take a tip from me, Ruth, the more you scream the louder they'll talk. *Make* 'em listen!"

Years later—oddly enough, at Barney Josephsen's Cookery—I was about to finish a medley that included Billie's "Good Morning, Heartache." Just as I reached the last line, right at the climactic point, with the band quiet and my voice accompanied by a lone guitar, a waiter at the table directly under my nose said, "You folks all right? Can I freshen your drinks?" I almost blew up, but I smile about it now. What can you do? Billie was right, but it's not only interruptions from customers you have to look out for!

After one critic heard me doing "Good Morning, Heartache" he said, "That song's always belonged to Billie in my mind, but Ruth Brown owns a piece of it now." Rightly or wrongly. I always believed Billie was singing about her drug habit in that number. I learned a lot from her. From Dinah too. They had a way of projecting, paying attention to what was coming out of their mouths. What made Billie so great was her singing about her life. I believe it's true to say she *sang* her life. But when I do turn to wonderful songs like "Heartache" and "God Bless the Child"—and how could I not?—I'm still able to reach deep inside and let that emotion pour out. Straight from the heart and soul of no one but Ruth Brown.

As HOWELL'S MEETINGS with Ahmet and Warner's representatives continued through 1987, he and Gerry Bursey compiled a list of over a dozen accounting "irregularities" they wanted explored.

The list included foreign royalty rates, so-called free goods, packaging allowance deductions, returns, foreign tax deductions, improper reimbursement for pension and health fund contributions and, most importantly, unreported and underreported sales. Ultimately, Ahmet and his colleagues agreed to test the validity of their claims by conducting their own internal audit of just four of the alleged abuses: foreign royalty rate, free goods, packaging and foreign tax deductions. As far as unreported and underreported sales were concerned, we were by implication asking for the moon. The audit extended to just seven of Howell's clients: myself, Clyde McPhatter, the Clovers, the Coasters, the Drifters, Chuck Willis and Ivory Joe Hunter.

We were handed the results in May 1987. In total the "discrepancy" thrown up amounted to $250,000. "Okay," they finally admitted, "we got a problem. And it appears to be across the board."

Although it was a major breakthrough, there remained a lot to be hammered out. What about the session costs? Would they continue to be charged against any payout? Then there was Atlantic's claim that several years of accounting had simply disappeared. How could that be compensated? And how did we proceed from the seven artists initially chosen to cover the whole spectrum?

Ahmet was adamant on the selection process. He and he alone would do the choosing. Fine, Howell agreed, so long as it was clearly understood that every other artist not covered would have the same rights of redress based on the resultant settlements. And he insisted on a further crucial point. Whatever sums were dispensed would not interfere with the artists' ability to hold out for more if they still felt shortchanged. (Howell, you surely are a rebel and you'll never ever be any good!)

This almost stopped the show, for their acceptance of this term meant that Atlantic would be unindemnified, exposed to the possibility of further claims. In fairness to them, they swallowed it. Just as well, for Howell would have refused to have anything to do with talk of a "full and final settlement."

While Howell was often accompanied to the sessions at Warners by aides from both Jesse Jackson's Operation PUSH and Mickey Leland, the company's executives conducted their own separate meetings with Jackson and Leland. In one of them Leland suggested that as part of any settlement, since it was clear that the settlement itself was never going to be anything like fully comprehensive, some kind of grant-awarding music foundation be set up with Warner money. The idea seemed to strike a chord with Steve Ross. It grew, took hold, and when Howell and I discussed it we could see two major advantages.

First it would ensure that money found its way directly into artists' pockets. The problem with a straightforward back-payment of royalties was the slice liable to be hijacked by ex-managers and agents emerging from the woodwork at the smell of new money. There was nothing in the grant suggestion, for example, for a Chuck Rubin. Sorry, Chuck!

Second—Mickey Leland's point in the first place—was that there did not seem to be any realistic way to expect that whatever money paid out in royalty recalculations would approach the sum actually due. Money dispensed through a "Rhythm and Blues" foundation would at least begin to make up for the lost years. And the grants could be tax-free. Yep, it was a brilliant notion.

I HAVE SAID it before and I will say it again. Willis Jackson was the love of my life. I know, I *know* it was not a relationship that worked too well. So what else is new? Looking back I can see why. We were two volcanic egos, and when we both erupted at the same time, it was too much for either of us. Nevertheless, we had a love that endured through the years, on both sides. Whenever we saw each other, no matter what the circumstances or what had transpired in the meantime, we always made time to talk, and we could relate to each other and what we were going through.

I'd heard bits and pieces of his activities in between our meetings over the years, for in the tight little world of the business many people had felt it their bound duty to fill me in, as well as assuring me that Willis knew he'd made a mistake in letting me go. Maybe they thought that was what I wanted to hear, maybe they were right, I only know that whenever someone told me something like, "He says he really misses Shorty," my insides just melted. When I heard that, I could bypass all the stuff that was not so hot and remember only the good things. And every time I listened to the music we made together, naturally I thought of him.

I had the strangest encounter with someone close to Willis soon after returning from Paris in 1986. I was walking my little Yorkshire terrier Miss Bebe around the block—the cast of *Black and Blue* had presented me with the pet at the end of our run—when a lady came walking towards me with a chihuahua. Their leads got all tangled up as we drew alongside, and we laughed and stopped to talk as the two little critters skittered around each other. At the same time I had the strangest feeling that I should be careful what I said.

"Cute little dog," I remarked.

"Isn't he?" she replied. "I got him from Paris."

"Oh? I just got back from working there."

"Really? You're in show business?"

"Sort of."

"That's interesting. My husband's in show business. You probably know him. His name's Willis Jackson."

My heart turned over. "I heard the name," I managed to reply. "He's a musician, right?"

"Yep, he plays tenor sax."

Somehow I got through the next twenty minutes or so of small talk, although my mind was racing. Willis and she were still living in the house on 163rd and St. Nicholas we had shared all those years ago, just a few blocks from my 165th Street apartment.

Six months later I was out exercising the dog again when I saw a man walking in front that looked so much like Willis. Except oh, he had lost so much weight. His overcoat just hung around him, and under the cap he wore even his head looked shrunk. A week or so later I saw the same man, and this time I could not resist calling out his name. It was Willis, and he really had shrunk to skin and bones.

"Shorty!" he hailed me. "What the hell're you doin' here?" It was quite a contrast to the last time we had seen each other, on a Circle Line jamboree on the Hudson River with my band. He was sitting in with Red Prysock—the two were buddies as well as rivals—and although I could see he had lost a little weight, he had never sounded better. He gave no signs then of having fallen on hard times, and I only heard later he had been forced to pawn his precious horn and sell his car. He played that night with a sax borrowed from Red. We did not talk, for he was on the opposite side of the boat from me. And I suspect his wife must have been on board with him. When he got into "Can't Help Loving That Man" and our eyes met, however, words were unnecessary. When the boat approached the Statue of Liberty he managed to sneak a friendly wave.

Now he was on the way to the hospital for dialysis treatment, but we stopped and sat for a while on a park bench. "Where you livin' now, Shorty?" he asked. "Hey, I'll bet you're down on the East Side where all those rich folks are."

"Is that right? No, Gator, I'm right around the corner facing your hospital door."

"You married, Shorty?"

"No, Gator, there's just me."

"You pullin' my leg? Fine-lookin' gal like you? I'll bet you're fightin' them off!"

"If I am, I just don't know it."

From then on I looked for him on the days of the week, Mondays, Wednesdays and Fridays, when he went for treatment. One day he said, "Shorty, would you mind if I dropped by your place after the hospital?"

"Why?" I asked, teasing him. "You got something on your mind, Gator?"

"I have," was his unexpected reply. "Shorty, you still got a wire to God? I really need some help. I need to know if it's still possible for me to be favored in God's eyes."

"All you gotta do is to ask and it shall be given."

"But you know what my thing has been over the years," he protested. "I ain't been no prayin' person."

"Gator, you have nothing to do at this point except to say you are sorry, ask for forgiveness and start again. That's all you got to do. The Lord says if you acknowledge Him secretly, He will reward you openly."

That was the beginning of our inspirational talks, on the park bench, sometimes in my little apartment, often on my stoop, just as we had done in the old days at Uncle Monk's. One day he burst out laughing after several moments' silence. "You know, you're funny, girl," he said. "What the hell is it after all these years that keeps us runnin' and bumpin' into each other? Why can't I stay out of your life and you stay out of mine?''

"Good question," I replied.

I never asked him about his domestic arrangements and he never offered, we really had gone beyond that. Our companionship was all that was important, and it truly seemed a miracle in my life that I had my man back again. I questioned neither the circumstances nor the lack of physicality, and there was no jealousy involved in knowing he was living with another woman. It was just pure, true love, and it was purely, truly beautiful.

One day I waited and waited on the park bench and he never showed. After an hour or so I went back to my apartment, and that night I got a call from Willis in the hospital. "They kept me in," he explained. "Well, it'll save me dragging myself back and forth three times a week. Shorty, why don't you come 'round and let's talk some?"

Although it was after visiting hours nobody stopped me as I followed his instructions and made straight for his floor and ward. A skeletal figure in a bathrobe was sitting on his bed, an I.V. drip dangling alongside. "Oh, excuse me," I said, heading for the door, "I must have the wrong room."

"Shorty," came the voice, "do I look *that* bad?"

"Gator," I replied, turning quickly, "you know perfectly well I know you. I was just trying to be funny." It was the bathrobe that had thrown me, for in it he looked so decimated.

"I didn't think you recognized me"—the ghost of a smile—" 'cause I've put on so much weight."

We both laughed, but he knew the truth. "Shorty," he went on, his deep voice dropping, "the day you don't recognize me is the day I just ought to be dead."

"Come on, I wasn't doin' nothin' but playin', I knew you! Hey, let's face it, you ain't no cuter!"

That really cracked him up, and as we touched hands I added, "You'd do anything to get attention, wouldn't you?" He chuckled again, then winced as he gestured at the I.V. "Hey, don't make me laugh so much," he pleaded. "This thing hurts!"

"Sorry."

"Okay. Listen, I know we've been through the Scriptures together, but I have to tell you there's one line in there I just can't swallow. It says *ashes to ashes, dust to dust,* but Shorty, I don't never want to be put in no fire. The thought makes me real scared."

"I have no control over that," I told him. "Besides, you ain't gonna die, you're way ahead of yourself. You're too mean for that. And you ain't goin' away and leave me. How you gonna manage without your Shorty somewhere 'round?"

The subject of Drew Brown's re-emergence never came up, and as far as Willis knew it was status quo with Ronnie. My son called him up in hospital, and when Willis got too morose Ronnie told him, "Hey, you'd better not die, 'cause you and I ain't had time to do nothin' together." Willis told me that had really lifted him up.

One night, early in October 1987, he phoned from the hospital. He sounded terribly low. "Shorty, I can't read no more," he told me. "I got the Bible here, but my eyes are goin'."

I went round and read a few passages for him, like the Book of Proverbs, the 139th Psalm: *Lord, you know my going and my coming, You know every bed on which I lay my body.* It was his favorite, and we talked and talked until he got too tired.

A few days later I took a call in my apartment. It was Ivan "Loco" Rolls, Willis's friend from boyhood. "Ruth, they amputated Gator's legs this morning," he told me. As I put the phone down I knew that was it. Willis would give up, he was too proud and independent to live that way.

The following Sunday I attended the little Emmanuel Baptist AME on 155th and Amsterdam that I often sneaked into just to hear the choir. The service was almost over, the preacher was doing the recessional and preparing for the benediction, when I clearly heard Willis's voice calling me. Riding home on the bus I heard it again. "Shorty, Shorty . . ."

Mama had always told me never to answer a voice like that, but I had to. Although it was my first visit to the hospital during regular visiting hours, I made straight for Columbia-Presbyterian and presented myself at reception, where I gave my name. The clerk looked through her records and shook her head. "I'm truly sorry, Miss Brown"—she could see how upset I looked—"but I have a list of approved visitors here and you are not included. I cannot allow you to go up."

"It's got to be a mistake. I've known—"

"It's no mistake," the clerk told me. "I didn't want to say this, but your name's marked down special *not* to be admitted. It's more than my job is worth to let you in."

As soon as I got home I took my hat off and called Willis's room. There was no answer. It was like a rerun of my mother's death, for I was calling from the same apartment. Swallowing hard, I looked up his number and dialed Loco.

"Ruth, Gator's gone," he told me.

"Gone *where?*" I screamed.

"He passed an hour ago."

I wept, I prayed for him, I wept again, I called my boys, I wept and prayed.

Willis's funeral service was held in St. Peter's, the church where all musicians, entertainers and peddlers of the 'Devil's music' are accepted. My wreath was a bleeding heart of roses, with an arrow through the center. Pastor John Gensell, the famous "jazz priest," was conducting the service and I sent ahead a eulogy Ronnie and I had composed that I hoped would be read out. When I arrived at the church Pastor John took me to one side. "Ruth, I hate to tell you this," he said, "but I've been asked by Willis's wife not to read your eulogy. Nor is your name to be called. And she wants you seated right at the back of the church."

My first reaction was outrage. What the hell did she mean? Was she going to act as if I had never existed as far as Willis was concerned? I had known there was no question of my singing at Willis's service, that Melba Joyce was doing that, but a simple little eulogy? Then I calmed down as I thought about it. If that was what she wanted, maybe that was her privilege. It was not kind, but who said she had to be kind?

I took my place at the back while one by one new arrivals greeted me with, "Ruth, what're you doing back here? Come on up with us." I shook my head each time until a face from the past made me an offer I could not refuse. It was the face I had last seen backstage at *Staggerlee,* the face of the man Howell and I were threatening with court action.

"Are you kidding?" Ahmet asked when he saw me sat there. "You come here, Ruth, you sit with me, and don't dare argue."

This time I meekly obeyed, taking his hand and walking down the aisle with him.

Up there with Ahmet in the dignitaries' pew, raised three levels high, there was no way anyone could miss us. After all the unpleasantness we were going through, it was like old times sitting by his side, brought together in mourning as if the intervening years had never happened. On the altar of flowers was the photograph of Willis in his prime, the one he had signed, "To Shorty with the big brown eyes, eyes I'll be looking in 'til the day I die."

I might have accepted not having my name called in deference to his widow's wishes, but without exception every single musician who stepped forward to deliver their own tribute mentioned the name of Ruth Brown. Ahmet capped it all with his speech.

"It was a lucky day for the world and for all of us at Atlantic Records the day that Ruth Brown brought Willis Jackson to us," he declared. "Not only did she bring him, she gave us an ultimatum. No Willis, no Ruth. She insisted we sign him, we really had no choice. She had the power then and called the shots, but let me tell you how happy we are that she did. The sound behind Ruth on all her great records was the tenor sax of Willis Jackson, and he laid down some mean tracks on his own as well."

When he paused and turned to me at this, the tears were streaming down my face.

"Thank you, Ruth," he said, "for allowing me the privilege to have known Willis Jackson."

Truly the Lord works in mysterious ways!

ALMOST SIX YEARS after Willis's passing I recorded an album in March 1993, at M&I Studios in New York. I called it *The Songs of My Life,* for it featured many of the songs that had meant so much to me personally over the years. I included the number that started it all for me back at the Apollo's Amateur Night, "It Could Happen To You," the song that was Daddy's favorite, "They Say," Billie's "God Bless the Child," the beautiful song Eric Clapton introduced, "Tears in Heaven," Lena's "Stormy Weather"—and naturally, "Can't Help Lovin' That Man," the tune that Willis had made our own.

The only accompaniment on the last tune was Rodney Jones's acoustic guitar and a tenor saxophone, and let me tell you, when Robert Kenmotsu came in with his horn it was like a ghost had entered the room. The musicians were so moved we had to stop the session and start again.

The lyric that says it all, though, was reserved for the final number. *I'll be seeing you* . . .

24

ATLANTIC SETTLES

A MAJOR SURPRISE for me in the late fifties was the re-emergence of a name from the past. None other than Mr. Lavoisier Lamar. I called him after hearing he was in charge of the Newark, New Jersey, YMCA, having served his time for Alvin's killing. I explained that little Ruthie Weston was now Ruth Brown, how grateful I'd been to have had the benefit of his early encouragement, how sorry I was that things had turned out the way they had. "It's all right," he told me, "you were just a kid and it was nothing to do with you. I've served what was required of me, now I'm just concerned with getting my children through college. When that's done I'm going to take off and try to see the world 'fore I die."

He was back in the business of helping young children—one of his protegés went on to become mayor of Newark—and he said he was busy organising an annual benefit lunch, the proceeds intended to send needy kids to summer camp and other such endowments. I attended that lunch every year until he retired, and nobody could understand why I did that. It was simple. He had paid a terrible price for the perfectly innocent encouragement he had given me, and what was done was done and never could be undone. But that was in the past, and there was no reason why he should keep on paying.

A WEEK BEFORE the Bottom Line gig for Showtime in February 1988, Annie Groer invited Howell and myself along as guests to the annual Washington correspondents' dinner at the White House. It's customary now, I believe, for an eclectic group of guests to be asked to these affairs. It was much less common then, and I asked Annie as we drove over why she had invited me. "Believe me, Ruth," she said, "if I had to choose between spending an evening chatting to the assistant deputy under-secretary in charge of paper clips, or spending time with Miss Rhythm and Blues, it's no contest. Besides, the more you're seen around, the better. And there's one guy in particular tonight you've simply got to meet."

With *Hairspray* making waves and Motormouth Maybelle the current toast, I felt a bit like a split personality. Whatever that was, following President Reagan's speech we had a visitor at our table, ushered over by Annie in no time flat. Lee Atwater was a dashing young man who professed to be both an R-and-B fanatic *and* an ardent John Waters fan; naturally he had seen *Hairspray* and was simply bubbling over with enthusiasm. He was also, of course, George Bush's campaign manager, and kept staring at me admiringly. "We really should try to organize something, Ruth," he declared. It seemed another case of yeah, yeah, yeah. He was obviously genuine, but at the time I regarded the incident as an interesting diversion, nothing more. Sure, it was election year, but who knew that Bush would win? A surefire bet named Michael Dukakis was beginning to hit the headlines at the time.

Howell flew to New Orleans a couple of months later to rendezvous with Bonnie Raitt, set for a guest date at a Little Feat concert, part of the city's annual Jazz and Heritage Festival. Seeking Bonnie's agreement to become involved as an active member of the Rhythm and Blues Foundation when it was officially formed, he took with him the list of thirty-five artists Ahmet had just produced as a dramatic illustration of how far the battle with Atlantic had progressed. Names in there like John Lee Hooker's did much to persuade Bonnie to sign on.

Little Feat's outdoor concert, unfortunately, took place in the middle of a torrential downpour, thinning the crowd down to a few diehards. One who was standing a yard or two away from Howell, a trash bag protecting him from the worst of the elements, looked familiar. Lee Atwater had claimed to be a great fan of the music.

Here was proof that he was the genuine article. On this occasion business cards were exchanged. Well, it was progress of a sort.

ATLANTIC VIRTUALLY HANDED US a locked-in timetable for a settlement when, six months before the event, they began to trumpet their Fortieth anniversary gala. Planned for Madison Square Garden in May 1988, it was to be a fourteen-hour megashow, featuring all their leading artists, past and present. My Showtime buddy Ken Ehrlich was one of the producers, with an HBO special planned for cable, followed by a network airing on ABC.

When Howell broke the news of the upcoming marathon, my reaction was, "Well, they sure can't do that without me!" How could they be trumpeting their enormous artistic success with a gang of impoverished people standing outside, noses pressed against the windowpane, chorusing "We, Who Have Nothing"? Sure enough, they called about my appearing. Despite what was going on, there was no reason to play dog in the manger. This was one gig I had no intention of missing.

Just before Atlantic's bash Howell finally reached agreement with Warner on all the details of our royalty recalculations. Like many great victories, it was a compromise. All of our "debts," our session costs, would be wiped out. In exchange for that, as well as for the setting up of the Rhythm and Blues Foundation—capable of awarding grants to both Atlantic and non-Atlantic artists—the backdated repayment would be for only eighteen years, from 1988 to 1970. This, of course, neatly excluded our best-selling period in the fifties. Nevertheless, $250,000 had been set aside for payment to the initial seven artists and their estates, and Atlantic had agreed to begin immediately to conduct the same limited audits on behalf of twenty-eight additional pioneer artists who'd recorded for the label in the fifties and sixties.

When I got my check it was just as well I was sitting down, for otherwise I'd have *fallen* down. My first money from Atlantic since that handout in the sixties! Thirty-thousand dollars may not sound like a fortune, but it's nearly forty times more than the figure that had been yanked out of the air in 1983. And now I get royalties *each year* that multiply many times what Atlantic had claimed covered *twenty* years. One reason: every artists' master is now on their data-processing system.

And there was more welcome news, for a number of artists affected by Atlantic's recalculations, including me, suddenly discovered they had health insurance again. Under AFTRA rules health insurance is stopped when an artist's earnings drop below $5,000 a year. The pity is it arrived too late to save Big Joe, who had been forced to keep performing long after his strength was gone.

Even with all this good will swilling around, Howell felt unable to relax. The Rhythm and Blues Foundation would be set up to present tax-free grants in recognition of artists' contributions to their music. They would be non-refundable, and able to be handed over in cases of need, to pay for medical or funeral expenses, whatever. And there would be cash awards presented annually for trailblazing music pioneers. There would also, of course, be a concerted effort to get every other label in the industry to commit to the royalty recalculation process Atlantic had agreed to, as well as gaining general industry-wide support.

All that was fine in principle, unless Warner Communications Inc., believed that the foundation would be a mere puppet organization, with them pulling all the strings. And Howell had been unable to get the company to put a figure on the extent of their charitable contribution.

Not only that, but with the countdown continuing to the Fortieth Anniversary Gala, Warner continued to hold back a formal announcement of both the recalculations and the establishment of the foundation itself. We came to realize that once the bash was over much of our clout would be gone. The opportunity for backtracking simply had to be closed off.

HOWELL SOUGHT AN URGENT MEETING at Warner to discuss the potential composition of the Rhythm and Blues Foundation board of trustees. Their nominees were Vice-president of Community Relations Tom Draper and, naturally, Ahmet.

With that under his belt Howell went off on a recruitment campaign of his own. He'd gotten to know Judy Belushi at Martha's Vineyard since their first meeting at the Hard Rock launch. Along with Bill Murray and Michael Douglas, Dan Ackroyd was set to em-cee Atlantic's fortieth anniversary party. What better chairman of the board if Dan could be coaxed into taking over? Judy agreed to be the initial co-chairperson and was instrumental in bringing in Dan.

Like Dan and Judy, the other appointees Howell wooed and won, with considerable help from the resourceful, won't-take-no-for-an-answer Joyce McRae, were calculated to convey the message to Warner that this was no paper tiger they were creating. The names encompassed industry-wide experience:

Bonnie Raitt

Ray Benson, Grammy award-winning singer/songwriter of "Asleep At the Wheel"

Jay Berman, ex-Warner executive, now president of the RIAA (Recording Industry Association of America)

Phyllis Garland, professor of journalism at Columbia University

Gerri Hirshey, freelance music writer and author of the ac-claimed history of soul music, *Nowhere to Run*

Reverend Jesse Jackson of Operation PUSH

Congressman Mickey Leland, who had provided such a vital link

Dave Marsh, feature writer for Rolling Stone, music critic and Bruce Springfield biographer

Kendall Minter, entertainment attorney and executive director of the Black Entertainment and Sports Lawyers Association

"Doc" Pomus, legendary songwriter and lyricist, composer with Mort Shuman of over a hundred hits, including "Save the Last Dance for Me," "This Magic Moment," and "Suspi-cion"

David Sanborn, eminent jazz/blues musician

Isaac Tigrett, founder of the Hard Rock Cafe and owner of the largest collection of rock 'n' roll memorabilia in the world

Dionne Warwick, Arista Records veteran with a career span-ning four decades

Louise West, music publisher and active member of the Black Music Association

Howell Begle
Joyce McRae

People like myself and other early artists were purposely excluded during the early stages of the foundation, to avoid conflict of interest when grants policy was on the agenda.

With only days to go before the Atlantic bash would remove the pressure on Warner, Howell contacted the Washington *Post*'s Richard Harrington, who had earlier written a not-unflattering profile of Ahmet. When Harrington approached him again Ahmet must have assumed it would be more of the same and agreed to talk. Instead, Richard managed to pry from him a declaration of the amount of Atlantic's contribution, as well as confirmation of the recalculation deal. Then he was off like a bat out of hell, garnering quotes from other startled Warner executives.

At last, with just forty-eight hours to go, there it was, officially, undeniably, unbacktrackably in big, beautiful, bold Washington *Post* print:

ATLANTIC'S BOW TO THE BLUES HERITAGE:
Label Is Recalculating Past Royalty Payments and Committing $1.5 Million to Rhythm and Blues Foundation

I had to look again to make sure it wasn't $15,000 or $150,000. No, it was a cool *$1.5 million.*

Bob Morgado was at pains to stress that the company was merely responding to a combination of artistic merit and financial need, and admitted to no deliberate wrongdoing. "There is no obligation on the part of companies to entertain audit challenges that are twenty and thirty years old," he declared, blithely overlooking that RICO, if pursued, would have neatly overstepped these limitations. He conceded that Atlantic had been "founded on black music at a time when the business was neither as sophisticated nor as economically healthy as it is today. Many of the artists who had a lot to do with the development of modern pop music, and with the creation of the business for us, never really participated in the economic fortunes of that business. Now there is a way to compensate for

their contributions, either through adjustments, through re-re-
leases we put out, or the foundation to handle grants.''

While some referred to Atlantic's old ways of dealing with their
black acts as ''plantation accounting,'' Howell was magnanimous
enough to give them their due. ''No one should think that Atlantic
was any worse than other folks,'' he declared. ''It's just that with
management still in place there we at least had a hope that we
could approach people and they'd understand what happened because they were there. Anybody else, all they bought was a catalog.''

If Howell had impressed me up to that point, it was nothing
compared to seeing him in action at Madison Square Garden. He
constantly amazes me, not only with his business smarts, but because he really is one of the kindest and most caring people I've
ever met. With potentially millions in back royalties secured, properly calculated future royalties guaranteed, vital health insurance
reinstated and $1.5 million set aside for the foundation, you might
be forgiven for thinking he'd be content to rest on his laurels.
Don't you believe it!

In the electric atmosphere generated by the impressive parade of
past and present superstars, a euphoric Dan Aykroyd—fresh from
performing a knockout ''Soul Man'' on stage with Sam Moore
(''Sam and Dan'' ride again!) as well as tearing it up with Phil
Collins—was collaring every reporter in a five-mile radius and telling them all what a wonderful organization he'd be chairing.
Amidst all this it seemed to dawn on Bob Morgado that, hey, this
could really be something worthwhile! I'm sure he had sudden visions of the acres of good press being generated, and I watched as
he leaned over to Howell.

''Gee, Howell, you're going to need some money to operate this
organization of yours,'' he murmured. ''What good is one and a
half million if you don't have any operating capital?''

So quick it took my breath away, Howell responded, ''A very
good point, Bob. Do you have a figure in mind?''

''Oh, something like four hundred fifty thousand,'' Morgado replied, a little taken aback at this literal response.

''Right!'' said Howell.

''Over a three-year period, of course—''

''Of course!'' Without missing a beat Howell looked around, saw

Receiving the first Rhythm & Blues Foundation Achievement Award, November 1989, from Congressman John Conyers.
(Courtesy of Ruth Brown)

Richard Harrington nearby and hauled him over. "Would you care to repeat that, Bob?" he asked. Morgado did, and next day there it was in the Washington *Post*, rapidly becoming my favorite paper: "Warner Pledges $450,000 to Run Rhythm and Blues Foundation."

I believe it's called striking while the iron is hot.

My cup was full and running over. "Hey, we really started something back in 'eighty-three," I remarked to Howell.

"No, Ruth," he replied, *"you* really started something twenty-odd years ago!"

After my involvement in the dispute with the label for close on two decades, and being repeatedly told—even warned—how ill-advised it was, there was a sense of relief as well as triumph in the welter of emotions I felt now that it was over. Howell had brought off the seemingly impossible. He had fought the good fight for me, he had fought for my fellow artists, he had fought for the music he had grown up with and loved. There was so much more involved than money, and it was a feeling I find hard to put into a single word or phrase. I had held out for what I was convinced was my due in monetary terms, but there had always been that greater consideration.

Atlantic had tried to deny the very existence of the people who'd made them worth the $17 million plus that Warner/Seven Arts had paid, the artists who'd provided them with a matchless catalog of lasting value. The company hadn't produced these records in a vacuum, twiddling the knobs on some computer. Their sounds had soared from the throats of real people, artists who had suffered for their art, who had been dirt poor and may have mismanaged the sudden rush of money and fame that came their way—most of the former, God knows, from performing, not from royalties—but who nonetheless needed a fair deal now to compensate for their being shortchanged in the past.

Token recognition is one thing, but you can't take that to the bank, it don't buy no groceries. Ahmet hadn't settled for token recognition when he'd sold his company in 1967. So why should we? Now the record had been set as straight as it was ever going to be. My dignity, and that of dozens of fellow artists, had been restored at last.

COME JUNE all the foundation had received in funding was a $5,000 contribution from Isaac Tigrett, on the strength of which Howell had hired Gloria Beck, a former Al Gore aide, as a full-time staffer. A month later I headlined a benefit concert in Martha's Vineyard that Howell put together with Dan and Judy. When Warner's checks still hadn't been received by September, four months after their extravaganza, Howell called a board meeting.

Chairman Dan Aykroyd, looking like a refugee from the set of *Easy Rider,* was accompanied by Larry Bilzarian, a leather-clad motorcycle buddy who announced he was acting as Isaac Tigrett's proxy. Others in attendance included Judy Belushi, Bonnie Raitt, Joyce McRae, Ray Benson, "Doc" Pomus, Dave Marsh and Gerri Hirshey. Judging by the reaction of the Warners contingent, their august boardroom had never seen anything quite like it. Unabashed, Howell produced a snazzy press kit listing the aims of the foundation. It was in the form of a twelve-inch album cover displaying a record more than slightly warped. The heading, "Setting the Record Straight," was followed by our manifesto. It ran:

In the beginning there was Rhythm and Blues. Way back, long before Billy Joel was touring the Soviet Union, before Michael Jackson was moonwalking across Japan—even before the Beatles had half the free world glued to the *Ed Sullivan Show,* you had Ruth Brown rocking 'em dead from the flatbed of a tobacco truck. Ray Charles was rolling out some of the sweetest gospel harmonies ever heard from a church in Greenville, Florida. James Brown, LaVern Baker and the Drifters were making jukeboxes sing like never before. An extraordinary group of musicians was laying down the beat to what was to become the soundtrack to our lives.

Back then it was called Rhythm and Blues. Today it's better known as Rock and Roll. But what it really has become is big business. Popular music is now a $5.5 billion industry with an enormous international following.

It was a whole different world when the Coasters were recording classics like "Searchin' " and "Charlie Brown." A world without major arena tours. Without mega-hype and national media blitzes. Without MTV. It was an industry in its infancy.

Today popular musicians are backed by teams of lawyers, agents and accountants. But artists like Wilson Pickett and Sam and Dave had little more behind them than a tight rhythm section. After all, who would have thought this crazed new music would be around for more than a few years anyway?

To make matters worse, over the years most original recording companies have merged, been bought out or gone out of business. Contracts have been lost. Catalogs have changed hands. Inflation has taken its toll.

And the bottom line is, the people who began it all have very little to show but memories. That's why the Rhythm and Blues Foundation was created.

The Foundation has a board of trustees comprised of a broad range of people, all sharing a common interest in rhythm and blues. One of our first goals is to establish a grantmaking program to recognize the achievement of these early artists. We expect to work closely with existing labels, in fact Atlantic/Warner has already pledged generous support to this end.

A spin-off of this program would be the creation of a professional support system for previously overlooked artists, whereby the Foundation would underwrite such things as press kits and booking agents, as well as set up tours for these artists.

As Dan Aykroyd puts it, "We all enjoy the music, but there hasn't been a method to go back and materially appreciate what the music has brought us. The Rhythm and Blues Foundation provides the method."

It's the way we can start to set the record straight.

"Stunned" would be a fair way to describe the reaction of the Warner contingent to the presentation. Whatever their vision for the foundation had been, Howell had seized the initiative and run with it, turning Mama's "stumbling blocks into stepping stones, problems into challenges."

Howell went on to announce the scheduling of the foundation's first major fundraiser, a concert to be held in Austin, Texas. Willie Nelson, he explained, had donated the use of his Opera House, and set to appear were Bonnie, Stevie Ray Vaughan, Nick Lowe, the Fabulous Thunderbirds, Chuck Jackson, the Clovers and Ruth Brown.

If Atlantic had entertained the notion that the Rhythm and Blues Foundation would be a tame poodle, Howell was clearly intent on building a different beast. "Oh, by the way, Ahmet," he added, "we'd like *you* to be our emcee in Austin. And it sure would be good to have Atlantic's contribution by then."

Ahmet Ertegun has been responsible for selling a lot of records in his lifetime. If the expression on his face could have been captured at that moment, it too would have sold a million copies.

Wonder of wonders, the $1.5 million check arrived from the mighty Warner three days before the Austin concert. There was no sign of the first $150,000 pledged for running costs. That didn't turn up until a full nine months later in June 1989. For now, though, the heat was off.

The show itself was a blast. Although we had never rehearsed together, Bonnie joined me on stage when I sang "Since I Fell for You," playing slide guitar and duetting. We raised $45,000 that night and grabbed a lot of attention. Newsweek did an article headed, "One for the Soul Survivors: Righting Old Wrongs in the Music Business" that really touched my heart.

Reporter Bill Barol led off with a plea from Howell that all record companies take a leaf out of Atlantic's book and accept the same moral responsibility, whether or not they were on safe ground legally. "Other maturing industries that have had dramatic salary increases," he argued, "like football, baseball, whatever, have all found a way to take some of the profits from today and funnel them back to the people who made it possible. The labels that are profiting from this very successful business ought to find a way to do that. You just have to look at the dollars these people got. When the Coasters did "Searchin'," which went on to sell 2 million copies in its first year of release, they got a $65 advance. *Four guys split 65 bucks!* It isn't hard to figure out that maybe if the song still has legs twenty-five years later, something else is in order."

Chuck Jackson put it another way: "A lot of guys never got theirs. What they got was like drippings from a beehive full of honey. What we're trying to do here is attack the beehive and get some of the *real* honey."

Barol was lyrical about the program's highlights, but still managed to pick out the small, eloquent moments that for him showed how blues and R and B can bring people together against tough times: young Joe Harris standing in with the Clovers for Bill, his gravely ill dad; Bonnie's deeply felt slide work behind me. He quoted Bonnie as saying, "There's a lot to do. You can't change everything overnight, and there are wrongs that have been going on for years. But what we can do is try to get some recognition from the younger generation for these great musicians we grew up loving."

Watching us embrace at center stage as the audience went crazy, Barol reported he couldn't help feeling that both the present and the future of rhythm and blues were in good hands. Finally, he signed off, it was time now to take care of the past.

Amen to that!

25

"AIN'T NO BAND PLAYIN' THIS TIME"

MY LIFE HAS BEEN FILLED with so many unforgettable characters. One, I'm proud to say, was the awesomely talented Lester "Prez" Young. Another was the wonderful Charlie "Bird" Parker. Then there was my own Dave Crew.

Prez was a gent who never bothered anybody. Long as his red plaid carpet bag was stocked with his favorite Johnnie Walker Red, he was happy. He addressed everyone as "Lady," regardless of their sex. I was Lady Brown, Chickie was Lady Horne, Mr. B was Lady Eckstine. Chickie wondered for a while if Prez was "in the life" himself, but there was never any sign of it, and I'm sure Effie Throckbottom would have known had it been the case.

Prez invariably wore a porkpie hat and straw shoes that creaked like crazy. You could hear him coming a mile away. Thelma heard his unmistakable "e-r-k, e-r-k, e-r-k" one night as he creaked his way along to our hotel bathroom, clad only in his trademark hat, shoes and a pair of boxer shorts covered with signs of the zodiac. Before they passed each other she couldn't help noticing an amazing bulge on one side of his shorts that was hanging mighty, mighty low. He caught her looking and said, "Oh, don't worry, Lady Manley, that's where I keep my stash."

We had a nickname for Prez that derived from an incident in

Austin, Texas. The sign outside our hotel said, "Rooms With, $15; Without $12." We assumed, reasonably enough, that it meant with and without private bath, and I was determined, being the big cheese that I was, to have me a $15 special. Prez got to reception ahead of me. "Look, I'm tired," he explained to the clerk. "Just give me a twelve-dollar room and let me get up there to sleep."

As the rest of us checked in, we heard the distinctive "e-r-k, e-r-k, e-r-k" of Prez's shoes as he made his way back downstairs. "What in hell's goin' on here?" he yelled at the clerk. "That room you've given me has no damn window! You've put me in a goddamn closet!"

It dawned on all of us what the sign meant—with and without *windows!* Thereafter, as far as our troupe was concerned, Prez was known as "Fifteen With, Twelve Without"!

While all this was going on, young Thelma was, just possibly, on the brink of womanhood. I tell you, her date with Charlie Parker had us all on edge. Would she or wouldn't she? If she did, Bird had himself a real scoop, for Thelma, bless her, had acquired a third nickname by this time, "the Virgin Queen." (This made Chickie really cross. "That title should be mine!" he protested. Way too much, some of us felt.)

Bird was experimenting with string accompaniment at the time and on the bills we shared he'd really taken a shine to our Thelma. I knew she was fond of him too, for when Bird wanted to, he exuded an old-world charm that was devastatingly effective. I saw her out walking with him and his small son one afternoon. They made a fine-looking couple, and that night she obviously had something other than ironing my dresses on her mind. "Miss B," she finally began, "Charlie's asked me out to dinner after the show. Is it okay for me to go?"

"It depends," I replied. "Are you asking me as Ruth Brown, entertainer, or as someone your parents put their trust in?"

"Don't worry," said my little dresser. "I'll behave, you know me. I like Charlie's company, that's all."

"In that case," I told her, "go and enjoy yourself. But be careful, I hear he's a lot to handle."

"That's okay," Thelma replied. Then, absolutely deadpan: "Believe it, I won't be handlin' anything that don't belong to me."

Next day we got the whole story. Bird had been charming company all through dinner, which for him had been two dinners, and in the taxi afterwards he suggested a nightcap in his hotel room. Nervous as she was, Thelma decided she would go that far. Once they were settled he poured their drinks, eased himself down into a big, comfy sofa next to the stiff-backed chair she chose, produced his stash and began rolling a joint. "Care for a smoke?" he asked my poor innocent. Thelma shook her head. "No? Well, why not take your shoes off and relax a little bit?"

"I'm fine."

"Aw, c'mon. Relax, we've got all night." He patted the cushion beside him. "An' why don't you come over here and get comfortable?"

The phrase *all night* immediately started red lights flashing for our girl. And *comfortable* was the exact opposite of how she was feeling. "I think I should be going," she told him.

"But I told the guys at reception that you're my wife. C'mon, Thelma, don't let me down."

"You told them *what?* Well, you'll just have to tell them your wife got angry and left."

That produced a deep-throated chuckle from Bird, on whom it was rapidly dawning that the game was up. Shrugging, he lifted his considerable bulk from the sofa, walked Thelma downstairs like a true gentleman, gave her a gentle kiss on the lips and put her in a cab.

After she had related her story, I mischievously suggested that maybe she had shortchanged Bird. "Oh, no," she protested, "I ain't goin' home with nuthin' I didn't come here with!" That was my Thelma. When she did eventually fall she fell hard, but that's her story and I guess you'll have to wait for her book to hear about that.

With Dave Crew, unfortunately, there will be no book. Preparing to drive from New York to the Paradise in Detroit in 1959, with Brook Benton on board, Dave asked to be excused. "I don't feel well," he explained, "and I just can't face the journey." I knew right away something had to be far wrong, for this was a man who drove fifteen hours at a stretch without complaint. "Don't worry," was the last thing he told me. "I'll get a later bus and be there before you open tomorrow."

As soon as we checked in to our hotel I phoned Dave's home to see how he was. Dave was dead. He had, it seemed, suffered from edema and high blood pressure, and he had collapsed soon after reaching home. We were all devastated, Mama too, when I broke the news. It turned out she'd had a quiet crush on Dave, the true gentleman who'd been my close friend and adviser, as well as road manager, for close on a decade.

MANY TIMES WHEN I TALKED to Howell in 1988 one name kept popping up: Lee Atwater. After their April meeting in New Orleans he had invited Howell along to a picnic being held on George Bush's vice-presidential lawn for their campaign workers. He had already contacted the Clovers' Bill Harris to organize a band for the occasion, and Bill, bless him, turned out from his hospital bed, still wearing his blue plastic I.D. bracelet, for the gig.

Accompanied by Annie Groer, Howell watched Atwater take the stage and was blown away. Although he'd discovered that he once had been featured in Percy Sledge's band, the sight of Bush's campaign manager playing guitar on his back, then leaping to his feet and performing nifty James Brown splits, was something else again. This guy wasn't just a fan, he was a *fanatic*.

Come August, Lee asked Howell to help him put together a blues bill for the Republican Convention in New Orleans. This was the major jamboree for press heavyweights, and as he watched the likes of Diane Sawyer and Ed Bradley jivin' and arrivin' to the sounds of Johnny Adams, Irma Thomas, Snooks Eaglin and Benny Spellman, Howell couldn't help reflecting on the music's timeless, classless, across-the-board appeal. They all seized the opportunity to let their hair down, and all had a great time.

All these events, it turned out, were mere practice runs as far as Atwater was concerned. Following Bush's election victory in November, he called Howell once again. "Now we're *really* pulling out all the stops," he declared. "We're going to have the greatest inauguration ever. And we've got to have Motormouth Maybelle as one of the stars."

The *Celebration for Young Americans: A Special Tribute to Rhythm and Blues Artists and Their Music* was set for Saturday, January 21, 1989. Slated to appear with me was an incredible list of top talent: Joe Cocker, Etta James, Billy Preston, Percy Sledge, Albert Collins, Steve Cropper, Bo Diddley, Eddie Floyd, Chuck Jackson, Dr. John, Delbert McLinton, Sam Moore, Koko Taylor, Stevie Ray Vaughan and Ron Wood.

This was a big story in the U.S. press, for it was seen as hardly a typical Republican line-up. (I believe Don Rickles was the headliner on the previous occasion, and it was quite a jump from Don to Ruth Brown and friends.) It was a tremendous showcase for R-and-B music, a watershed in our struggle to gain respect. If it was important enough for the President of the United States . . .

Howell was jubilant, for he could point to the Rhythm and Blues Foundation, which many still hoped would simply curl up and die, as the current, alive-and-kicking keeper of the flame. To our friends in the press who'd supported us in the past and the waverers who might do so in the future, he could say, *"Keep pushing.* You're on to an issue that matters."

What he said to me was important as well: "If it hadn't been for you and Motormouth back at the Press Corps dinner, none of this would be happening. And that's the truth, Ruth."

Unfortunately, instead of the inauguration, the painful truth for me was hospitalization with the angina attack that darned near polished me off. I do not believe the God I have loved, worshipped and respected all these years is a vengeful God, but I do believe we tend to get carried away by a sense of our own importance in the great scheme of things. "The Lord will put you on your back sometimes, and that way you'll have to look up at him," my mama used to say. I kept remembering that as I lay in that hospital bed, staring up at the ceiling, trying to re-establish my spiritual connection.

For someone of my independent nature I found it difficult being forced to rely on others so completely. I simply could not fathom another individual having to take me to the bathroom, leave me there, decide when I'd had long enough, come back and haul me off, turn me on my side and wash me. Even worse was having to put up with someone approaching me with a bad attitude and being forced to take it without responding. Only one thing got me through the experience: the knowledge that Mama's spirit was in that hospital looking after me.

So while I missed the excitement of the inaugural, I was there in spirit. And I heard it went wonderfully well, with Joyce McRae's support enlisted once again by Howell, all the way from procuring the artists to helping produce the event. I believe, however, there was some concern expressed within the Republican ranks at the sight of George Bush up there on stage surrounded by a sea of black faces in the *Celebration for Young Americans*. What kind of message was this sending out? A positive one, I'd say!

While convalescing I was bracing myself for the next big test, the Broadway opening of *Black and Blue*. Hector and Claudio, as I knew they would, kept their word and followed David Hinckley's advice to hold that curtain. *"Black and Blue* really sizzles," Howard Kissel declared in the New York *Daily News*. "Color it great!" Clive Barnes raved in the *Post*. "Big, glamorous and glittering," said *Women's Wear Daily*. Time magazine described it as "Gorgeous fun." David Patrick Stearns called it "A red-hot number" in *USA Today*, adding, "When Ruth Brown sings 'St. Louis Blues' you realize what we've been missing all these years, the *bruises* of the blues." Hallelujah, we were a hit!

There was more good news for *Black and Blue* farther down the line. No less a director than Robert Altman planned a version for television. He did a lot of work backstage to capture the activity behind the scenes as well as what the audience saw, and turned out a dynamic program.

In all the excitement after the Tonys I was not only booked to sing on *The Tonight Show* with Johnny Carson, but for a full interview as well. It was an unbelievable high. Why? I'll tell you. Back in the fifties, when Ed Sullivan was king, I had about as much chance of appearing on his show as I had of flying to the moon in my Caddy convertible. Patti Page and Georgia Gibbs could sing their cover versions of my black chart hits on Sullivan's show. I was denied that exposure and the opportunity to break through to the white public.

I told Johnny backstage how I always watched his show but had long since abandoned any thought of being invited to appear before he and I were too arthritic to lift hands and say, "Good eve-

With an old friend—
Cissy Houston
(Whitney's mom).
(COURTESY OF RUTH BROWN)

ning." On the air I was truthful about what I had done to survive throught the sixties and seventies. Why shouldn't I tell the world I was a school bus driver and a domestic? All those good ladies in the world, like my mama before me, did those things for just one reason. To keep on keeping on. Me too!

"I'm not an educated woman," I told Johnny straight out. "I narrowly graduated from high school. But I feel I'm educated with what my mama called good old mother wit. Street learning. Experience. With a fierce instinct to survive no matter what life throws at me. Besides, I've always believed that what Ruth Brown was will *always* be. I've always felt there would be a place for me and my singing. Good soul singers sing the way they do because they are singing out of personal experience, be it tragedy, joy, dissapointment, whatever. If they couldn't express it through music, somebody going that deep into themselves would probably end up in a cell block somewhere."

When Johnny asked if I felt resentful about the old days when my music was covered by white artists, I replied, "I look at it this way. They were taking away a bone that belonged to me. Well, now that I've got that bone back, nobody's ever going to take it away again. *Not ever.*"

No matter who I talked to, the subject of my settlement with Atlantic came into the conversation. It was the same with Johnny.

Many tried their darnedest to conjure up where I had this hatred going for Ahmet Ertegun. I told them that was not and never had been the case. Anger and resentment, undoubtedly, and a burning sense of injustice. For every Picasso he had hanging on his wall, I had a damp patch on mine.

But hatred? Never.

WHEN I HEARD about Sarah Vaughan's sudden hospitalization in Los Angeles during the run, I called her from my dressing room at the Minskoff. I never had gotten to know Sarah all that well, for we'd never worked together and had only met briefly through George Treadwell, then again at Redd Foxx's home, until she stopped in at La Cafe, a little club in the San Fernando Valley, in the early eighties. Sarah quietly slipped in one night and was very complimentary, and I was just thrilled she'd turned up to hear me sing. I got to know her well enough after that to call her "Sailor," the name by which she was fondly known by her closest friends. Sure, she's far better known as "Sassy," but I'd been aware of her alternative, private nickname for many years. "You wanna know the best gigs in town?" Mr. B asked me once. "Ask the Sailor." All I'll say is that Sarah earned the name, for her command of the vernacular rivaled Dinah Washington's. And that's *really* sayin' somethin'.

"This is a rough one, girl," she said when I asked how she was.

"Yeah, but you've been through rougher than this and got through," I replied.

"I know," she told me, "but Ruth, there ain't no band playin' this time."

That's when I knew we were about to lose another of our greats.

AFTER THE OUTER CIRCLE AND TONY AWARDS the money men got into a feud with Claudio and tried to prevent him from coming backstage. "If he's not here, neither am I," I told them, "for he's the reason I'm here." Gradually I began to feel it was time to move on. My contract was about to expire in any case, and all I needed was one simple excuse to call it a day. Those pesky financiers gave me two beauties.

Earlier in the run the Lone Star Cafe in the Village had booked me for their Monday night slot during my night off from *Black and Blue.* I think they were expecting okay business on what was normally an off-night, and the crowds that turned up took them completely by surprise. After a couple of return bookings I approached them with an idea. My proposition was simple: "Look, there's an incredible pool of talent out there being ignored. Plenty of the greatest rhythm-and-blues artists are still around, just waiting for another chance to strut their stuff. Like Jimmy Scott. You've never heard of him? Well, let me tell you, you got a treat comin'. And there's the fabulous Charles Brown, the great Chuck Jackson, hey, there's a whole list."

The upshot was their asking me to host their Monday show as "Ruth Brown Presents . . ." The Lone Star became known as Ruth's Place once a week and the venue was the only game in town on Monday nights. Apart from Charles, Jimmy and Chuck, others who did great were Irene Reed, another wonderful, underrated singer from Harlem who once had a record with Basie, my good buddy Doris Troy, Jack McDuff, Panama Francis and the Savoy Sultans, Houston Pearson, Etta Jones and Arthur Prysock.

The success of the Lone Star gig really got under the skin of *Black and Blue's* backers, who didn't have the brains to see that far from detracting from the show, the extra favorable publicity did a power of good all round. They asked me to drop the date. I refused, they threatened legal action, Howell told them they didn't have a leg to stand on. They backed down, but it caused a lot of needless bad feeling.

That to-do followed a charity date organized by Governor Cuomo's son Andrew for the city's homeless. It was taking place just one block from the Minskoff, at the Sheraton Centre Ballroom. I worked it out so I wouldn't miss any of my solo numbers, just one ensemble item, where anyone who had paid to see Ruth Brown wouldn't even notice my absence. On that basis I promised to do my bit. Once again the purse-watchers behind *Black and Blue* brandished the prospect of an injunction, once again Howell rode in there, guns a-blazin', and this time we had one of the headliners, Paul Simon, threatening to organize a posse of homeless kids to

With the great Panama Francis, backstage at "Black and Blue."
(COURTESY OF RUTH BROWN)

picket the Minskoff if I was prevented from appearing. In the end it boiled down to, "Okay, go. But if you do, don't come back."

I decided to ignore their ultimatum. Did you ever doubt it? I don't know which school of PR these guys attended, but it must have been a pip. I followed Robin Williams on the show and woke up next morning unsure whether I still had a job or not. I decided to turn up anyway, and when I did the financiers were nowhere to be found. "Don't anybody try turning me around," I warned, marching toward the dressing room. DON'T MESS WITH MISS RHYTHM was the headline that day of another press stalwart, the *Daily News'* Mike McAlary.

Governor Cuomo, accompanied by his wife Matilda, son Andrew and Ethel and Bobby Kennedy's daughter Kerry, had been among the dignitaries in the charity audience at the Sheraton. I guess he must have liked what he saw, for next thing I knew he asked me to sing at his sixtieth birthday party. And when Andrew subsequently married Kerry Kennedy at Hickory Hill I was right there too, singing a number specially composed for the occasion. Jacqueline Kennedy Onassis was kind enough to approach me afterwards to tell me how much she'd enjoyed my singing. "You have a great gift," she told me. I was deeply, deeply touched that this most gracious, charming lady had seen fit to acknowledge me in this way.

As for *Black and Blue*'s accountants, they deducted one night's pay for my absence during the charity gig. On balance I have to say it was worth it. First, to enable me to keep my word, for apart from my voice that's all I have. Second, we raised $600,000 for a worthy cause. Third, for giving me an introduction to such terrific people.

Soon after the Tonys I indicated my intention to move on from

At Kimbals East Club,
Emeryville, California.
(Courtesy of Ruth Brown)

Black and Blue, and suggested LaVern Baker as my replacement. The powers-that-be were initially unenthusiastic about the choice, for the last they'd heard of LaVern she was doing disco retreads in Manila. However, the Rhythm and Blues Foundation helped arrange a showcase booking at the Lone Star, where she was given a chance to really cook with a terrific fourteen-piece band backing her. The gig brought about a swift change of heart. She did a wonderful job in the show, as I knew she would, and her success in the Big Apple encouraged her to consider picking up the threads of her career in the States.

My stint in *Black and Blue* provided the theme for my next Fantasy album, *Blues on Broadway.* Meantime I was invited to be spokesperson for Seagram's Gin, sponsors of the Taste of the Blues festivals around the country. I ended up being handed the keys to several cities, places I'd scarcely been allowed on the sidewalks once upon a time—Birmingham, Jackson and Memphis, as well as Cleveland, Detroit and Tulsa. I was inducted into the Hall of Fame in Tulsa, and down in New Orleans at the Mardi Gras I performed the honor for B. B. King.

The news of Hector's death while I was out there came as a wrenching blow to everyone, most poignantly to Claudio, who called and asked that I sing at his partner's funeral. I performed his favorite, "Body and Soul." The death left a terrible gap in Claudio's life, and I know there's still a lot of healing to take place.

If anyone had asked, I'd have honestly said that *Black and Blue* and the recognition I'd gained through that show would have represented the peak of my "comeback." Instead, it just seemed to grow and grow. I was invited to appear at the Kennedy Center in Washington and at Lincoln Center in New York. A concert we called "Three Divas," in the company of Etta James and LaVern, blew the roof off the 15,000–seat Wolf Trap Center for the Performing Arts in Washington. The awe-inspiring Carnegie Hall beckoned with the JVC Jazz Festival; I played the Hollywood Bowl as part of the Playboy Jazz festival, then the beautiful Bob Hope Performing Arts Center in Palm Springs. Under the auspices of George Wein, the brains behind the Newport Jazz Festival, I traveled to Europe to take part in the Montreux, North Sea and Umbria Jazz festivals, in Switzerland, Holland and Italy. Back in the States I shared the bill with B. B. King at the 60,000–seat Black Expo Convention in Indianapolis. "B. B.," I said, 'it's a long, long way from the eighty-seat Baby Grand."

'Ain't it the truth!' he replied.

On a return engagement at the Hollywood Roosevelt's Cinegrill, Bruno Fava asked if there were any other artists I could recommend to follow me. I put forward the names of Charles Brown and the extraordinary Jimmy Scott. I'd first met Jimmy in Newport News while I was running around with Jimmy Brown. He was "Little" Jimmy Scott then and touring with his mother, the original Caldonia, a contortionist whose real name was Estella Young. Both Charles and Jimmy really made their mark at the Cinegrill, re-

Hallelujah—made it at last! My induction into the Rock and Roll Hall of
Fame. (COURTESY OF RUTH BROWN)

launching both their careers. I'd been given a second shot and was
only too happy to pass it along.

DAN AYKROYD personally chipped in $60,000 in January, 1989, to
initially fund the Rhythm and Blues Foundation's financial assistance program. Warner's check for the first third of its promised
$450,000 finally arrived in June, the day before the Tony awards
ceremony.

Howell, meanwhile, had been pressing ahead, scheduling the
first presentation of the Foundation's Pioneer Awards for November. Bonnie and John Conyers were among the hosts at the Smithsonian's National Museum of American History in Washington, our

permanently established headquarters. You cannot ask for a more prestigious home than that, and it was all part and parcel of Howell's master plan to let everyone know that we'd arrived, that we mattered, and that we were in for the long haul.

Once again he turned to the redoubtable Joyce McRae to help organize something special for the foundation's first awards presentation. Working with their staff, Joyce produced a series of three concerts under the heading, "The Smithsonian Celebrates Stax Records and Soul Music." Presented in conjunction with our awards ceremony, that brought us Isaac Hayes, Sam Moore, David Porter, Carla and Rufus Thomas, together with a group of the original Stax session musicians.

It would have helped had more of the trustees made the short trip from New York to Washington to elevate the occasion even more. Alas, those busy, busy schedules! Neither Ahmet, Tom Draper nor any representative from Atlantic or Warner showed up. Of the recipients only LaVern Baker was unable to attend. She was still in Manila—this was before the Lone Star booking that eased her into *Black and Blue*—but she spoke to Richard Harrington by phone from the base where she'd been entertainment director for nineteen years after playing in Vietnam.

"When I first heard about the grant I ran everybody out the office with my screams," she told him. "It's so near Christmas and I've got four adopted kids, so it's really wonderful." Was she angry about the belated nature of the award? "I was never bitter," she asserted, "because *somebody* has to pay the dues. Even the ones before us, they were never rewarded. We were just lucky enough that somebody remembered us."

Together with LaVern, the other seven recipients—Charles Brown, Etta James, Jimmy Scott, Percy Sledge, Mary Wells, the Clovers and myself—shared awards totaling $145,000.

After the ceremony Bonnie talked with Harrington as well, listing the lack of career guidance, the racist nature of society and the opportunities lost to the original music-makers when their material was co-opted by others. "To me it's an imperative payback for those of us who make our living doing this kind of music," she said. "Lip service is one thing, but this is a real program with real musicians that need help right away. This music is alive, these people are

Signing and having a good time with Little Jimmy Scott in Berkeley.
(COURTESY OF RUTH BROWN)

viable and as long as I've got a breath in my body I'm going to try to get this music out."

One of the faces unfortunately missing at the event was that of the Clovers' Bill Harris, who had succumbed after a long illness. The other was that of Mickey Leland, tragically killed in a plane crash during a visit to South Africa in August. He was a man who'll be remembered for many wonderful things, not least for dreaming up the idea of the foundation.

In my acceptance speech I described the arrival of the foundation as nothing less than the realization of a dream. And no matter who the recipients were, I declared, I could stick my chest out just a little. I confessed, though, that I was still scared I'd go to sleep and wake with someone saying, "No, it's a mistake, we've got to go back." It had been a long time coming, but it was a reality now. And right on time.

I went on to express the hope that it would be just the beginning of something important, with every other record company following suit to pay tribute to the artists responsible for laying down the foundations of today's multi-billion-dollar record industry.

Was that asking too much? More so, it turned out, than any of us thought.

26

LONG LIVE ROYALTY REFORM

STEPPIN' LIVELY, steppin' proud—leastways, as lively and proud as my legs would let me. Memories of Harlem, the way it *was,* often come creepin' back, usually when I least expect it. Lord, it was a *time.*

I could have given a guided tour of Harlem at the drop of a hat. Come to think of it, I did just that when the Johnny Otis Show hit the Apollo in 1950 and Little Esther Phillips, born plain Esther Mae Jones, found herself in urgent need of a new dress. Enter Ruth Brown, Harlem guide extraordinaire. Off we went to 125th Street, taking in the flavorful sights and sounds along the way, scoping out all the juke joints, clubs, restaurants and bustling stores. At that time you could walk out of the Apollo, take a left on Seventh Avenue, and meet people like Joe Louis and other sports heroes of the day. How come? Simple. That was their beat, their turf, the place they came to be ogled and idolized. Young bucks could spend time in Sugar Ray Robinson's bar, then get their hair cut and processed in the barber shop he owned next door. Here reigned the King of the Process, Roger Simon, a guy male entertainers would travel miles out of their way to get to, often flying in specially for an appointment. An application of white potato and Red Devil lye, the stuff used for cleaning toilets, was the deep, dark secret of the hair-straightening process. It had to be washed off right quick, no more than a minute after being massaged in, otherwise it burned right through the scalp. The "konk" became the "process," then simply a "perm" as science moved on by leaps and bounds. Long before "Which twin has the Toni?" there never was any doubt which professional had been processed by Roger Simon. Trust me! I even arranged for my brothers, Leonard and Benny, to study under Roger, in between accompanying me on tours.

On 135th Street and Seventh was Small's Paradise, a club that boasted its own chorus line. A block up was Count Basie's bar, which had a restaurant nearby named Jimmy Lou's that served great home-style cookin'. The Red Rooster was on 138th and Ninth, with Bowman's Club up the hill on 155th and St. Nicholas, and between them was the Savoy Ballroom on 143rd and Lenox, where you really could stomp to your heart's content.

Esther was only fourteen years old at the time and her eyes were just a-poppin' as we continued our circular tour. We enjoyed a great morning together and ended up back where we started, buying her dress at Bloomstein's, the famous department store on 126th Street. First came lunch, with a choice between Frank's Steakhouse and the Palm Cafe, both on 125th and neon-lit although it was broad daylight. Esther picked the Palm for our meal, and a tasty blue satin number for the dress.

Her idol, she shyly told me, was Dinah Washington. She hardly needed to, for you only had to listen to the girl for half a minute to realize that. Esther really was something, a child wise and experienced way beyond her years, a sweet kid who thought she knew all the answers. Maybe it was the questions that eluded her.

Esther was just one of a host of performers I got to know through the Apollo, where the crowds in the second balcony—the infamous Buzzards Roost—either pronounced your sudden death sentence or passage to glory. Seldom was there an in-between. The veteran comedienne "Moms" Mabley became a great friend. That gravel voice comin' out with stuff like, "The only thing an old man can show you is where it's at!" cracked everyone up. And she'd take her teeth out between homilies right there on stage. She said that one of her favorite songs, "My Ship," would be just right for me. She'd been a virtual fixture at the Apollo since it first opened its doors in 1934, and I guess another great comic, Pigmeat Markham, came not far behind. He began the routine Sammy Davis, Jr. later adopted, "Here Come the Judge." With sentence about to be passed, the prisoner pleads, "Judge, Your honor, don't you remember me? I'm the guy who introduced you to your wife!"

"Life!" thunders the judge, banging his gavel on the stand.

And there were many others, like the little Jewish comedienne Totie Fields, and Marge McGrory, Pearl Williams, Slappy White (LaVern Baker's first hubby), Irving C. Watson, George Wilshire and Spo-dee-o-dee. All, I regret to say, long since bundled off to vaudeville heaven.

You never knew who you were going to bump into at that theater, either out front, on stage or backstage. Having admired them on screen as a kid, can you imagine how I felt being introduced to Mantan Moreland, the bug-eyed chauffeur in the Charlie Chan series, the wonderful Hattie McDaniels from *Gone With the Wind,* Louise Beavers from the movie that had torn Mama apart, the original *Imitation of Life,* legends like Paul Robeson, Pearl Bailey, Eddie "Rochester" Anderson and Bill "Bojangles" Robinson? Aspiring young actors Sidney Poitier and Dane Clark were fellow students at Lee Strasberg's academy and frequented the shows before visiting our dressing rooms, often in the company of the Bowery Boys' Huntz Hall, their third partner in a Harlem burger joint. When Harry Belafonte appeared on a bill with me, a number he sang that really struck home was "I Want Recognition As a Man." Boy, he surely got it. He wasn't into calypso at the time; that arrived later. I even saw him play Birdland before he found his ticket to the top. A bit like yours truly, I guess, the balladeer turned "Miss Rhythm."

The Apollo, the still-beating heart of a once-proud Harlem, provided the most emotional return gig of all, early in the nineties. Once again I was in the company of B. B. King, together on this occasion with Bobby "Blue" Bland. The theater had, it seemed, turned its back on me for two entire decades before that; the last time I'd appeared there was on that traumatic date in the late sixties when we lost Frankie Lymon, and Frank Schiffman had to beg me to get Clyde to leave the stage.

Oh, the ghosts that walked as we revisited that legendary place! Little Esther, Little Frankie and Little Willie John, three innocent, fresh kids, kept peekin' round various corners while I rehearsed

With my beloved B.B.—no
longer two skinny-minnies!
(COURTESY OF RUTH BROWN)

with B. B., while Clyde, Sam Cooke and Jackie Wilson shot the
breeze with Bobby Bland. That first evening Blanche Calloway,
looking fine and elegant in her prime, and Dinah Washington—
matching her inch for inch from her mink stole down to her alliga-
tor shoes—eyed me from the front row of the stalls in friendly, if
decidedly hypercritical manner. Later I spied Willis in the wings,
with "Moms" Mabley at his elbow. "Come on, honey. Sing 'My
Ship' for Moms, I could almost hear her ask.

NOW THAT LABELS like Atlantic had everything in their computers
and sales were being properly tracked, they—and other record
companies too—began to cotton on to the true value of reissues. It
became a self-perpetuating thing, with more material than ever being put out in compilations and boxed sets. In turn this led to an
increased willingness to record surviving legends today, safe in the
knowledge there was a market out there. This became part and
parcel of the rejuvenation of many careers previously consigned to
history. Unfortunately it arrived too late to help some performers.
    When Dee Clark suffered a stroke in 1987, it was friends like
Chuck Jackson and Sam Moore who dug deep to help out with the
medical bills. Jackie Wilson and Esther Phillips were buried without
headstones. Supremes member Florence Ballard died a welfare re-

cipient. Rock and Roll Hall of Fame inductee Jimmy Reed died penniless in 1976, having received precisely nothing in royalty payments for eighteen Top Twenty rhythm and blues hits between 1957 and 1963. Scott A. Cameron is a Burbank artists' rights advocate whose company negotiated a settlement on behalf of Jimmy's widow with the publishing company that controls her husband's catalog. As he put it to Los Angeles *Times* reporter Chuck Philips before Jimmy's posthumous induction into the Rock and Roll Hall of Fame in 1991: "The tragic irony of pioneers like Jimmy being honored is that many of these artists and their families were abandoned to live and die in destitute conditions by the same industry now singing their praises. For that, the music industry should be ashamed of itself." The title of Jimmy's last big hit, the classic "Shame, Shame, Shame" echoes the sentiment.

I first heard Mary Wells was ill through Spooky, a little guy who puts out a newsletter called *The Ladies of Blues*. "I don't know how any of your readers can continue purchasing the old Motown hits," Mary had told a reporter. "Look at the condition Motown left Mary Wells in." Joyce McRae did a great job for her friend Mary, publicly urging people all over the country to send their donations to the Rhythm and Blues Foundation. Through her efforts we were able to pay the rent on Mary's apartment in Burbank and contribute some $130,000 to pay bills and make her more comfortable in the eighteen months before her untimely death from throat cancer.

Joyce added her voice to Scott Cameron's: "Most of these artists are living without the benefit of health insurance, for God's sake. Every year the industry pats itself on the back at these award shows for honoring rock's royal heritage, but in the meantime these people are suffering."

The foundation, first and foremost, is a giving organization that does not require people to bare themselves before a grant is awarded. There are no announcements about sums handed out unless permission is given, a procedure that enables the recipients to retain their dignity. Folks may be hurting, but they do not necessarily want everyone knowing their business. I detest self-serving presentations that are run like circuses, with twenty-five cameras around and all the hoopla, someone being handed a check for

$25,000 and you just know it has cost another $25,000 for the rental of the hall, celebrity invites and buffet.

I am sure Howell never thought it was going to be easy roping in the rest of the industry to follow Warner's example, but the stone wall of indifference he came up against at first surprised even him. Top record executives like Dick Asher at Polygram, Jheryl Busby (Motown's president) and EMI's Joe Smith all conceded the vast sums they had at their disposal to follow hunches and sign new acts. But there was, it seemed, no provision anywhere to make restitution for the past. Charitable contributions? Get real! So Atlantic had been "suckered" into it? So what?

Not a single soul chose even to come close to Atlantic's commitment until Irving Azoff stepped forward in February 1990. I guess Howell and Dave Marsh must have caught him on the right day. About to leave MCA to start his own Giant record label at Warner, Azoff agreed to up royalties on the Chess/Checker catalog MCA had acquired from five to ten percent, doubling overnight the potential reissue income for artists like Etta James, Chuck Berry, the Dells, Koko Taylor, John Lee Hooker, Memphis Slim, Percy Mayfield and Jimmy Witherspoon. And with old "session costs" canceled, they'd actually see some real money.

Some Chess artists, Muddy Waters among them, had settled for flat payments of a few dollars a side back in the fifties and sixties. Regardless, the company had still debited session costs, leaving people like Muddy permanently in debt. His account still showed a negative balance of $56,000 in 1986, so although he earned $25,000 that year in royalties, he had not been paid a dime. Now he too was on ten percent, joining fellow artists in the same boat—Buddy Guy, Howlin' Wolf, Bo Diddley and the Soul Stirrers.

Richard Harrington of the Washington *Post* saw MCA's action as even more far-reaching than Atlantic's in that Atlantic had benefited for years—and were continuing to benefit—from the old five percent royalty rate paid to their artists. MCA, after all, had only recently taken over the Chess/Checker riches, yet they had still chosen to cough up—and at ten percent.

"When we purchased the Chess catalog," said Bruce Resnikoff, MCA's vice-president, "one of the most disturbing things was that virtually all of the accounts showed substantial unrecouped bal-

Koko Taylor, me and Irma Thomas at the 1990 "Three Legendary Ladies" concert at Lincoln Center.
(COURTESY OF HOWELL BEGLE)

ances. From an ethical, moral and historical standpoint, everybody at MCA believes that these artists, because of their importance to the history of rock and roll, to blues and in general to the history of music, deserve to be recognized. By doubling the royalties, we're compensating them for money they may not have received in the past to which they were entitled. We've also issued them with new contracts directly with MCA, which obligate us to pay them semi-annual royalties. We are not talking about recording artists who made the millions of dollars that are made by today's superstars. In many respects, these artists are just as great, and if it weren't for them, you wouldn't have a lot of the superstars you have today. So anything we can do to help them from an industry standpoint is just wonderful.''

Ahmet's reaction to the news was, by any yardstick, incredibly po-faced. "When a record company buys a catalog," he decreed, "I believe they also inherit the duty to pay the artists on the records that they release. These people deserve to be paid." Ain't it the truth, Ahmet, ain't it the doggone, downhome, copper-bottomed truth!

The only bad news out of MCA, and it was a real oddity, was their refusal to spread the largesse right across the board and include their in-house Decca label in their recalculations. Maybe, despite all the rhetoric, it was just too much to contemplate backpayments from before time began for the estate of people like Billie Holiday. They must have made a fortune several times over from her recordings, as well as from early Ella, Louis Jordan, Count Basie, Joe Turner and dozens of others. Still, half a loaf was better than none at all, and both Howell and I echoed Resnikoff's last statement: "I just hope every label recognizes its obligation to its own history."

Looking back from today's perspective, it's easier to compare the way various labels treated their artists in the fifties and sixties. Chess, by any reckoning, had to be near the bottom of the totem pole, grouped in close proximity to Aladdin, where Charles Brown suffered in the trenches; Savoy, whose Herman Lubinsky single-handedly hogtied Jimmy Scott's recording career; and King, Syd Nathan's domain. When the Rolling Stones arrived at Chess back in the sixties, they were astonished to find one of their all-time heroes, Muddy Waters, painting the studio to make ends meet. You have to give credit to Atlantic for more than that. Everything, though, has its logical progression, and I marveled at the way Motown groomed, choreographed and nurtured their artists, although they charged a hefty price for what they termed "Charm Enhancement." Thank God for at least giving me Blanche! Regardless, all those labels had one thing in common. They all did their level best to deny their artists royalty payments.

By October 1990, alas, no other record company had followed Atlantic in pledging any new money to the foundation. Warner's response was a shocker. Although their money had supposedly come without strings attached, they now questioned why they should be the sole contributors to the running costs of the foundation—and flatly refused to pay the last third of their $450,000. Their action served to remind us yet again that any commitment, even of the charitable variety, was subject to revision.

The individual who did most to meet the challenge was Bonnie Raitt. After sweeping the boards at 1990's Grammy Awards, Bonnie's amazing, many-splendored debut album for Capitol, *Nick of Time*, multiplied several times over the million copies it had already sold. My buddy, the superstar! The irony is that Bonnie had hardly been welcomed to Capitol's family of artists with open arms (O, ye of little faith!) Her manager, Danny Goldberg, had felt obliged to offer to refund personally the company's session expenses if the album failed to sell 150,000 copies.

For our next awards event in February 1991, co-hosted by Bonnie and myself, Howell obtained the participation of several industry executives, Ahmet among them. CBS provided substantial underwriting for the evening, courtesy of Lebaron Taylor's efforts, and the tremendous amount of press coverage we achieved seemed to impress industry insiders. Atlantic's stubborn reaction? The withdrawal of their last contribution still stood.

In September, 1991, Bonnie exercised her clout and enlisted Capitol/EMI president and CEO Jim Fifield's involvement in the foundation as both a member of the board of directors and chairman of the development committee. One of his first acts was to commit $150,000 on behalf of EMI, neatly filling in for Warner Communications Inc.

Now Warner's decidedly shamefaced reaction was to "restructure" rather than cancel their remaining $150,000 and commit to $50,000 a year over three years. Grateful as some of us were for the change of heart, it was hard to believe we were now dealing with the multi-billion-dollar Time-Warner giant, to whom our much-needed infusion could not be more than a few days' lunch money.

Dave Marsh felt strongly enough about their behavior to resign from the foundation. Warner's attitude, he maintained, represented the thin end of the wedge. "Is this a result of Time-Warner's failed stock offering?" he wondered aloud in his *Rock & Roll Confidential* newsletter.

> Or is it just a reassertion of the record industry's plantation mentality, in which music makers are treated like sharecroppers to be paid what the companies want, when they get around to it? Either way, it's intolerable . . . Three years ago, Time-Warner's Atlantic Records took deep bows for endowing the Rhythm and Blues Foundation with $1.5 million for the benefit of the great artists on whom today's rock world is based —artists the company had cheated out of royalties for the pre-

With B.B. and
Bonnie, two greats.
(COURTESY OF
RUTH BROWN)

vious three decades. Atlantic also agreed to recalculate royalties for the primary Atlantic artists, paying them some fraction
of what they'd been owed, and to contribute $150,000 for each
of the following three years to the foundation's operating expenses. There were no strings attached to any of this, but last
fall, Atlantic chairman Ahmet Ertegun told the board that unless substantial fundraising in the rest of the record industry
was received before the final $150,000 came due in June 1991,
Time-Warner was backing out of the deal.

The foundation raised more money, [mainly] a three-year
pledge of $150,000 from EMI. Time-Warner's condition was
phony and several trustees screamed. So rather than welshing
on the whole deal, the company announced that it was "re-
structuring" its last payment, giving $50,000 for each of the
next three years.

This is unacceptable . . . If Atlantic's parent company is
screwing the foundation out of a mere hundred grand, what's
it doing about the several times that much it owes in royalty
recalculations? . . . And how the hell is the foundation supposed to get any other company to give it money if it can't get
Time-Warner to keep to the original bargain?

Joyce McRae conveyed her deep concern to Billboard, the industry bible: "This is a throwback to the same mentality that has
always existed with black artists. They say, 'We're going to give it to

you, but *when* we want to, and *how* we want to.' And that's unpalatable.''

Dave and Joyce had voiced the fears of many of us.

Never one to let the grass grow under his feet, and forever the guy to accentuate the positive, Howell took the opportunity of the new dialog with Jim Fifield to initiate discussions on an across-the-board clean-up of Capitol/EMI's royalty practices. Fifield's announcement of sweeping reforms was preceded a month earlier by Bonnie's second Grammy sweep in February 1992, this time with her five-million-copy-selling *Luck of the Draw*. He followed Irv Azoff's lead in increasing royalty rates to ten percent. EMI had a lot further to go in some cases than either Chess or Atlantic, since the rate they had been paying several of their older artists was as low as three quarters of one percent. Once again, thankfully, them old devil "session costs" were wiped out.

The decision covered all labels owned and acquired by EMI, including Capitol (Peggy Lee, Ella Mae Morse, Kay Starr, Nellie Lutcher), Imperial (Fats Domino), Aladdin (Charles Brown), Liberty (Jan and Dean, Julie London, Gene McDaniels, Timi Yuro), Pacific Jazz (Art Blakey, Miles Davis), and Sue (Ike and Tina Turner, Charles and Inez Foxx). And before the end of the year Fifield had secured a further $1 million in new industry pledges for the foundation. EMI TO PUT THE GOLD BACK IN THE OLDIES was the headline the Washington *Post* offered its readers.

By the time the third awards presentation of the Rhythm and Blues Foundation came around it had become an official part of Grammy week activity, and accepted, for better or worse, as part of the music industry establishment. The good news: Jim Fifield's efforts had ensured it could never be regarded as Atlantic's puppet. The bad news: many now regarded the entire music industry as pulling the strings. Believe it or not, the revised gospel according to Tom Draper, Atlantic's Chairman of the foundation, was laid down in a letter to Howell dated October 3rd, 1991: Thou shalt not seek further royalty reform from the industry.

The redoubtable Howell's answer: Royalty reform is and always has been a fundamental objective of the Rhythm and Blues Foundation.

And so say all of us, especially newly-elected member of the Foundation's Artists Advisory Board (as of February, 1995)—did you guess?—Ruth Brown. As Howell put it to Rolling Stone: "Consumers ought to know that if they buy an EMI reissue, the artists get something, but if they buy a Sony reissue, the artist is getting stiffed."

With Grammy week coming up a few weeks after my appointment, ABC's "Nightline" contacted me about contributing to a program they had planned to examine the continuing plight of R and B pioneers signed to labels like Sony, Polygram and BMG that were unwilling to join the ranks of Atlantic, MCA and EMI in instituting royalty reforms.

Many felt the combination of the Grammy week publicity and the upcoming threat of a "Nightline" exposé brought Sony up to the plate. On February 17 they informed the Rhythm and Blues Foundation that after conducting a "thorough, ongoing investigative process," reviewing their "extensive artist roster and catalog of recorded music" on the Columbia, Epic, ARC, OKeh, Brunswick and Vocalion labels, which they described as being "at the cornerstone of popular music today," they had identified an initial group of more than 60 artists to be included in a royalty reform program: artists with royalty rates below 10 per cent, or no royalty rate at all (the result of a buyout, which was commonplace in this century), would be awarded a 10 per cent royalty rate; all unearned balances would be eliminated. Another big fish had been landed!

This still left a couple of industry giants holding out: the Germany-based Bertelsman Group's BMG (RCA Victor and its original subsidiaries Bluebird, "X", Vik, Camden), and the Dutch-based Polygram, controllers of Verve/MGM (Ella Fitzgerald, Louis Armstrong, Billie Holiday, Charlie Parker, Jazz at the Philharmonic), Mercury/Wing/EmArcy (Sarah Vaughan, Dinah Washington, Billy Eckstine, The Platters), and Motown (Diana Ross, the Supremes, Martha and the Vandellas, the Four Tops, the Temptations, Marvin Gaye, Smokey Robinson and the Miracles). On a local level there was Fantasy, with access to valuable reissue material on Stax/Volt/Enterprise and Specialty, amongst others.

Although Chris Wallace of "Nightline" skillfully spotlighted Polygram's position, what he got in response from their representative was vague talk of helping out with "medical expenses" for pioneer artists. It seems that "plantation accounting" is still with us. I only wish my reply to that particular piece of flannel had been broadcast in full!

Since then things have moved on quite a bit at the Rhythm and Blues Foundation, with myself, Jerry Butler and Chuck Jackson made fully-fledged trustees, and Jerry appointed chairman following Tom Draper's resignation in August, 1995. The "Ice Man" has cometh—and for the first time in its history an *artist*, rather than an *industry exec*, is actually in charge! This sent Howell straight into overdrive, right back on his royalty reform platform. Following a meeting convened at the end of October where this original purpose of the Foundation was re-affirmed, he agreed to chair a Standing Committee consisting of Ruth Brown, Jerry Butler, Chuck Jackson, journalist and record reissuer David Nathan, and Bonnie Raitt. Its purpose—to consolidate and extend royalty reforms on labels already in the fold, and to prepare a full-scale assault, PR-assisted, *the works*, in the early months of 1996, on every hold-out. I tell you, if that boy has his way, we'll end up having some form of identification, like a green sticker, on all reissues where reform has been instituted. That way, the customer can make up their own mind which labels to support, with the full and certain knowledge that the original artists are being fairly compensated. I feel we're really about to turn that last corner.

THERE WERE THREE REASONS for my move to Southern California in December, 1990: my sons, Ronnie and Earl, and Brandon, my grandchild.

I had sung at Ronnie's wedding—no, I could not just be the mama—and when a divorce loomed the question of visitation rights for Brandon became the number-one issue. After Ronnie's first court appearance, in a brand-new suit I had bought for the occasion, we were granted forty-five days before representatives from juvenile court visited his accommodation and pronounced it fit or otherwise. It took me most of that time to find a place in the Hollywood hills, leaving precisely one and a half days to have it furnished before the inspection. With the help of a thrift shop you'd better

With dear Nipsey Russell at Sam's Restaurant between shows of "Black and Blue!"
(COURTESY OF CHARLES ADAMS)

believe I had it looking great, with a separate room set aside for my grandson—and granny too. We passed with flying colors.

Meanwhile Earl had settled back in Los Angeles after his hospitalizations in New York, for the sunshine and open air helped his skin condition. I desperately needed a business manager to organize my revived career, but still hesitated before offering Earl the job. Riding on his mama's coattails? Hardly the thing to boost his self-esteem. Earl had his answer: "Don't hesitate. Fire me if it doesn't work out. If you don't, I'll fire myself." After a stormy first year—I'll blame the agony I suffered with my legs—it worked out wonderfully. Earl does an incredible job, his psoriasis is under control and I have the great pleasure of a big handsome son with me wherever I go. I spent years trying to figure out why his father had played the role he had in my life, why I'd had to suffer through that. The legacy of that relationship, Earl Jr., is the answer and one of the great joys of my life. He was the reward, he was the gift. I thank God for giving me both my boys.

THROUGHOUT 1991 the problems with my legs increased, and gradually it got to the point where I faced the prospect of spending the rest of my life in a wheelchair. Unless, that is, something was done. Earl and Howell both tried to coax me into knee replacement surgery. I was reluctant, despite the promise of the new life they held out. Earl laid it on the line: "Mom, we go to places like Acapulco with the band, and we all have a great time and enjoy the place—all except you, confined to your hotel room, which could be any place. I'm the one who sticks these enormous needles loaded with cortisone into your knees, right to the bone. I'm the one who hears you screaming with pain, I'm the one who sees you unable to move for hours afterwards, still lying on your bed in the dark while we're out enjoying yourself. Mom, it doesn't *have* to be that way!''

I finally gave in to the inevitable and had the operation performed in New York in February 1992. I badly needed physiotherapy during my convalescence and called Joe Molloy, the department head at Harlem Hospital. Although I'd attended school with Joe back in Portsmouth, our paths hadn't crossed in all these years. ''I need help, Joe,'' I told him. ''I'm sure the operation will make a difference eventually, but right now I'm in agony.''

I still had the lease on my one-room apartment in Harlem, but when Joe discovered that my sister Delia lived in Hempstead, just one expressway exit from him, he asked if there was any way I could stay there; if that could be arranged, he was prepared to drop in every night. Delia did have a little apartment in her basement, a one-room studio with its own bathroom and kitchen. It was perfect, even had its own entrance.

My first sight of Joe reminded me of one of Dad's favorite sayings, ''I cried 'cause I had no shoes, until I saw a man with no feet.'' I was feeling pretty sorry for myself as I sat awaiting Joe's arrival, then as he made his way down the steps I saw for the first time he was a double amputee. He drove a specially equipped truck and explained that he'd lost his legs through diabetes.

Even with two artificial limbs Joe is the most cheerful and optimistic person alive. Through rain, sleet and snow he came every night, easing, probing, soothing, mending. He had me back on stage by the end of April, albeit sitting down, and although I still need regular therapy I've never looked back. After a lifetime of suffering the consequences of that car crash in 1948, I enjoy more mobility now than I've known for years.

Faced with his steadfast refusal to accept financial payment for his services, I racked my brains to think of something special I could give him. I finally found the answer after performing at President Clinton's inaugural in 1993, when I was presented with a mag-

Meeting President
Clinton.
(Courtesy of Ruth Brown)

nificent leather jacket with a little thank-you message sewn inside. "I can't take this," was Joe's initial response, but I could tell he was tickled pink and I refused to take no for an answer. "Without you, Joe," I told him, "I'd never have made that date. So if there's anyone in the world who deserves it, it's you."

We had been children together, we had grown up together, now here was this friend from the past reaching out all those years later with his healing hands. It was eerie, for like so many things in my life it represented another full circle.

A ceremony a few weeks earlier had provided another, courtesy of Ahmet Ertegun.

27

MY WAY OF EVANGELIZING

IF BEING NOMINATED for a Grammy for *Blues on Broadway* was the icing on the Tony cake, winning it was the cherry on top. Anita O'Day was up in the same category, which caused some confusion since Alan Eichler represented both of us. Busy working in New York at the time, I had been been unable to attend the awards ceremony in Los Angeles in 1990, and it was a call to my dressing room from Alan that told me I'd won—with Anita professional and sport enough to stand alongside him as he made the call. Armed with my Tony and Grammy, there was just one more mountain to conquer.

After being nominated for five years for induction into the Rock and Roll Hall of Fame, I found myself dropped altogether for two years, 1990 and 1991. Nobody had a chance to vote for me, for I was not even on the ballot, and no biographical material, essential for filling in younger writers, was sent out. "Ahmet is being vicious and vindictive," I was told repeatedly. "This is his retribution. He'll never forgive you for getting the better of him. It'll be Leiber and Stoller all over again."

Certainly the common knowledge that the organization was his personal baby—"an $80 million tribute to Ahmet" is how one writer described it, referring to the hefty estimated cost of the orga-

325

Backstage at the 1989 Tonys
after winning for "Black
and Blue."

nization's Cleveland showpiece—led to speculation that I had indeed been blackballed. Apart from anything else, surely the last thing Ahmet wanted was for all us old skeletons to come tumbling out of his closet into the clear light of day. Hey, we're talking the *new* Ahmet, one writer pointed out, the Ahmet daily accepting Humanitarian of the Year awards, the deeply respected, unimpeachable elder statesman of the music industry, benevolent benefactor, all-round good egg. Why, of all people, would this whiter-than-white, noble figure wish to raise the profile of a bunch of forgotten, down-and-out, no 'count, so-called artists the *old* Ahmet had stiffed so many years ago? No, Ahmet wished the Rock and Roll Hall of Fame to reflect *his* version of music's story, the rock gospel according to Ahmet, with neither embarrassing loose ends nor loose-cannon apostles.

I was informed many times, and from many sources, that Ruth Brown *in particular* would never be granted admission to the Hall of Fame's magic circle, that my mouth was too big, that I rocked too many boats. What I never anticipated was my family's being affected. My son Ronnie was under contract writing music and producing at Warner, was highly thought of and doing real well. Until suddenly they let him go, that is. Rightly or wrongly, I believe to my heart it was because they discovered he was my kid. Ronnie still lives and breathes music, working as a producer and writer as well as performing, and I would like to believe he will make it in the end despite that major setback.

What Ahmet hadn't reckoned with was the power of the press. With every single interviewer asking, "Why aren't you in the Rock and Roll Hall of Fame?" I had one particular champion in good old David Hinckley of the *Daily News*. Every year when the list came out he would write something like, "Where *is* Ruth Brown?" and refer to the organization as "the Boys' Club." I used to call and thank him and ask, "What makes you love me so much?" His reply: 'Because the truth is the truth, and you belong there.' One of his headlines was HALL OF SHAME.

Along the way, please do not imagine I harbored any illusions about the institution. A remark made by Billy Joel summed up not only the annual event, but what my entire battle with Atlantic had been about. "If you ever go to these Rock and Roll Hall of Fame dinners," he said, "where they induct the Drifters and the Coasters, these old guys come out, they don't have a nickel. They don't have anything. And the heads of the record companies stand at the side and chuckle about how little they paid them. I'm not going to be one of those artists." Billy, as one who *was,* I sincerely hope you're *not!*

When they finally did vote to induct me in 1993, the notification was sent to an old address. I didn't hear about it for a month, just read it in the papers like everyone else, and I had to write and apologize for not responding sooner. The night of my induction, which was performed by Bonnie Raitt, we duetted on "Mama, He Treats Your Daughter Mean." And they ran a load of old film clips from the fifties, some of which were new to me.

Ahmet got up to talk about my arriving at Atlantic in the forties, how glad they had been to get me, how strong I was now and how I had maintained my dignity . . . the whole spiel. Then he handed over to Bonnie, who gave a short speech of her own before presenting me with the award. In reply I thanked everyone for their support, then cracked, "I really don't think there's much more to say at this point . . . except where's my gold record, Ahmet?"

I did go on after that, describing how Ahmet had come to the hospital with a gift back then, now the award represented another gift and yet another full circle in my life. And I said how grateful I was that nobody had had to go up and accept the award for me, because once again I was fresh from a wheelchair and not walking as fast as I might. "Ahmet," I said, "it seems like every time something happens where you and I are concerned, it's something to do with these legs. The only thing left for me to do now is to record for Atlantic again."

This really brought the house down, but a few weeks later I got Ahmet's reply. It came after he watched Bonnie and me repeat our duet at the Rhythm and Blues Foundation, where we were again co-presenters, handing out Lifetime Achievement Awards to Little Anthony and the Imperials, Wilson Pickett, James Brown and the Famous Flames, Charles Brown, Solomon Burke, Martha and the Vandellas, Panama Francis and Erskine Hawkins. Ahmet was highly complimentary after the show, describing it as the best presentation of all the awards he'd seen that year. "You know, Ruth, you're wonderful," he said. "Maybe we *should* record again." If he doesn't like me or resents what happened, he certainly does not show it. I don't think he feels intimidated at this point, nor should he, and I'd like to believe Howell's description of us as "good-natured ex-combatants" fills the bill nicely. This certainly came across in April of '93 when Ahmet invited me along to the Hall of Fame's groundbreaking ceremony in Cleveland.

There was, I regret to say, a sting in the tail. A sting that went all the way back, that took me completely by surprise, that raised many, many questions, that reached forward with icy fingers from the late forties. Any reasonable person, probably even Ahmet at this stage of the game, would admit that I was never recompensed properly for my record sales on Atlantic, let alone the part I played in building the company up. The rationale back then was that at least on the road I was earning good money, subject only to a deduction of promoters' fees and, of course, Blanche's cut.

The sting hit home courtesy of a Billboard clipping that came into my hands in the spring of '94, when the following item, dated July 1949, was brought to my attention:

CALLOWAY ASSOC. FORMED: New York—Herb Abramson, president, and Ahmet Ertegun, vice-president of Atlantic Records, have joined with Blanche Calloway in forming Blanche Calloway Associates, an artists management organization. The first artist pacted is Ruth Brown, vocalist currently appearing at Cafe Society. Miss Brown records for Atlantic Records.

This was the first I had heard of any such arrangement, for none of the principals in Blanche Calloway Associates had ever mentioned the alliance. What did it mean? Only that every time I had sung my heart out on the back of a tobacco truck, suffering slings and arrows while making far from an outrageous fortune, the boss men back in New York, not content with giving handouts instead of proper royalty accounting on my records, had been systematically collecting their pound of flesh from the road as well. Who do I blame? Blanche, for surrendering two-thirds to Herb and Ahmet of the ten percent I paid her? Certainly she could and should have told me, for the association raises all sorts of questions of conflict of interest. I tell myself she had to play along, for who would voluntarily accept one-third of her due? Let me put it this way: I think we can be fairly sure the suggestion of the "Associates" did not come from Blanche. As for Ahmet and Herb, well, at least with the likes of Morris Levy you knew going in to expect statutory rape. With Atlantic it was a case of date rape.

Incredibly, there was more, reaching even farther back. And now that I had discovered Blanche's ties with Ahmet and Herb, the new revelation made perfect sense. The well-established Capitol Records, I was now informed, had come talent-scouting at the Crystal Caverns at the same time as Atlantic. They had offered a contract and had been turned down, completely without my knowledge, in favor of Atlantic, a company with no track record to speak of. Why would Blanche have come to that decision? You tell me. All I can say is that I was nineteen years old, trusting and just glad to be getting signed up by anyone at all. And who's to say what would have happened if I had heard about Capitol and insisted on going with them? Well, there might have been no car accident, for one thing. And instead of Kay Starr, it might have been Ruth Brown singing "Side by Side" or "Wheel of Fortune." Speculation along those lines will take you wherever you want to go, I guess. And life's too short to dwell on it.

A COUPLE OF DAYS after my Rock and Roll Hall of Fame induction I guested with Bonnie on Arsenio Hall's show. "I'm so proud to be doing this," I told him in the green room before I went on, "but you've been running an ad all week, flashing photos of your guests, and when you came to Ruth Brown . . . that was not my photo! You've been advertising me with a picture of Etta James!"

"Oh, no!" he said.

"Oh, yes," I insisted.

"My people messed up your promo?"

"Yep. Hey, I know we all look alike!"

Arsenio was mortified, but he's a good guy and took it well.

THE MOST FULFILLING TIME for me ever is when my brothers and sisters get together. We sit around on the floor and talk about Mama and Daddy, the days we spent working in the fields, the simple pleasures that will never fade from memory. We visit Mama's grave every Mother's Day, form a circle and say, "Look, Mama, every one of your children is here. Nobody's in jail, nobody's on drugs. Mama, we're all here."

In January 1990, to coincide with my birthday, the city of Portsmouth had paid me a wonderful tribute, holding a Ruth Brown weekend with parades, banners, marching bands, honor guards and marquees. It was the most joyous four days ever. Every business in town had "Welcome Home, Ruth" emblazoned outside, every schoolkid was given a hat embroidered with my name and a butterfly motif, a favorite of mine. Two streets were named after me. There was a class reunion, a church visit—the chair I used to sit on has my name engraved permanently—and a dinner thrown by Mayor Gloria Webb in my honor, attended by my whole family, Bobby Jean and Bunky.

Goldie took the stage to speak on behalf of the family. I had no idea, no understanding whatever of the kind of pride they felt for me until she got into her speech. "I want to speak to my mother

Portsmouth Mayor Gloria O.
Webb making me one proud
lady. (Courtesy of Ruth Brown)

and father," she declared, "because I know they're listening tonight. It's because of Ruth that every one of us made an effort to be
something. They always wanted so much for little Ruth, and Daddy
thought she had the greatest voice in the world." She paused for a
moment, lifting her eyes to the sky before continuing, "Well, Mama
and Daddy, I know you're smilin' tonight, 'cause Ruth is still out
there doin' it. And the main thing is she's still just our sister, she's
never made any of us feel one iota smaller because of who she is.
The world is still looking at her, Mama, just like you always said it
would. And you know what? The street where you brought us up is
now Ruth Brown Avenue!"

It was the most emotional scene. I just came apart as my sister
spoke those words, for my concern through all the years had been
that none of them should be ashamed of me. What she said about
how they felt raised me to a different level. When I looked at them
all sitting there, all the men in tuxedos, all the women beautifully
dressed, it seemed so unreal. Was it really more than half a century
ago since we slept together as children? One thing was certain, for

The exact moment my sister Goldie said she was sure my mama and dad were watching from heaven. (COURTESY OF RUTH BROWN)

my dear sister's words had just proved it—that mysterious connection that only brothers and sisters enjoy had never been lost. A commendation from the White House that night capped it all, although I have to say it took some doing.

WHEN RONNIE WAS ABLE to find a place of his own for his girlfriend Debbie and Brandon, I took a look at the empty space in my house in the Hollywood hills and began to plan a move. I was so isolated it was next door to impossible even to get a pizza delivered. I was looking through the curtains one night when I was on my own, and I saw a pair of coyotes peeking back at me from the garden. With Earl's help I located a cozy apartment off Ventura Boulevard in the San Fernando Valley. It was a move of less than two miles, but it landed me smack in a well populated strip with shops, restaurants and clubs nearby. As for the actual address, Willis Avenue, what *can* I tell you?

I moved in just before Thanksgiving 1993, and it seemed ideal. I was on the second floor of a pleasant apartment building with an elevator, and a pool that I told myself would prove wonderfully therapeutic for my legs. Earl had it laid out beautifully, with an office area complete with fax, telephone and filing cabinet at the opposite end of the room from the entrance to the kitchen.

Lynn Palmer, my astrologer, set me wondering soon after the move when comparing the area numbers with my signs. "Not good, Ruth," she told me over the phone from her residence in Las Vegas. "You'll be out before next February."

"What *is* that?" I spluttered. "Why, I've just moved in. And if you could see it, Lynn, you'd fall in love with it too. Earl has worked wonders. I have a spare bedroom for guests, a patio overlooking the pool . . ."

"Before next February," Lynn repeated.

"Well, they're goin' to have to *carry* me out!" I declared.

Man proposes, God disposes. I should have been made to write it out a thousand times, I should have had it set to music and chanted it morning, noon and night. Unfortunately, some lessons we never learn.

I had my family 'round me in that apartment for Thanksgiving and Christmas, as well as for my birthday on January 12. When I had been hospitalized with angina back in New York, Lynn had adopted my Yorkshire terrier, treating it as the child she never had. I could have asked for it back, but I would have felt like a monster. Now Earl presented me with an adorable three-month old Yorkie pup for my birthday. I called him Encore, and Ronnie promised to take care of him in February when I left for London with Earl and the band to open at Ronnie Scott's, the city's number-one jazz club. I was excited about it, for incredibly this would be my first visit to England.

My bedroom furniture at Willis Avenue was French Provincial, something I had always wanted, and as I lay in bed in the early hours of a January morning, Encore started making one heckuva ruckus, barking, yapping, running round in circles. My first thought was: Is someone trying to break in? Dressed only in a blue nightgown, I gingerly made my way through to the living area to check the doors. Nope, everything seemed okay, although Encore was as agitated as ever. I started back to the bedroom, then turned back and looked at the TV console in front of the patio window. Aw shucks, what the heck, I thought. I settled down on the couch and picked up the remote—now I was up, I might as well have me a dose of American classic movies on TV. The only problem was shutting Encore up. He wanted to join me on the couch, but he was so tiny he was unable to get up there on his own. Reaching down, I picked him up and deposited him beside me, his little body still trembling badly. After a couple of minutes I must have dozed off for a few seconds. I was due the rudest awakening of my life.

There is a sound concrete makes when scraped by metal, a hideous, screeching sound second cousin to the squealing of brakes. That's the noise that jerked me awake, that and the instant, unmistakable impression of a building in the throes of wall-to-wall agony. Concrete was being racked and cracked, beams were being forced by some terrible power from their moorings. I screamed as I felt myself being levitated, suspended, then hurled to the floor like a rag doll. Oh, my God, I thought, as the word flashed through my brain. *Earthquake!*

Lying on my stomach, I could hear glass shattering all around me, pots and pans a-clatter in the kitchen. Then the lights went out, I heard the noise of electricity spitting; there was a strong smell of gas. I felt the building lurch and roll, rupturing walls and ceilings, dipping the floor. I heard and felt objects—paintings, light fixtures, ornaments—dropping all around me, and I waited for one to score a direct hit while frantically trying to figure out where I had landed in the room. I had but one thought, to reach the hallway, for I remembered someone telling me you should always try to get between two walls in an earthquake.

I got my bearings by reaching out with my right hand and touching the straw settee near the office desk in one corner of the room. Next thing I knew, the big desk began sliding toward me. I held it off as best I could and managed to crawl over to the door leading to the hallway. It was shut, and I could not reach the doorknob. Then the floor dropped again.

I knew right then that I was not going to live. Something was going to hit me, I was going to be crushed. I called on Mama to help me and said my prayers. "Lord," I cried, "if this is it, make it quick. Don't let me suffer."

There followed the eeriest silence, no sound whatsoever for a split second. It truly was like time stood still while the Lord considered my request. Then I heard the sound of a big dog howling fit to bust, together with a woman's voice uttering a prayer. In my mind's eye I pictured an old woman, and she was on her knees with her hands pressed together in supplication. "Lord Jesus, help me," I said.

For a moment I was certain I had died. And I was in hell, for there was no way this terrible chaos could be heaven. Then, like a miracle, I heard a voice: "Mama, Mama, where are you? I'm comin' in." It was my son, Earl, in the hallway outside my door. Next thing I knew he had the door open, and I saw the flickering of his flashlight. My mother's words echoed once more in my ears: "When you see the light at the end of the tunnel, it ain't no train a-comin'!"

"Mama, we've got to get you out of here," I heard Earl say.

"I can't walk," I told him.

"Mama, you've *got to*," he replied.

Somehow he managed to get me up and out into the hall. I screamed, for coming at me through the dark and dust was a second light. It was Phil, our Scottish super, who had seen Earl enter the building and had come to help. I pleaded with Earl to go back and find little Encore. "Hold my mother," Earl told Phil, then dashed back into the apartment. He emerged with a trench coat to cover my nightgown and a pair of shoes to put on my bare feet. "What about Encore?" I asked. "Mama, let's go," was all he said. I knew better than to ask again.

Supported by the two of them, I groped my way along the hallway. "Forget it," Phil advised when we reached what looked like an empty elevator shaft. The staircase too had detached itself from the building, but there was no other way down, and I had to be lifted on as it swayed perilously. Down we went, to find the hallway covered with shattered glass. Outside the pool had split in two jagged halves, its contents flooding the pathway. The smell of gas was stronger than ever, and beyond our block I could see water pipes shooting up and bursts of flame leaping up to illuminate Ventura. A neighbor, one to whom I had briefly nodded a couple of times, came up to me and offered to share her blanket. Others stood around in groups, looking every bit as stunned and bewildered as I felt.

The quake had hit at 4:31 A.M. precisely. Time takes on a whole new attitude in a crisis, when it's possible to live an entire lifetime in fifteen minutes. I had never felt so helpless, and if we needed reminding of who the power is, how little control we have over our lives, there was the proof. Out there on the street, facing the gray light of dawn, shivering in a neighbor's shared blanket, wearing a pair of mismatched shoes on my bare feet, my world, like that of thousands of others, turned upside down, I realized that it did not matter how much you had or did not have, nobody could give a damn whether you were fat or skinny, ugly or beautiful, whether you were black, blue, brown, yellow or white, all that nonsense was stripped away, masks ripped off. The name of the game was *I want to live—and I know you do too!*

Earl's automatic reaction when the first shock hit had been to run outside, leap into his car and come get his mother. Even so, I shall never know how he got from his apartment two miles away in Van Nuys so quickly. Now my immediate concern was to find Ronnie, Brandon and Debbie. I had never sat in Earl's pride and joy, his natty, low-slung little sports coupe. The thought of squeezing myself in there, despite his repeated invitations, had been too much to contemplate before. Not now. Not on this, the first day of the rest of my life. Now *anything* was possible!

As we sped towards Ronnie's house in Studio City, Earl told me that the big settee where I had been watching television had been overturned, crushing little Encore to death. In the time it took to drive to Ronnie's, through the war zone that the San Fernando Valley had become, all I could do was pray that everyone had been spared. When we arrived we found the same extensive damage we had fled, and I frantically searched the sea of faces. Debbie spotted us and ran over. "Where's Brandon?" I screamed. "Where's Ronnie?"

"Brandon's safe," Debbie assured me. "And Ronnie's gone lookin' for you."

I looked at Earl and did not have to say a word. "We'll go straight back," he told me. "C'mon, Mama." Within an hour, thank God, we were all together.

In the days to come there were constant aftershocks to remind us that we might not be out of the woods yet. There was no fresh water or power supply. Unable to return to our homes, seven of us slept on the floor at Debbie's sister's house. And all of a sudden I had pains everywhere, all over my body, especially my legs.

Still I was thankful. I had been spared through the grace of God and my son.

WITH WILLIS AVENUE TOTALLY CONDEMNED, Ronnie and Earl ignored warnings and went back in, coming out with some of the wardrobe I needed for London and not a whole lot else. In New York for a week before the flight to Europe, the worst snowstorm of the winter whipped up. With flights canceled all over the place, what could be next? Would I be able to leave for my date at Ronnie Scott's before the plague of locusts arrived?

I did get out, together with Earl and my six-piece band, and we arrived in London to be met by their worst winter storm in seven years. I should have known better than to kid about those locusts! After all I had been through, our two weeks at the club were simply out of this world. We played twenty-four shows, and filled every seat for every performance. I had a change of costume for each and every show, and don't even *ask* about the excess charge to haul my luggage across the Atlantic! Ronnie, his partner Pete and their staff could not have been nicer, with "Is there anything you need, Miss B?" the constant cry and fresh-cut flowers waiting for me every night. And the audiences . . . ! What *is* all that nonsense I've been fed over the years about English reserve? I've been asked back twice since—first in November, '94, then in October, '95, for three sold-out weeks on each occasion, with a "Live in London" album in the can for good measure, recorded at the club. Ronnie and Pete? Good people.

I had a date with one more snowstorm during the first week of March, back in New York at the famed Roseland Ballroom, where once again Bonnie Raitt and I co-hosted the Lifetime Achievement Awards of the Rhythm and Blues Foundation. Checks for $25,000 each were handed out to Little Richard, Ben E. King, the Shirelles, the Coasters, Otis Blackwell, Jerry Butler, Clarence Carter, Don Covay, Bill Doggett, Mable John (Little Willie's sister), Johnny Otis, Earl Palmer (the fabulous drummer behind so many hits, including those of Little Richard, Fats Domino, Shirley and Lee and a host of

others) and Irma Thomas. It was another amazing night, with almost everyone talking about Ruth Brown in their acceptance
speeches.

Doris Jackson of the Shirelles talked about that first tour of theirs
with Brook Benton, where I had virtually been entrusted by Florence Greenberg with the chaperoning of "her girls," how I had got
them to dump their high heels and fancy clothes for those long
daily bus rides, just to relax, be comfortable and save all the glitz for
the customers. And to keep their ears closed tight whenever
raunchy tales were being swapped!

Little Richard, in between commanding the audience to "Shad-
dup!" when they applauded or laughed too enthusiastically, and
having his brother hand out hundreds of free religious instruction
books, repeated yet again that his squeal at the end of "Lucille"-*uh!*
had come from "Mama-*uh!* He Treats Your Daughter Mean." "I
idolized Ruth Brown!" he told the crowd when the cheering
stopped for that. "I wanted to *be* Ruth Brown!"

Mable, who had gone from a solo career to Ray Charles's Raelet-
tes, to pastor at a church in Los Angeles, recalled her first appearance at the Apollo, when I had invited her along to my apartment
before the show. I had showed off some of my stage dresses, and
she fell in love with them one by one. She was especially thrilled
with three of them, and I encouraged her to try them on. When we
discovered that they all fitted perfectly, I insisted that she take them
all. Like that loan to Redd Foxx back in the stone age, I had completely forgotten the incident. I'm just glad she didn't seem to recall my knocking out two of her brother's front teeth!

After watching his wife and me sway in unison like a couple of
moonstruck kids to the Shirelles singing "Dedicated To the One I
Love," Michael O'Keefe, Bonnie's handsome and talented actor
husband, asked, "Ruth, how does it feel to have so many people
love you?" I couldn't answer him, my heart was too full. All I could
do was shake my head from side to side and smile like a happy
clown.

With the collapse of Willis Avenue I began to think about a return to Las Vegas to live. Earl went ahead to check out apartments

With Little Richard and Howell Begle at the 1994 Rhythm and Blues Foundation Pioneer Awards.
(COURTESY OF RUTH BROWN)

and called me in New York to say he'd found one on the ninth floor of a condo that seemed eminently suitable. You're not going to believe this, but when I called Lynn Palmer to check out the numbers, it turned out she was living just one floor above me. The numbers were great, so that was settled.

Sure enough, soon after moving in I got a call from Bonnie Raitt. Would I care to join her as a "Special Guest" with Charles Brown on her '95 Summer Tour? Would I! It was during the space of that tour—on which, I don't need to add, we stayed in all the best hotels, travelled in unbelievable luxury—that I got to thinking how far one person can travel in the space of a lifetime . . . from the back of a tobacco truck in the fifties, changing in the headlights, washing with witch hazel, paid if we were lucky enough or smart enough to extract the money in advance, to playing with a true friend like Bonnie, someone who worked her butt off each night, sang her

On stage with
Bonnie Raitt.
(COURTESY OF
RUTH BROWN)

heart out—then turned around and gave you the most glowing and gracious introduction imaginable.

I have an old friend who is forever telling me I need a male image in my house. I cannot buy that. Sure, there comes that moment after you have been out performing, with people as far as you can see standing up to applaud. That's wonderful. Then you close the door of the hotel room behind you, and there's nobody there to tell it to. Many women feel there has to be someone waiting, but there comes a time you have to be realistic about it. Sometimes I think it would be nice, but hell, I don't want to have to get up and fix someone's breakfast every morning either. (Somedays I don't feel like getting up at all.) The way I am, I can please myself. I feel wonderful, I can stay up all night if I want to, it's my choice. And let's face it, along the way I've tasted everything that was on offer.

With the Broadway superstar John Raitt (Bonnie's dad).
(COURTESY OF ROBBIE TODD)

With Charles Brown and comedian Robbie Todd in Denver on Bonnie Raitt's Summer '95 tour.
(COURTESY OF ROBBIE TODD)

Live in concert at the Red Rocks Outdoor Theater in Colorado on Bonnie's Summer '95 tour. (COURTESY OF ROBBIE TODD)

Believe me, I ain't got nothing coming to me. A new man? Looking I'm not!

I am a strong woman from a long line of strong women, and that has its pluses and minuses. I know it has not been easy for a man to be Mr. Ruth Brown, and that's what happened most of the time, but I have two fine sons and a whole bunch of good memories to help me overlook that other stuff.

Billie, Dinah, Sarah, the Count, the Duke, Sammy, Dizzy, Mr. B, Clyde, Brook, Roy, Jackie, Blanche, my dear Willis . . . so many days I remember the faces of those who have gone before me, so many nights I find myself wondering where all my good friends have gone, the dear ones who accompanied me on my journey. As for me, we are promised only three score and ten. I check the obituaries every morning, and if my name ain't there I phone my agent and tell him to get going!

I feel Mama's presence with me every day of my life. As for Dad, there are so many times I wish I could look around and talk to him now that I am a woman, for I was just a kid last time we sat down. He did not live to see either of my children, and hardly any of his grandchildren. All my brothers have outlived him, even Alvin, the baby Mama thought stillborn. I would like to ask my father how he feels about the things I have achieved. I am almost sure he creeps into my spirit sometimes.

A year or so ago I attended the Abyssinian, the top Baptist church in Harlem, and I know he was up there singing with me that night, because I pulled out some tunes I had not done for years, not since I was a child in church with him playing the piano beside me. My physician, Dr. Erin Wells, had asked me along to help out with a membership drive they were having, and I have to admit I hesitated. Why? Hey, those card-carrying Christians still have this funny thing about the Devil and his tunes. "At this stage of my life," I spelled out, "I'm not into setting myself up."

I went along anyway, and took my whole band with me. "I know everybody's wondering what I'm going to do," I told the Reverend Butts. "So am I, but I'm just going where the spirit leads me." I need not have worried, for what followed was one of the most amazing concerts of my life. "The Lord's Prayer," my finale, was greeted by a rapturous standing ovation. That night, like the one back in

Still singing for
my supper.
(Courtesy of
Ruth Brown)

the fifties with Little Richard, Sam Cooke, Billy Eckstine and the
rest of the congregation, was for my Daddy.

I know that what I do is blessed, for after all I have come through
it seems obvious that somebody bigger than me has been keeping
watch. People leave my performances a little bit happier for seeing
me, and that's my way of evangelizing. Now I have reached the
stage where I am ready to sing about my experiences, to reflect on
my life and pass on the message, to clear the spirit and soul.

How has it been? Lord have mercy, it's been like a dream.

But oh, what a dream . . .

DISCOGRAPHY

Reissues:

MISS RHYTHM: GREATEST HITS AND MORE
(Atlantic 2-CD 7 82061-2)

Executive Producer: Ahmet Ertegun,
Reissue produced by Bob Porter

So Long
Hey Pretty Baby
I'll Get Along Somehow (Part One)
Sentimental Journey
R.B. Blues
Teardrops From My Eyes
Standing On the Corner
I'll Wait For You
I Know
Don't Cry
The Shrine of St. Cecilia
It's All For You
Shine On
Be Anything (But Be Mine)
5-10-15 Hours (Of Your Love)
Have a Good Time
Daddy, Daddy
Mama, He Treats Your Daughter Mean
Wild, Wild Young Men
Ever Since My Baby's Been Gone
Love Contest
Oh, What A Dream
Old Man River
Somebody Touched Me
Mambo Baby

344

I Can See Everybody's Baby
As Long As I'm Moving
It's Love Baby
I Gotta Have You*
Love Has Joined Us Together*
I Wanna Do More
Lucky Lips
One More Time
This Little Girl's Gone Rockin'
Why Me?
I Can't Hear A Word You Say
I Don't Know
Takin' Care of Business
Don't Deceive Me

* Duet with Clyde McPhatter

BLACK IS BROWN AND BROWN IS BEAUTIFUL
(DCC Jazz DJZ-620)

Produced by Norman Schwartz. Recorded New York City, 1969.

Yesterday*
Please Send Me Someone To Love
Looking Back
Try Me
Miss Brown's Blues
My Prayer
Since I Fell For You
This Bitter Earth

* Grammy Nominee "Best Female Jazz Vocal"

FINE BROWN FRAME
(Capitol Jazz CDP 0777 81200 25)

RUTH BROWN with
the THAD JONES/ MEL LEWIS ORCHESTRA

Produced by Sonny Lester (Originally on Solid State label.
Recorded at Plaza Sound, New York City,

on June 18 and July 2, 1968
Produced for Reissue by Michael Cuscuna

Yes Sir, That's My Baby
Trouble In Mind
Sonny Boy
Bye Bye Blackbird
I'm Gonna Move to the Outskirts of Town
Black Coffee
Be Anything (But Be Mine)
You Won't Let Me Go
Fine Brown Frame

HELP A GOOD GIRL GO BAD
(DCC Jazz DJZ-602)

Arranged and Conducted by Peter Matz, Produced by Bob Shad,
Recorded in December, 1964 (Original Title: RUTH BROWN:
'65, on Mainstream Records)

He's A Real Gone Guy
On The Good Ship Lollipop
Help A Good Girl Go Bad
Porgy
What Am I Looking For?
Here's That Rainy Day
Hurry On Down
Table For Two
What Do You Know? (Quien Sabes Tu?)
Whipering Grass
Watch It
I Know Why

LATE DATE WITH RUTH BROWN
(Atlantic Japanese Import AMCY-1055; Originally Atlantic 1308)

Arranger-Conductor: Richard Wess. Recorded New York City,
1956

It Could Happen To You
Why Don't You Do Right

Bewitched
I'm Just A Lucky So and So
I Can Dream, Can't I?
You and the Night and the Music
You'd Be So Nice To Come Home To
We'll Be Together Again
I'm Beginning To See the Light
I Loves You, Porgy
No One Ever Tells You
Let's Face the Music and Dance

Current Recordings:

BLACK AND BLUE
(DRG CDSBL 19001)

ORIGINAL BROADWAY CAST Recording produced by Hugh Fordin, Arranged and Orchestrated by Sy Johnson ("I Can't Give You Anything But Love" Arr. and Orch. by Luther Henderson)

Recorded and Mixed at Clinton Recording Studios, New York City, November-December, 1989

Ruth is featured on the following tracks:

I'm A Woman
St. Louis Blues
If I Can't Sell It, I'll Keep Sittin' On It
T'Ain't Nobody's Bizness If I Do
Body and Soul
Black and Blue

HAVE A GOOD TIME
(Fantasy FCD-9661-2)

Produced by Ralph Jungheim, arranged by Bobby Forrester.

Recorded Live at the Cinegrill, Hollywood Roosevelt Hotel, June 10-11, 1988

Gee Baby, Ain't I Good to You
You Won't Let Me Go
5-10-15 Hours
Have A Good Time
Teardrops From My Eyes
Always On My Mind
Yes Sir, That's My Baby
When I Fall In Love
Mama, He Treats Your Daughter Mean
What A Wonderful World

BLUES ON BROADWAY
(Fantasy FCD-9662-2) *

Producer: Ralph Jungheim

Arranged by Ruth Brown, Ralph Jungheim ("I Don't
Breakdance" arranged by Rodney Jones)

Recorded at RCA Studio C, New York City, June 12-13, 1989

Nobody Knows You When You're Down and Out
Good Morning Heartache
If I Can't Sell It, I'll Keep Sittin' On It
T'Ain't Nobody's Biz-Ness If I Do
St. Louis Blues
Am I Blue?
I'm Just A Lucky So and So
I Don't Breakdance
Come Sunday

* GRAMMY WINNER "Best Jazz Female Vocal Performance", 1990

FINE AND MELLOW
(Fantasy FCD-9663-2)

Produced by Ralph Jungheim, Arranged by Frank Owens

Recorded at Sage and Sound Studios, Hollywood, April 1-2, 1991

Fine and Mellow
Ain't Got Nothin' But the Blues

A World I Never Made
Salty Papa Blues
I'll Drown In My Own Tears
Knock Me a Kiss
It's Just a Matter of Time
Don't Get Around Much Anymore
Nothing Takes the Place of You
I'll Be Satisfied

THE SONGS OF MY LIFE
(Fantasy FCD-9665-2)

Produced, Arranged and Conducted by Rodney Jones for New
Tide Music

Recorded at M&I Studios, New York City, March 1993

Song of My Life
I've Got the World on a String
While We're Young
God Bless the Child
It Could Happen to You
Tears in Heaven
Stormy Weather
They Say
Wonder Where Our Love Has gone
I Know Why
Can't Help Lovin' That Man
I'll Be Seeing You

Ruth guests on the following albums:

B.B. KING: BLUES SUMMIT
(MCA Records)(Grammy Winner, "Best Blues Album", 1994)

MANHATTAN TRANSFER: TONIN'
(Atlantic Records)

BONNIE RAITT: ROAD TESTED
(Capitol 2-CD LIVE)

BENNY CARTER: THE BENNY CARTER SONGBOOK
(MusicMasters)

A SEASON OF GIVING
(HQ Charitable Foundation: In Support of Children's Hospitals across America)

Ruth's Latest Solo Release:

LIVE IN LONDON
(Jazz House Records JHCD042)

Recorded at Ronnie Scott's Jazz Club, London, November-December, 1994

Produced, Recorded and Mixed by Chris Lewis
Executive Producer: Pete King

I've Got the World On a String
I'm Just a Lucky So-and-So
Have A Good Time
Fine and Mellow
Lover Man
Good Morning, Heartache
Secret Love
Fine Brown Frame
It Could Happen To You
5-10-15 Hours (Of Your Love)
Be Anything (But Be Mine)
Since I Fell For You
He's A Real Gone Guy

(Thanks to FOOTLIGHT RECORDS, 113 E. 12th Street, New York City, for their help in research, also CHRIS LEWIS of JAZZ HOUSE RECORDS, London. All CDs mentioned are also available on cassette format).

INDEX

351